JOHN HEYL VINCENT
A Biographical Sketch

THE MACMILLAN COMPANY
NEW YORK · BOSTON · CHICAGO · DALLAS
ATLANTA · SAN FRANCISCO

MACMILLAN & CO., Limited
LONDON · BOMBAY · CALCUTTA
MELBOURNE

THE MACMILLAN CO. OF CANADA, Ltd.
TORONTO

PREFATORY NOTE

THE chief sources of this biographical sketch are Bishop Vincent's journals, and other private papers (now in the possession of his son, Dr. George E. Vincent), his printed books, the *Autobiography,* and an article entitled "How I Was Educated," written for *The Forum.*

The suppression of all but necessary references to Bishop Vincent's associates has been deliberate. It was important to keep the matter within reasonable limits, and it would have been superfluous to tell over again what has already been told elsewhere. *The Story of Chautauqua,* by Dr. Jesse L. Hurlbut, is full, accurate, and accessible; not a name has been omitted of the many hundreds of people who had an intimate or a passing relation with the Assembly. There is a history of the International Lesson System, by Simeon Gilbert, and numerous accounts of the movement have been recorded in the current bibliographical manuals.

To Bishop Vincent's son I am indebted for most of the striking anecdotes of his father, and to Dr. Hurlbut for many facts of the utmost value. And I should be wanting in common gratitude if I failed to thank Miss Mary Warren Allen for her admirable work in going through and classifying the mass of letters, manuscripts, and clippings that was turned over to her for this purpose.

CONTENTS

ILLUSTRATIONS

JOHN HEYL VINCENT

A Biographical Sketch

CHAPTER I

ANCESTRY, PARENTAGE, AND BIRTH

JOHN HEYL VINCENT traced his ancestral line to one
Levi Vincent, who was born at Charente Inférieure on
April 10, 1676, and emigrated to America after the
Revocation of the Edict of Nantes. He lived for a
time at New Rochelle, New York, and then settled on
a farm in Essex County, New Jersey. His wife, Esther
Debue, may well have been of his own race and faith.
The little record from which these facts are taken men-
tions a son by the name of John, but has nothing to say
of other children.

If Levi Vincent came to this country at the time of
the first great scattering of the Huguenots he would
then have been a nine-year-old boy. He must therefore
have come under the protection of some kinsman. The
Huguenot monument at New Rochelle bears the names
of certain early settlers, and among them a Vincent,
possibly the father of this same Levi. Surnames only
are engraved on the stone.

John Vincent, the son of Levi and Esther, should be
the man who figures in the disputes over their respective
rights between the Essex County farmers and the Pro-

[1]

prietors (1745). He was indicted, along with Levi Vincent, Jr. and others, for "Riotous Conduct and Treason."

The Proprietors had surveyed and offered for sale not only unimproved lands but cultivated tracts as well. When notices of ejectment were served, the farmers began to stand for their rights. Their spokesmen were seized at the instance of the Proprietors and put in jail. A body of farmers, three hundred strong, broke open the jail and released their men. The two Vincents, John and Levi, Jr., may have been ringleaders in an affair which, after all, was merely an episode in a quarrel that lasted some five years.

John Vincent was about thirty-six at the time of the riot in question. He had married in 1733, Elizabeth Doremus, of the stock of Wolpfert Webber. Dutch by descent, she was unmitigatedly Dutch in that she could speak no English. John Vincent, on the other hand, spoke English only. The lover must have courted his mistress after the manner of Dirk Waldron (in Washington Irving's story) who, it will be remembered, "said little but sat long." Yet Dirk was able to speak to Amy Webber in her own tongue.

John Vincent and Elizabeth Doremus had a family of nine children, among them a son named Cornelius. On arriving at man's estate Cornelius took to wife a certain Phebe Ward. They likewise were blessed with children to the number of nine. Bethuel, their third son, was the grandfather of John Heyl Vincent, the subject of this memoir.

Meanwhile members of the tribe (Bethuel was one of them) had migrated to a valley of the Susquehanna, and may be accounted Pennsylvanians from now on. The date of their removal from Essex County is given as 1772. They made homes for themselves near the mouth of Warrior Run Creek, to the north of the settlement that became the town of Milton. Bethuel Vincent met his future wife, Martha Himroth, at Milton. She was a daughter of Simon Himroth, or Himrod, as the name was latterly spelled.

Martha Himrod Vincent sustained the family tradition by bearing her husband four sons and five daughters. The sixth child in order of birth, John Himrod (Bishop Vincent's father), was born at Milton, Pennsylvania, on April 20, 1798, and died at Erie on August 13, 1873.

These genealogical details will interest only those to whom they are interesting. They were collected by Bishop Vincent himself and may be found, in a less condensed form, in a privately printed pamphlet that he brought out to commemorate the centenary of his father's birth. Their principal source would seem to be the records compiled by Bethuel Boyd Vincent of Erie,[1] but he undoubtedly overhauled a large number of books and documents on his own account. He had a lively curiosity as to his forebears, and was pleased when he unearthed anything that threw light on their doings and sayings. The study of one's ancestry was, he thought, a pursuit worth any man's while. The man might, to be sure, run across some disagreeable episode. In that case it was permitted him to make amends for it by a stricter ordering of his own life.

During the Revolution these settlers by Warrior Run Creek suffered many inconveniences and were at times in

[1] The father of the Rt. Rev. Boyd Vincent, Bishop of Southern Ohio.

must have presented itself. Jackson appointed him to be Registrar of the Land Office; but this would be subsequent to 1828. An advertisement in a local newspaper calls attention to the fact that he was empowered to act as agent for "the Bank of the State of Alabama." He was also a member of the firm of Vincent and Pitcher, merchants.

On one of his journeys between Tuscaloosa and Mobile, Himrod Vincent met at Demopolis a Philadelphia girl, Miss Mary Raser, the daughter of Bernard Raser, a sea captain. Orphaned at an early age, she had been brought up by an uncle and aunt; she was now visiting a brother who had settled in the South. The two young Pennsylvanians fell in love with each other and presently were married.

Whether or not, at the age of twenty, Mary Raser would be accounted a pretty girl, is now unknown. That she had a natural and laudable partiality to articles of feminine adornment admits of no doubt. She was the present writer's grandmother, and he is pleased to find her ordering from Philadelphia, August 18, 1821, a large tortoise-shell comb, a pair of earrings with drops, "a good quality," and a bunch of curls. One admires her good sense. No bride of less than a year's standing can afford to be indifferent to gewgaws, curls not excepted. What mother of a bishop was ever the worse for a touch of coquetry in her dress?

Himrod Vincent and his wife had a large family—for the fourth and last time we meet with the mystical number nine. All but three, the three youngest, were born in Alabama. The first four children died in infancy. John Heyl Vincent survived the perils incident to childhood in that unscientific age and lived to be eighty-eight.

He was born at Tuscaloosa on February 23, 1832. A sentence in one of the many letters written by his mother to her Philadelphia relatives brings out two points—that there is danger of their "making an idol" of the boy, now in his eighteenth month, and that the fear of losing him is ever present. But not because he was frail. He had a good start in life, and his mother could describe him at two years of age by the phrase "as hardy as a pine knot."

A few anecdotes of his life in the South are set down in the *Autobiography*. He recalls, for example, how he once played at being a preacher, and exhorted a group of blacks, children as diminutive as himself. "My little hymn book in one hand and a rod in the other, I was fully prepared to keep order and impart instruction." He might have added—it is a well-known family tradition—that he also tore up a small Testament, bound in red leather, and distributed the leaves among his ebony-hued congregation, so that every one might have, as it were, a service book. He was duly admonished by his parents that this was no way to treat the Scriptures.

A letter of Mrs. Vincent's gives a picture of the budding pulpit orator at the age of three. She writes: "I wish you could now see John; he is standing beside me with his Bible and hymn book before him, his hands spread out, preaching. He says he is preaching in Greek."

No less amusing is his own account of his elopement with a girl playmate; the two infants were presumably of the same age, about four and a half years. They knew where they meant to go and actually reached their destination, the house of Professor Tutweiler (John's Sunday-school teacher) at the University. A servant was dispatched to bring the runaways back home.

The house in which the Vincents lived was a roomy one-storied structure with a broad veranda, a homelike dwelling and unmistakably "Southern" in aspect. When, in 1871, John Vincent was shown the church to which he had been regularly taken by his parents, he was able at once to turn in the right direction to find his birthplace; he had not been in Tuscaloosa since 1837.

Three negro servants were attached to the place; by what sort of tenure does not appear. It was a modest retinue but adequate, and had the merit of being fixed rather than migratory; the problem of hired help, so vexing to housewives, had not arisen, at least not in that part of the world.

Conscious as she must have been of the advantages of her situation, Mrs. Himrod Vincent was not altogether happy in the South—her son says, "chiefly on account of slavery." There is no hint of this in her letters. She complains of nothing, has no criticism to offer, is cheerful, occasionally humorous, and evidently busy every waking moment of the day. But on almost every page there is some expression of an almost passionate longing to be within reach of her own people. She mentions each one by name, sends specific messages to each, wants not to be forgotten, and apologizes meekly for any delay in answering letters or acknowledging gifts.

One concludes that she had not taken root, that her heart was still in the city of her girlhood, and that the only fault she had to find with Tuscaloosa was that it was not Philadelphia. She does not say so—of invidious comparison her letters are totally innocent. But it is evident that the ties that bound her to her old home were too many and too strong to be broken; at best they could only be stretched.

She made three or four visits to the North, always under her husband's protection. In the letters written after her return, she invariably voices the fear that this particular visit may turn out to be the last. If so it would be because God had willed it; they were one and all in His hands.

Whatever may have been the causes that led this family to remove to Pennsylvania, it is pretty clear that the change was made in 1837. It had been contemplated a year earlier. In an advertisement in a Tuscaloosa paper, under the date of June 11, 1836, John Himrod Vincent offers for sale "the House in which he now resides, together with all his Furniture." He will likewise sell "an excellent pair of family Carriage Horses— young and in fine order. And also an entirely new Barouche." Of the house, he says: "There is perhaps no residence in Tuscaloosa possessing more conveniences than the one now offered for sale."

In an issue of the same paper appeared, on February 20, 1837, a notice of the dissolution by mutual consent of the firm of Vincent and Pitcher. This meant the severing of the last link, exclusive of warm personal ties, that bound these people to their pleasant Alabama home. At the time the journey northward was made, John Heyl Vincent would have been about five years of age. He had companions in the shape of a brother, Bethuel Thomas Vincent, two and a half years younger than he, and of a cousin, Ann Raser, somewhat older.

JOHN HEYL VINCENT

To small John this presumably tedious expedition
counted for a prolonged holiday; there was much to
entertain a boy, and the annoyances and drawbacks were
few. A seasoned traveler at five (having already made
the journey between Alabama and Pennsylvania at least
twice) he was prepared to extract fun out of everything.
An incident that always stuck in his memory was of
his finding, on a river steamboat, an empty wooden box
just large enough to hold a boy of his size. Getting
into it, he propelled himself about the deck, somewhat
to the annoyance of the passengers in general and of one
sour-faced lady in particular. Conscious that he was not
giving pleasure he, nevertheless, persisted defiantly in his
sport. The moral he draws from the incident concerns
parents, not children.

In the letters of this period that remain no hint is
given as to the route taken by the travelers. They might
have gone from Tuscaloosa to St. Clair Courthouse, then
in a northeasterly direction to the state line, crossing the
Tennessee River at Calhoun, and so on to Morgantown
and Knoxville. From Knoxville the road would take them
through Abingdon, Newbern, Staunton, and Winchester
to Harper's Ferry, and thence to Washington. The
point is of no importance except as it might throw light
on modes of travel in 1837.

The *Autobiography* makes mention of stagecoaches
and steamboats, yet leaves the impression that a large
part of the journey was made by private conveyance.
The hotels are praised. To a boy, the worst of them
would seem delightful. There must have been many that
deserved praise. An intelligent English farmer who
wrote an account of his wanderings about the United

States in 1819 had always a good word for the inns at which he stopped. The cuisine pleased him. Everywhere he found the food not only palatable but abundant. By 1837 the inns on the great post roads should have improved rather than fallen off.

The travelers met with a hearty welcome at Mrs. Vincent's old home in Philadelphia. There the mother and children remained for a number of weeks; the father went on to Northumberland County to make all ready for their coming.

Himrod Vincent's acquaintance with Alabama and its people was extensive and intimate; he had lived in the state for not less than eighteen years. His famous son lived there but five years, and only retained such memories of his birthplace as a child might be expected to retain. But John H. Vincent was a man of strong attachments and unswerving in his loyalty. "I have always felt a measure of pride in the fact that I was born in the South," he writes in the *Autobiography*. Until the close of the Civil War he had little chance to become well acquainted with Southerners. Nevertheless he was prejudiced in their favor, and one never heard him speak of them in terms other than those of affectionate admiration.

Alive to their many virtues, he keenly relished—as was natural in an eminently social being like himself—their open-handed hospitality. He did all that he could, all that lay in the power of one man, to heal the wounds left by the great struggle. It was characteristic of him early to instill into his son's mind an idea such as this—that one should be especially considerate in one's dealings with Southern people because of their disappointment over the outcome of the war. He had a contempt for politicians who, to further their own ends, kept alive the feeling of sectional jealousy and distrust. He wanted to see a united country, and he believed that "silence, patience, and charity" would be effective agents in bringing about the desired end.

CHAPTER II

THE HOME ON THE SUSQUEHANNA

HIMROD VINCENT had taken a farm, not far from the river, at a point designated by the unmelodious Indian name of Chillisquaque. Either from restlessness or because he thought to better himself he afterwards exchanged this farm for one nearer the Susquehanna. In 1839-40 he built a new flouring mill on the creek, the old mill having fallen into decay. This he operated for about three years and then put it into other hands while he made a trip to Mobile.

This journey of 1843 would indicate that the South had not lost its attractions, and that he had more than half a mind to return there if a good business opening presented itself. Some months elapsed before he became satisfied that a change was not advisable. In the early summer of 1844 he was back in Northumberland County.

Removing across the river to "the smart village of Lewisburg," as an old resident has called the place, he opened a shop for the sale of such commodities as dry goods, groceries, hats, and so forth. Having been active and prominent in Freemasonry at Tuscaloosa, he was naturally interested in the welfare of the order at Lewisburg. He was one of the five men who reorganized the local Masonic lodge, acted as secretary at that time and afterwards, and held for one year the office of Master.

[13]

His business did not prosper to the degree he hoped it might. Either for this reason or because he had a promise of the postmastership at Chillisquaque (he had formerly held it), he decided to return to the earlier home and open a country store there. This was the store in which young John Vincent worked when he was not at school.

There is nothing in the scanty household records to show that Himrod Vincent was much affected one way or another by his somewhat frequent changes of residence and occupation. He was never rich and at no time was he actually poor. The necessaries of life he could command. For luxuries he cared little or nothing. Once he complains (to a correspondent) of the scarcity of money and once of the number of guests. Living at a time when guests came, not for a week-end but for a month, or for the entire summer, he may have found hospitality expensive. His family increased. Three more children were born to him after the migration from the South to Pennsylvania.[1] It was in the nature of things that he should have moments of anxiety.

John Vincent retained vivid impressions of his first home at Chillisquaque, the one to which he was brought as a child of five. A stone house, it stood on a rise of ground at no great distance from the point where Chillisquaque Creek joined the West Branch of the Susquehanna. Back of it towered the Montour Ridge. To his boyish imagination the Ridge, well wooded to the summit, resembled a gigantic grave; he used to call it "the grave of Napoleon."

[1] Frank Lyon, 1839-89; Thomas Raser, 1841-43; Mary Elizabeth (Mrs. Farovid), 1842-1924.

Another object that excited his curiosity at first was the dilapidated mill on the creek. When the new mill was finished the old one was turned into a chapel. Here the itinerant preachers held forth on Sunday afternoons. They were an interesting breed of men—forceful, democratic, good talkers, and endowed with plenty of mother wit.

The grassy open spaces about the house made an ample playground for the two boys, John and Bethuel. At Philadelphia their father had bought them a marvelous plaything in the shape of a miniature coach. Needless to say that they put it to good use as long as it lasted. One may conclude that this toy had something to do in fostering the future Bishop's love of travel.

All through his boyhood he was eager to be on the road. He liked to picture himself as away on an extended tour, now at this place and now at that. To give a realistic touch to these fantasies he would make up a bundle of mock paper money, and on each day of the imaginary journey destroy a part of it—"for expenses."

Your born traveler cannot see any kind of a public vehicle without longing to be in it and off. The canal that ran from the mouth of the Juniata River to Farrandsville, above Lock Haven, was in plain sight from the Vincent house. To young John no spectacle was more fascinating than that of the approaching packet, a long, narrow craft, painted white, with many windows, green blinds, and an upper deck crowded with well-dressed passengers. Drawn by three horses that actually trotted (not walked) along the towpath, it looked one of the pleasantest of contrivances for getting about the world. If not so scrupulously clean as it might have been

—"Every traveler is a self-taught entomologist," said
Doctor Holmes—the packet had a high reputation for
the excellence of its table. It carried the mail sacks. An
event of the day for country boys was the regular advent
of the packet, and they listened eagerly for the blast of
the horn that announced its approach.

Of the two brief character sketches that John Vincent
made of his father, one runs thus: "He was an attractive
man—social, genial, full of humor, considerate of others,
magnetic and sympathetic." Exactly this might have
been said of Himrod Vincent's three sons; they resembled
him in each of these characteristics. Other traits' are
recorded in the following sentence: "As a father he
was almost perfect—firm, just, tender, sometimes severe,
but careful not to punish in anger." In no sense conten-
tious, he enjoyed an argument and was well able to hold
his own. The boys pestered him with various questions,
to which he did not always give a categorical reply. One
of them interrupted him in the midst of his reading to
ask what an aristocrat was. Himrod pushed his spectacles up over his brow and said, "Remember, my son, that
there is no place to which a Vincent may not go," and
then resumed his book, leaving the boy in doubt as to
whether, in the event of his wanting to go to any particular place, it might not be more convenient to go in
his own quality than in that of an aristocrat.

In 1871, when on a visit to Tuscaloosa, John Vincent
took pains to search out and talk with the people who
had known his parents. One old resident said to him,
"Your father was a rare disciplinarian with both children
and servants. He always accomplished what he undertook. Used to rise before daybreak. Always made his

own fire. Had the servants get kindling and wood ready, but preferred to set them the example of promptness and industry. Often ate breakfast by candlelight. He was the most popular man in Tuscaloosa. He was Sunday-school superintendent for many years. I never knew a man who could manage a school as well. We hardly knew what we should do when he left."

A pleasant saying of Himrod Vincent's about his wife was long remembered by the two older boys. There was frequent talk in the household concerning the doctrine of "holiness" as expounded by Wesley. Now Mrs. Vincent never professed to have atttained the lofty height implied in the expression as then used, but her husband often said (though not in her presence) "that if any one had attained it certainly mother had."

A quiet, modest, almost shy woman, she was deeply religious and exerted a powerful influence over her boys. With seemingly no worldly traits or desires, she was nevertheless a practical body and a model housekeeper. She was both hospitable and charitable, much beloved by all who knew her. I have no reason to think that she preferred one of her sons above the others, yet am inclined to believe that John was the pride of her heart. Fortunate in being brilliant, he was still more fortunate in having self-control; and though, as we shall see, a problem to himself he was no problem to his parents.

Married at eighteen, Mary Raser Vincent died at the age of forty-nine. Her last illness was brief. Aware that she had not many more minutes to live, she was anxious to keep her reason to the very end, "so that her children might see how a Christian could die." But one portrait of her is in existence. The face is sweet and

[17]

thoughtful; it is the face of a matured woman who has not, however, lost all her girlish traits. Her son remembers that she always dressed with Quakerlike simplicity.

The religious practices of the household were wholesome and regular—family prayers night and morning (never unduly prolonged, I should say), together with exact attendance on the mid-week and Sunday services. Himrod Vincent drifted naturally into the office of Sunday-school superintendent in a neighboring town just as he had done at Tuscaloosa. He liked to review the lesson for the day in the early morning by lamplight; many a time his son found him thus engaged. After breakfast he walked or rode the three miles that separated his house from the schoolroom, and began the session promptly at nine o'clock.

The Vincent home was well stocked with the books that old-fashioned Methodists were in the habit of reading. It may be assumed, therefore, that the atmosphere was on the whole fairly orthodox—orthodox yet far from narrow. Himrod Vincent, bred a Presbyterian, had at an early age revolted from a creed then taught in all its traditional rigor. His wife was brought up in a devout Lutheran family. Both became Methodists in Alabama. Were one to come on some letter or journal showing how great a relief they found in Arminianism one would not be surprised.

While the orthodoxy of the father and mother is not to be questioned, we cannot be sure of that of the grandfather, old Bethuel Vincent, the innkeeper of Milton. His views are believed to have been decidedly lax. He was an admirer of Joseph Priestley, who, as everybody knows, had settled at Northumberland in 1794, and whose teachings had a marked effect on all who were disposed to lean toward "liberality." Priestley's personal attractiveness made him many friends throughout the countryside. The Vincent boys were certainly not brought up to think ill of the famous English Unitarian. As a matter of fact, I have often heard John Vincent speak of Priestley in terms of warm admiration; he had no fear of evil as a result of difference of opinion.

When the boys were as yet too young to attend school, they were taught at home. A sort of governess, a Miss Faries of Milton, was engaged to train them in the rudiments. Under her they learned "reading, spelling, writing, arithmetic, and deportment," as well as "how to speak properly." As for speaking fluently, no less than properly, *that* was their gift. Neither of the two older brothers at any time knew what it meant to be at a loss for words; nor was there ever the least trace of ambiguity in what they said. The youngest of the three was an engaging and ready talker, but being a physician he was only now and then heard in a public address.

John Vincent mentions in their exact order, but without date, the several schools that he attended as a boy—the Milton Academy, the country school at Chillisquaque, and a school in Lewisburg. Much later (1852) he was a student at the Wesleyan Academy at Newark, New Jersey.

His early schoolmasters are briefly characterized in the *Autobiography*. One of them, Jesse Broomall by name, was a Quaker. He wore the customary attire of his sect, but did not use the customary locutions; at any rate, not in the schoolroom. At the first meeting with his pupils he told them that he had only one rule for their government and his own. Having worked their curiosity up to the proper pitch he then said, "The one rule, the wonder-working rule on which I shall base my administration, is this: 'Mind your own business.'" Broomall's notable peculiarity was that he never lost his temper.

Robinson, another teacher, was nearsighted and wore "strong spectacles." Their effect was to make the boy who was merely being looked *at* feel as if he were being looked *through*. Starke, the third, was a flogging master, very positive and over-strict. "He had the rare gift of expectorating tobacco juice from almost any part of the schoolhouse to the stove hearth, with an accuracy which excited the admiration of those of his pupils who had the temerity to look away from their books in order to watch his aim."

Young John Vincent was for a while under a man by the name of Pollock, who impressed him as being both a scholar and a skillful pedagogue. An Irishman, an energetic and impulsive fellow, Pollock was a bundle of nerves; he cannot be said to have chosen the calling best suited to his temperament.

The English grammar used by pupils in these schools was either Kirkman's or Murray's. Their literature was acquired by means of a "reader," a book of selections, and those of a high grade. Through elementary text-books (well illustrated) of astronomy, physics, and chemistry, they picked up some knowledge of those difficult subjects. John Vincent says that he mastered his grammar to the extent of having all the rules and definitions at tongue's end and was able to parse glibly. "I spent months in thus dissecting Milton's *Paradise Lost,* and I nevertheless still revere the poem and its author."

In Latin he went as far as schools of this grade undertook to carry a boy. He "knew the grammar well," and after translating the elementary reading lessons and Cornelius Nepos was put into Cæsar. All the students were required to write English compositions and to declaim.

Academic training of a sort went on out of school hours at the Vincent home. The father called his boys strictly to account in all that related to spoken English. No lapses in pronunciation escaped him. He encouraged them to correct one another. And he went so far as to allow them to correct any infelicities in his own speech, which proves that if somewhat rash he was fair-minded. The likelihood is that they were extremely deferential in their criticisms. One needs only to glance at Himrod Vincent's portrait to learn that he was not the type of man with whom one would take liberties.

They were a reading family. Here is a list of the books to which the boys had access in their father's library; the catalogue, if small, is by no means contemptible. On the shelves might be found the *Encyclopædia Americana* (this should be the work edited by Francis Lieber, fourteen volumes, 1839-47) ; Pitkin's *History of the United States;* Rollin, Gibbon, and Plutarch; Shakespeare, Milton, Bunyan, and *The Spectator;* the poems of Thomson and Pollock; Hervey's *Meditations,* and some book by Lardner, but whether by Dionysius or Nathaniel is not manifest. Himrod Vincent owned as a matter of course certain of Wesley's writings, and it is to be hoped that the *Journal* was among them; also

[21]

Clark's *Commentaries* and a fair collection of religious biography. Doubtless the usual amount of current (and ephemeral) denominational literature found its way to the house.

It will be observed that the above list contains no fiction. One would hardly expect to find the works of the Eighteenth-century novelists and Wesley's *Sermons* cheek by jowl. Scott and Cooper would not have been out of place. One can picture the entire household as absorbed in *The Spy* and *Old Mortality*. I have never heard that Himrod Vincent frowned on books of this nature; he merely regarded them as unprofitable. The boys read *Robinson Crusoe, The Swiss Family Robinson,* and *The Pilgrim's Progress;* the last of the three was not considered fiction.

What the mother liked best to read we know. Among her favorites were the lives of Carvosso, Lady Huntingdon, Lady Maxwell, and other evangelicals, and the writings of Richard Baxter and James Hervey. Her son says of her that "she was not in any sense a literary woman." It may have been so, but any woman professedly "literary" would have envied her the unaffected style of her letters and the grace of her penmanship.

The household was musically inclined. The father had a good singing voice and a correct ear. The boys were like himself in this particular. They could sing when mere children. One of them, on growing up, developed a bass voice of astonishing range, volume, and quality. The lower notes were something to hear and always remember. But he took no lessons and laughed at the suggestion that a talent so marked as his deserved to be cultivated.

It was a great day in the family annals when a piano arrived from Philadelphia and they were able to have an instrumental accompaniment to their songs. The piano belonged to a girl cousin who was staying with them, and who had been trained to an extent that would in a measure justify their estimate of her as "a fine pianist." They were probably not exacting. Of what is loosely called classical music they had little conception. Yet no one of them lacked fundamental musical sense, and their father would have brought the boys up standing had they failed to sing in time and in tune.

Ballads and hymns formed the staple of their domestic concerts. John Vincent never parted with the collection of old-fashioned melodies from which he used to sing when a boy. It was entitled *The Southern Harp,* and came from the publishing house of Parker and Ditson, Boston, 1841. The lyrics are all from one pen, that of Mrs. Mary S. B. Dana. The airs are by various composers, from Mozart and Haydn to the reigning American favorite of the day. Of *Volkslieder* there is a fair assortment. On a flyleaf are written the names of all the children who used to sing from that book.

On reviewing those days, John Vincent came to two conclusions: first, that he lacked boyish companionships and a fair opportunity to enjoy boyish sports—he does not say that he was wholly deprived of either. No two boys will agree as to the exact amount of diversion needed for their health, though they will deplore the inability of parents to see how great the need is. It was a busy life, that in the home by the Susquehanna, with little time for junketings. Amusement of a kind the boys must have had. One of them has been heard, by the present writer, to boast of how he used to skate until he was ready to drop with fatigue. It was a sensible proceeding on his part. Skating must be done when and where there is ice; in our capricious climate nobody can tell how soon a thaw will begin.

His second conclusion, that he was too early impressed by the severe and gloomy side of religion, is much dwelt on in the *Autobiography,* besides being used in many of his talks to young folks to point a moral. One excellent result this early training had, if indeed his state of mind can be referred to the training alone. It led him to employ all of his powers to convince so much of the world as came under his influence that religion, rightly understood, is essentially cheerful and optimistic, and that we do wrong to present it under the color of the lugubrious.

A part of the youthful morbidity of which he speaks may have been no more than the outcome of a strong disinclination to be cut off in his prime. No healthy boy, religious or otherwise, desires prematurely to quit this very amusing world. Yet at the time when John Vincent was about eleven years old general preparations were being made (in America) to leave the planet.

The Adventist excitement was at its height. Grave seniors, men who took no stock in William Miller's predictions, were a little uneasy, and this precocious, introspective lad may well have been so. Schoolboys scared themselves and one another by talking over the impending catastrophe. Recalling that time, John Vincent says: "I used to be filled with an anxiety which no 'consolations of religion' that I knew anything about were able to alleviate."

His fears, like those of other people, were aggravated by the looming up, night after night, of a comet. With that portent in the sky, and Miller proclaiming the end of the world on a near date, and the faithful getting their ascension robes ready, existence seemed rather precarious.

But even when the excitement was at its height there was no variation in John Vincent's daily round. He had his work to do, and it was not entirely confined to the schoolroom. He was active in ways in which a boy in his circumstances would naturally be active. Any boy whose father keeps a country store will, for a time at least, be eager to lend a hand. He will want to spend as many hours as possible at that focus of village life, and will take a keen delight in waiting on customers. This lad differed in no respect from the majority of his kind; and, young as he was, he must have been the sort of chap a busy man would like to have with him behind the counter.

He speaks in the *Autobiography* of having been a clerk in a drug store at Milton, that of his cousin John Raser. This would be subsequent to his first efforts at teaching school. It may be quite true that by the time he was fifteen he had made up his mind to become a minister, but he was well aware that many steps had to be taken before the goal so much as came in sight. One of these many steps was schoolmastering.

CHAPTER III

HE taught in the very schoolhouse where, only the summer before, he himself had been a pupil. A majority of the children were his juniors; there were about thirty of them all told. "I liked the youngsters, and I think the most of them liked me." He remarks that there was very little chastising to do. It is difficult to picture him with the rod in hand, except as a symbol of authority. One discovers by his account of the experiment that he was both methodical and thorough. He gave the pupils certain out-of-school tasks, which they may not have cared for at first, to encourage the habit of home study, and in addition to keeping a record of their work he also kept an accurate record of his own.

The following summer he taught a school at Watsontown, a few miles above Milton. Not far away was the Warrior Run Presbyterian Church, which most of the Vincents in that section attended. Of this second venture, he says: "I think it was a partial success. I know it gave me some experience and made me think that I had hidden away in me somewhere a measure of pedagogic ability."

Either this summer or the next he was captivated by the art of a peripatetic genius who went about the country teaching what was then called "Singing Geography." It seems a droll way of acquiring names and boundaries, as droll as some of our modern methods may appear when viewed with the ironic eye of posterity. John Vincent learned the man's system, and, having persuaded his father to buy him a set of Pelton's maps (to the tune of thirty dollars), went into the business for himself.

Himrod Vincent was not very sympathetic with this venture, neither was he out and out opposed to it; he made but one stipulation—that in his wanderings about the country the youth should always be comparatively near home. In the *Autobiography* are given the names of the four villages where the teacher of "Singing Geography" pursued his temporary calling—Selinsgrove, New Berlin, Lewistown, and McVeytown. To reach any one of them it was not necessary to go far afield.

The pamphlet containing the songs used by the class is a diverting document and undoubtedly rare. No collector of literary curiosities could behold a copy without yearning to possess it. We learn from the text that this adroit method of imparting knowledge originated in Germany. The book itself is pure American. The poet, whoever he was, has kept to the rules in so far as he understood them. One would rather read him than many a modern maker of free verse. He gives one both rhyme and reason. As the teacher migrated from place to place new editions of the pamphlet were struck off. To these the local versifiers contributed. Their effusions were apt to take the form of a parting song.[1]

[1] Their quality can be learned from a single stanza:
"On Pelton's maps by Vincent's aid, these many things we've learned,
And now we hasten to bestow the laurels he has earned.
May fortune's wheel e'er favor him, and may he happy live,
And while he lives, may he enjoy the pleasures virtues give."

The proofs John Vincent gave of being a born teacher led the school board at McVeytown to ask him to take charge of their academy. He accepted, gave a good account of himself, and always looked back on the period of his teaching there as one of the bright spots in his young manhood. The last school that he served was at Mechanicsville, near Colraine Forge. The date that he gives (1850-51) would indicate that he taught through the winter session, but not necessarily through the entire school year.

By this time he was fully convinced that his real vocation was the ministry; clerking and schoolmastering had been, after all, only stop-gaps. One might doubt the wisdom of a choice of profession made at the age of fifteen and have no misgivings as to a decision made at the age of eighteen.

At this point in his personal narrative he feels impelled to criticize somewhat the "home laxity" that allowed him to omit college training as an essential part of preparation for ministerial work. Elsewhere he notes that in that day it was the custom for young men to enter professions without first going to college. They read law in a lawyer's office, passed an examination, and were admitted to the bar. They studied medicine under a competent physician and became doctors. Those who had a call to the ministry (he is speaking of Methodists) "were on examination licensed as local preachers, traveled a circuit under the direction of a senior preacher, took a four years' course of study in theology, Church history, and so forth, . . . and became by vote of the annual conference, first deacons, and two years later, elders, being ordained to these orders by a bishop."

As a matter of fact the amount of preparation required was not inconsiderable, and in the case of a young man who had brains and conscience and a taste for study it was not inadequate. But this particular young man regretted all his life that he had not had a college education. He overestimated its value. He accomplished so much without its help that one cannot see wherein he would have been much better off for four years of grinding at Greek, Latin, and mathematics.

At eighteen he was licensed to exhort. The little document bears the date of March 17, 1850, and is signed T. Tanyhill. It lies before me as I write. John Vincent had a real regard for the man who, in an official sense, started him off on his career. Yet there are slips in the paper that must have caused him to smile. "This is to Authorize John H. Vincent, Jun. to Exhort in the Methodist E. Church so long as his Doctrine, Sperit, and Practice corrispond with the word of God, and the Disciplin of said Church. He being first recommended by the Society of which he is a member."

On June 15 of the same year he was "duly authorized to officiate as a Local Preacher" (this document exhibits none of the orthographical vagaries of its predecessor). The license was twice renewed—in December, 1850, and in October, 1851. The duties assigned him were those of junior preacher on the Luzerne Circuit; his superior was John W. Elliott, an Englishman "well Americanized." In this humble way, as a "circuit rider," he began a series of peregrinations that did not end till he was well past eighty.

The district he had to cover was large. To complete the round, leaving no place unvisited, took about four weeks. He had excellent health, ambition, and a good horse. Along with the usual impedimenta of a traveler he carried books in his saddlebags. While riding through the forests of Pennsylvania he read the *Divina Commedia* (probably in Cary's translation), committed to memory whole pages of Campbell's *The Pleasures of Hope,* and studied the articles on Comte's Positive Philosophy then appearing in the *Methodist Review.* Watson's *Institutes* was one of his roadside companions. When not reading he was outlining the sermons he proposed to give, and even practicing their delivery. He had a free field for elocutionary exercise. The district was thinly populated; a man might ride for hours without meeting another traveler or seeing a farmhouse.

The people to whom he ministered were of the plainest sort—farmers, mechanics, small shop keepers, and miners. They would be called American in a rather exact sense of the word; that is to say, they were the descendants of men who had settled there many years since. Among them was a generous sprinkling of newcomers, all from the British Isles—English, Welsh, and a few Protestant Irish.

The young preacher liked them. "I found," he says, "many a good book on the shelves of humble homes . . . heard many a pathetic story of separation, bereavement, struggle, aspiration." What with his sympathy, democratic friendliness, and humor, to say nothing of his genuine gift for public speaking (oratory of the manliest sort), his coming should have been looked forward to with unalloyed satisfaction.

Himrod Vincent had urged his son not to forget "that back of the pleasant manner and good voice and correct pronunciation there must be sound thought." The advice may not have been needed; it was gratefully remembered.

In after years the son deprecated the use of the word "sermon" as an apt description of the sort of discourse he regularly gave while on circuit; they were no more than "simple talks." They would be simple, sensible, and practical. Never at any time given to preaching above the heads of the congregation, he cannot be supposed to have done so in his period of apprenticeship. He remarks that preaching the same sermon over and over is not always a bad thing to do; "it is likely to lead to revision." Perhaps he agreed with Whitefield, who is said to have said that a sermon was good for nothing until it had been preached at least forty times.

The small square book in which he entered memoranda of the sermons preached before and during his term of circuit riding illustrates his methodical habits. In parallel columns are given the text, the place, the date, and the time of day at which each service was held. There are one hundred and eight of these entries, all in a hand as finished as copperplate. On the occasion of a protracted meeting he would preach on three consecutive days, at other meetings of a like character on alternate days. A preliminary page of notes enables one to follow him through the early stages of the career he elected to follow. They are as brief as they could be made. "Arrived at circuit on Saturday, May 3d, 1851. First sermon at Janesville." And again: "First Quar. meeting held at Beaver Meadow, Carbon Co., May 24th, 1851." And so on to the end of the book. Whatever faults this nineteen-year-old minister may have inherited or acquired, vagueness and garrulity were not among them.

John Vincent always had a good word for the system
under which he got his early training. Well aware that
the system could not be revived, he never failed to point
out its really admirable features, and to tell young men
who were entering the ministry that it was impossible
for them to know how much they had missed by not
having been born earlier. The chances are that they
were glad not to know, except through books and through
the reminiscences of their elders.

From his point of view, the mode of life seemed
touched with the romantic. As a boy he had admired
the traveling preacher both for his oratorical skill (often
considerable) and for his readiness in adapting himself
to his surroundings. The visitor's social gifts would
make a strong impression on any observant lad. And
if, as in his own case, the coming of the circuit rider
meant extra good cheer, the occasion would be none the
less pleasantly remembered. John Vincent does not deny
the mnemonic virtues of "a better supper than usual, a
huge bowl of popcorn in the evening, and an endless
string of good stories."

Circuit riding came to an end before or about the last
week of April, 1852. Two domestic events led to the
breaking up of the home at Chillisquaque, the death of
the mother and that of the adoptive sister, Ann Raser.
The younger woman (Ann Raser could not have been
more than twenty-five) died first; it was long known
that her health was declining. Two days later Mrs.
Himrod Vincent succumbed to what was thought to be
no more than a temporary indisposition. As the family
were returning from the cemetery they were met by a
messenger with the news that she had but a few minutes

more to live. Of all that took place during that unhappy week John Vincent has himself written in a way
to make anything beyond a bare statement of the facts
both unnecessary and presumptuous.

Himrod Vincent removed to Erie and connected himself with the firm of Vincent, Himrod, and Company,
iron founders. His son Bethuel and the two younger
children, Frank and Mary, went with him. John Vincent
went to Newark, "with no definite plan in view," though
confident that work might be found. He was also bent
on prosecuting his studies under conditions more strictly
academic than any he had yet enjoyed. This he could
not hope to do unless he obtained a church position of
some sort; that it was likely to be humble mattered little
to him.

As he packed his books for the last time he made a
list of the contents of each box. The half sheet on which
he penciled the titles of the volumes in "Box One" somehow escaped destruction. There are sixty-eight items;
one half theological, the other half miscellaneous. Con-
dillac's name occurs. The book, however, was not the
Traité sur les Sensations, but an elementary Logic, undoubtedly one of the series prepared at the instance of
Louis XV. A treatise meant for the especial use of the
Duc de Parma had become a common American school
textbook.

John Vincent was fortunate in having kinsfolk in
Newark who gave him a hearty welcome. His ecclesiastical superior put him in charge of the City Mission, and
he lost no time in enrolling himself as a student at the
Newark Wesleyan Institute. A comparatively new undertaking, the school had opened, in 1848, with two

hundred students. By the fourth year the enrollment had more than doubled. Sidera Chase was the principal. The preceptress was Mrs. Mary Fiske Green, the mother of John Fiske the historian. Students were graduated on completing the normal course. One writer speaks of the Institute as having been, in point of fact, "the first Normal School organized in the state of New Jersey."

The Wesleyan Institute was founded partly to counteract the quietly proselytizing influences of schools of other denominations. In New Jersey most of the fitting schools for college were conducted by Presbyterian ministers. These men were attractive, earnest, scholarly, and, strange to say, fully convinced of the immense superiority of Calvinism to Arminianism. The Methodist boys who attended these schools were more likely to matriculate at Princeton than at Middletown. It was hoped by the projectors of the Institute that when once they had a denominational school of their own in good running order fewer boys would stray from the fold in which they had their upbringing.

CHAPTER IV

MINISTRY IN NEW JERSEY

A FORMER registrar of the Wesleyan Institute has described how (in 1852) he made the acquaintance of a certain member of the entering class, and how at that very first meeting he was strongly drawn to him. Here are a few sentences from his narrative:

"One day in said year, as I sat in my little office, a young man about twenty years of age entered, desiring to become a student. I asked his name (to record), and he replied, 'John H. Vincent.' He was rather tall, slender, of fair complexion, of agreeable manners, dignified, self-poised—yet most affable and whole-souled. . . . Forty-four years have passed since that day. Through all these years our friendship has strengthened."

The writer of the above lines, George H. Whitney, was himself a student at the Institute at this time. He had undertaken the care of the office—as many a student is glad to do—to help defray the cost of his education. He prepared for the Wesleyan University at Middletown, Connecticut, was graduated there, taught for a few years, and then entered the pastorate. Later he became the head of the Hackettstown Collegiate Institute.

John Vincent and George Whitney studied their Greek and Latin together—the classes were reading Xenophon and Vergil. They belonged to the same society, the

"Philomathean," and to the same debating club. In their
free hours they took long walks, "and talked and laughed
and planned." The two would sometimes go away to
an outlying charge (Whitney was himself a local
preacher) and divide the Sunday services between them,
one taking the pulpit in the morning, the other in the
evening.

It was in the compact that they should afterwards mer-
cilessly criticize each other. And so they did. That
their friendship survived this test, and was stronger at
the end of almost half a century than when it began,
proves that it was really friendship, not something of
a transitory and superficial character. Whitney says of
his friend, "He was ever 'merciless'—and kind." It appears that he was also "generous," and from the context
one discovers that generosity in money matters is meant.
The young man was open-handed. Neither then nor in
later life was a dollar so precious in his eyes that he
would not gladly part with it if the doing so made for
another's pleasure or comfort.

Although his appointed work lay wholly among the
missions, he would be called on now and then to take
one of the better city pulpits for an evening; Whitney
would go with him and hear the discourse. At the conclusion of one of these services the two young men walked
up the street together. For some time not a word was
uttered. At last Vincent said, "Well?" To which Whitney responded, "You preached only seventeen minutes.
Why so short?" "Because," said his friend, "I could not
think of a single thing to say. I could not think what I
had just said, so I said, 'Let us pray,' and, after a hymn,
dismissed the congregation."

His text on that occasion was, "Ephraim is joined to his idols—let him alone." And if it happened to them afterwards to be passing the church, John Vincent would look up at the handsome edifice and remark, with a comical intonation, *"That* is where I let 'em alone."

As City Missionary he was expected to preach regularly to small gatherings of the faithful in various parts of town. There were too many of these groups for one man to serve. So he made a plan of the missions, enlisted a corps of assistants, and assigned one to each place that lacked a minister. This may have been the custom. Whitney speaks of it as though it were a novelty—at least in respect to completeness—and the sign of a marked gift for organization. It certainly shows John Vincent in a rôle in which he subsequently gained distinction, that of a leader, one who knew how to persuade a body of specialists to work to a common end.

Intimacy with a classmate who was preparing for college and the keen relish he had acquired for academic surroundings rather unsettled him. He half persuaded himself that he would do well to give up preaching for a few years and devote all his energies to "obtaining an education." The glamour of college life was very great, but hardly strong enough in itself to draw him away from the rather monotonous path he had elected to follow. It stood to reason, he argued, that with a collegiate training he would be able to do better work when, after four years, he returned to that same path.

Could he have done as he liked, and not as he must, he would have been found later at Middletown, with his friend Whitney. But he had to look to ways and means. His balance at the bank was probably small, and with all

[37]

his resourcefulness (of which he had an overflowing stock) it was not so easy to increase it.

His father, to whom he freely communicated his doubts and questionings, was sympathetic, though he declined to settle for the young man a point he ought to settle for himself. In reply to a letter in which John Vincent had set forth at length the advantages of a formal academic training, the father wrote: "I notice your argument in favor of a learned ministry; but, really, my son, the appeal is all labor lost. You are not one whit more in favor of a learned ministry than is your father. All he objects to is dependence on learning."

What Himrod Vincent seemed to fear was that his son would pursue bookish culture as an intellectual luxury, as an end in itself rather than as a means to an end. The son believed that he was misunderstood; never for one moment had he assumed that culture alone could be a source of spiritual power.

John Vincent wrote to Bishop Janes for counsel. That he always kept the bishop's reply hardly proves that the advice given in the four closely written pages determined his immediate future. He may have already determined to go on as he had begun, and have asked the opinion of his superior in order to be confirmed in his judgment. The bishop wrote: "I object to a young minister in your circumstances postponing the pastoral work to go to the college or the seminary for these reasons especially."

Then follow the reasons, four in number, the first two so naïve that they would not have convinced a boy of twelve. The other two were well enough. It *was* possible to get into debt for an education and be forced to stagger under the burden for years; and it was also possible for a young preacher to employ his time studiously while managing a church—practical knowledge he was sure to acquire. The bishop's really potent argument is put in the shape of an appeal; there was work to do *now,* and in this rapidly growing country it was difficult to get as many men as were needed.

The letter was dated February, 1853. The following April the young man to whom it was written was admitted on trial, as the phrase goes, to membership in the New Jersey Conference. He would now be styled, quite properly, the Reverend John H. Vincent. Long before this date he had become familiar with the appellation. It appeared regularly in his father's flowing hand on the backs of letters. The abbreviation "Jr." was always subjoined, notwithstanding the fact that the middle name of the one man was Himrod and that of the other Heyl.

There is a sequel to this brief tale of John Vincent's efforts to find a solution of the problem that most vexed him during the winter of 1852-53. For my part I cannot see that the problem did not in large measure settle itself. Some freedom of choice he had, though not a great deal. The state of his exchequer would hardly have justified his entering college. His father, now aiming to establish himself in a business new to him, might indeed have said, "Since you are positively bent on being 'educated,' draw on me for three or four hundred a year." That in the circumstances he should have made so rash an offer is inconceivable. Had the young man gone to Middletown it must have been at his own risk. This he would have minded little had he been sure it was his duty to go. He was not at all sure, and besides, there were opportunities for being immediately useful where he was. At all events he cannot be said to have taken the line of least resistance.

The sequel of the tale is that he had not been in active pastoral work three years when he began drawing up a scheme of study for "out-of-school theological candidates." It was to embrace courses of public lectures supplemented by private reading. Designed to stimulate those whose opportunities, like his own, had been limited, it was the earliest of the innumerable plans he made in the interest of self-culture. One of these plans, as we know, became popular.

He was sent to North Belleville (the name of the town was later changed to Nutley) and served the church there for two years. It was a small charge. When John Vincent took it in hand the rolls could account for only sixty-seven members and five probationers. At the end of the ecclesiastical year the membership had increased to seventy-five, with thirty-five probationers. That so diminutive a body could actually support a pastor is surprising.

At the close of the second year (and of his pastorate) the enrollment was only a trifle larger. Over against the small numerical increase may be set the encouraging fact that he had housed his people in a new church. The present handsome edifice at Nutley, built about 1911, was named in John Vincent's honor.

His bishop then appointed him to Camptown, now called Irvington (after Washington Irving), a village in 1855, but in time to become a populous residential suburb of Newark. He was now a deacon, and would attain to the dignity of elder the following year. Though he

began work with a larger membership than that at North
Belleville (it numbered about a hundred) he was fated
to see it reduced one-half by colonization. The outgoing
body, fortunately for him, did not migrate until the end
of the twelvemonth.

Their departure may have been one of the causes that
led John Vincent to seek a more promising field of labor
in the Middle West. This is mere conjecture; there is
nothing in his extant papers to prove it a fact.

He should have been pretty busy with his studies during these months, as well as with pastoral visitation and
sermon-making. The examiners provided plenty of work.
In the first year a candidate for deacon's orders took
up the doctrines (thirty-four in number, beginning with
"The Existence of God" and ending with "Rewards and
Punishment"), and qualified himself to state them accurately and to support them by Scriptural proof. During
the second year he took up the sacraments in the same
manner, explained the eight points specified, and de-
fended them by pertinent texts. So much of the course
at least meant a study of original sources. To what
extent a candidate would be able to divest himself of
prejudice and draw firsthand conclusions is a question.

He read, among other books, parts one and two of
Watson's *Theological Institutes.* He would not be required to peruse the *Observations on Mr. Southey's "Life
of Wesley,"* a famous work in its day. Even the Prince
Regent—who knew a good book when he saw one—
looked into it and remarked afterward, "Mr. Watson
has the advantage over my Laureate."

The *Institutes* have long since been dropped from the
list of required readings, and only those who are curi-

ous about polemics will spend any time on the *Observations*.

Fletcher's *Appeal to Matter of Fact and Common Sense* formed a part of the course, as did also Wesley's *Plain Account of Christian Perfection*. Collateral readings were provided for. The examinations were conducted by a committee of six ministers. Each candidate was expected to make a good showing in history, modern geography, and English grammar as well as in theology.

The chief subject in the course for the next degree was Bible history. Parts three and four of the *Institutes* were read, and a sermon or an essay presented to the committee. Whether the young men were called strictly to account or let off with a few comparatively easy questions must have depended pretty much on the examiners individually.

At Camptown, John Vincent inaugurated his "Palestine Class," a Saturday afternoon meeting, open to all who cared to attend, the object of which was the study of sacred history and geography. Doctrinal and denominational topics were strictly taboo, and the zealot who gave signs of being about to bring up such topics probably had short shrift. Not only was the time-honored method of question and answer employed, but a new feature was introduced. It consisted in the use of songs—the inventor calls them "chants"—as an aid to the memory. With a large wall map before them the class acquired knowledge by intoning it. The rhythmical swing and the strong body of sound produced by simultaneous repetition stamped the facts indelibly on the mind.

Here came into play the instructor's experience as a teacher of "Singing Geography." He could defy anyone who had fairly tried his system of mnemonics ever to forget the subdivisions of Asia Minor, let alone a multitude of other facts.

The Palestine Class was graded. Each grade had its name, a name indicative of the degree of progress supposed to have been made. The assignment of pupils to this grade or the next higher was not done by guesswork. Examinations were held, a record kept, and the candidates ranked according to their proficiency. A student who had attained the status of "Resident" was not exactly in possession of a sinecure. As a resident, not of Palestine in general but of a specified town, he was expected to make himself a storehouse of information as to that town's geographical position, history, and famous characters. His associates might draw on him *ad libitum*. This should have led to a great overhauling of Kitto's *Pictorial History* and similar works; Smith's *Dictionary* was not yet published.

As long as he stayed in the pastorate John Vincent made use of this device for awakening interest in what may be described as the secular side of the Bible, that part of it that belongs to general history, including the history of manners and customs. What a man of ten times his learning might have failed in he did readily. He was an ardent student, his knowledge was serviceable, his memory strong, and he had extraordinary verve. Meant primarily to attract young people, the classes drew in mature men and women of all ages. There was a good deal of sociability among the members. He himself once spoke of his Palestine Class as a "delightful fraternity," and then qualified the remark by adding that as a matter of fact it was "more nearly a sorosis."

CHAPTER V

HE was ordained an elder by Bishop Levi Scott at the meeting of the New Jersey Conference in April, 1857, and at his own request was immediately transferred to the Rock River Conference, Illinois. A personal motive entered into the business. Himrod Vincent had left Erie to take charge of the Chicago branch of his house. He wished to have his son near him. As the ecclesiastical authorities had no objection to offer, the change was made.

John Vincent was first stationed at Joliet, a church of a hundred and thirty-five members and twenty-three probationers. At the end of a year he had brought the total enrollment up to something over two hundred. He afterwards served churches at Mount Morris, Galena, Rockford, and Chicago. At no one of these towns did he remain more than two years. The extreme limit of service was just that, and no man was greatly astonished to find himself shifted at the end of a twelvemonth.

A Palestine Class was organized at each of these places but one. At intervals was held what the leader called an "Exhibition"; to wit, a miscellaneous program of recitations, music, responsive readings, together with a résumé of the work done. It was a public affair. The pupils were incited by the presence of outsiders to make

the best possible showing. The performance was anal-
ogous to the familiar close-of-school exercises, when parents were wont to be regaled with declamations, essays,
and the inevitable overture to the *Caliph of Bagdad*
or *William Tell,* rendered by the energetic fingers of
two well-meaning young girls.

A number of the old programs of these "Exhibitions"
have been preserved. One is headed "Life in the Mediterranean," another "Life in Egypt." The leader held
that to obtain the best results the class must be drilled
in a single topic until they knew it. He had many sound
pedagogical notions.

With his power of calling up a vivid picture of these
groups of young people with whom he was once associated, and even of the individuals composing them, John
Vincent was not likely to forget the class at Joliet.
Through some of the members he first heard of Miss
Elizabeth Dusenbury, who had recently taught there in
the high school, and had been forced to leave on account
of illness. "The praise they lavished upon her fidelity
and earnestness," he says, "prepared me to appreciate
her when we met."

His appreciation was so great that after no very
lengthy acquaintance he asked the young lady to marry
him. She consented, and the wedding took place at
Portville, New York, on November 10, 1858. The bride
was a daughter of Henry Dusenbury of Portville. Coming of an old and well-to-do family, she is said to have
met with some opposition on the part of her parents
when she took up the profession of teaching. And the
young ladies of her circle were not a little astonished that
she, who had been brought up in decidedly easy circum-

stances, should elect to share the lot of a young Methodist preacher living on a small salary.

A pleasant anecdote relating to the wedding is still current. The officiating minister was noted for his habit of giving advice on occasions such as this, of being both personal and prolix. Neither of the contracting parties had a mind to be married and lectured to, all in one breath. A wedding breakfast was to follow the ceremony. It was therefore arranged by the bride and groom that they two should stand at one end of the long breakfast table and the minister at the other. This disposition of the principals turned out to be perfect. It was possible to marry a pair at that distance; to buttonhole them afterwards was quite out of the question.

Of Mrs. John H. Vincent much might be written, and all in her praise. She had a strong intellect; she was even-tempered, generous, sympathetic. I should say that she was an absolutely just woman. Doubtless there have been many of her sex who resembled her in this trait, but one rarely meets her like. And furthermore, she carried common sense to the point of genius. She was an acute judge of human nature. I doubt whether she was ever imposed on. In the days of her husband's greatest popularity she had to meet, and dispose of, an endless procession of callers, each of whom had some private ax to grind. There were harmless charlatans among them—the most irritating specimen of the genus bore. She saw through them at once and was able to save her husband the time he might have lost by seeing through them for himself; it would have taken him longer than it did her. The pretenders departed, quite content with their reception and unaware that they had been correctly appraised.

A capital talker on a great variety of topics, Mrs. Vincent never uttered an idle word or made a loose statement; if she said that a thing was thus and so one might depend on her being in the right. Yet she was never dogmatic. Somewhat reserved at a first meeting—a dull-witted person might have pronounced her cold—she was the soul of kindness.

Of her almost passionate fondness for the best literature her acquaintances were well aware. All her life she was an indefatigable reader. No work was so formidable that she hesitated to attack it. She was the only person I ever met who had read Carlyle's *Frederick the Great*. We all read *in* it, very few of us see our way to going through the gigantic biography. But she read every line of it—for the pure intellectual pleasure of so doing. A friend once found her deep in Milman's *History of Latin Christianity*. It was the sort of reading she liked. She read aloud to her son, during the years of his boyhood and early youth, all the novels of Scott, Dickens, Thackeray, and George Eliot; this should have meant for her a second or third reading of the majority of them.

Her sister tells this characteristic anecdote of her. It seems that Elizabeth Dusenbury was addicted to books at a very tender age, and one is glad to learn that among her favorites were *Thaddeus of Warsaw* and *The Scottish Chiefs*, romances of which the present unenlightened generation of children knows nothing. There was a small circulating library in the town, and the little girl rifled it of these and other treasures. Taking her prize of the hour with her she would hide under a tall four-poster that had a valance about it. Safe from observation and interruption, she was able to take her fill of the literature she most enjoyed. She sought out this retreat simply from a wish not to be disturbed, and not because any objection was made to her reading stories. She wanted to give her whole mind to her book.

John Vincent and his wife began their married life at Mount Morris. To him the place was extremely attractive because of its being a sort of educational center, the seat of the Rock River Seminary. He relished the atmosphere of a town where students congregated. The school was denominational and many of the young people attended his church. This may account for the size of the membership—two hundred and twenty-five, with nearly a hundred probationers. And it would certainly account for the fluctuation in the membership. Students come and go. A class is graduated and the church as well as the school loses a dozen or so of members. The losses are not always made up at the opening of the next fall term.

With professors near at hand the new pastor hoped to find, and did find, an opportunity to do some private academic work. For example, he took lessons in New Testament Greek and attended all the lectures that were offered at the seminary. Had he been allowed to stay at Mount Morris the full legal term he would have been well pleased. But the bishop thought best to appoint him to the Bench Street Church at Galena.

The change was looked on as a promotion. If not large numerically, Galena was an active town; so promising in fact that at one time it was pronounced (by not wholly disinterested people) the rival of Chicago. The name it bears was given the town in 1826, presumably after the discovery of the deposits of zinc and lead in the vicinity. French settlers knew the place as La Pointe. It is picturesquely situated on rocky bluffs above the river. One of the first companies to enlist for the Civil War, the Jo Daviess County Guards, was recruited in and about Galena.

John Vincent recorded with his customary precision the moment when he took up his new duties. The last sermon at Mount Morris was preached on Sunday, October 16. "On the Tuesday after I went to Galena and was present at the prayer meeting on Wednesday, giving an address on 'Prayer' to my new people."

The references in the *Autobiography* to this period of his life are marked by a note of joyousness. He recalls the names of many parishioners and makes a thumb-nail sketch of this one or that—a lawyer, a bookseller, a fun-loving Sunday-school superintendent, and a certain staunch supporter of the Church who carefully avoided all the means of grace except the morning sermon. The roll of his Palestine Class lay before him as he wrote; he had preserved it carefully for nearly fifty years.

At Galena began his lifelong friendship with Ulysses S. Grant. Though not a member of the Bench Street Church, or of any church, Grant was a regular attendant. Shortly after settling at Galena, and before he had had time to become well acquainted with his congregation, John Vincent spent a few days at Joliet with one of his old parishioners. While there, he says, "I met a gentleman from Kentucky, a Mr. Grant, who said to me, 'I see that you have been appointed minister of the Methodist Church in Galena. I am interested in that place because I have a son there—my son Ulysses—who was for several years in the army, and is now in the leather business with his brother in Galena. I hope you will look him up and pay him some attention.'" The gentleman from Kentucky was, of course, Jesse R. Grant, who then lived at Covington, opposite Cincinnati.

John Vincent first saw the future Lieutenant-General and President at Dubuque, whither he had gone on a church mission of some sort. He arrived late on a Saturday evening and put up at the principal hotel.

"As I stood by the great stove just after breakfast on Sunday morning," he writes, "I noticed a short, compactly built man in an army overcoat, who at the time put me in mind of the familiar picture of Napoleon. . . . Almost immediately he came and spoke to me, calling me by name. He said, 'I hear you preach every Sunday. My name is Grant.' As I had been in Galena for a very short time I did not feel condemned for not recognizing him. I replied, 'I am glad to see you, for just before leaving Joliet I met your father, who spoke of you as being a resident of Galena.'

"He was going over to his home that morning, and knowing that my wife was somewhat anxious about my having to cross the Mississippi at night through islands of floating ice, and as Captain Grant lived but a short distance from my house, I asked him to call at the parsonage and assure Mrs. Vincent of my safe arrival. This he did.

"After that interview I did not fail to keep my

eyes on the 'little corporal' in the blue army over-coat. He always gave close attention, thanks to his military training. "

If not exactly loquacious, Grant seems to have been ready enough to talk when he had a subject and a listener of the right sort. At that first meeting at Dubuque, his comments on the stirring events of the day made a strong impression on the young minister.

When (on April 25, 1861) the Jo Daviess County Guards, accompanied by Captain Grant, left Galena for Springfield, it fell to John Vincent as representative of the townspeople to make the farewell address. He spoke from the top of a freight car. The speech was one of the sort invariably described by enthusiastic reporters as "ringing." One of the few surviving witnesses of the little scene (he was a boy at that time) remembers dis-tinctly all the details—the speaker's appearance, certain telling sentences that he uttered, the enthusiasm of the crowd, and how Mrs. Grant and her daughter stood at an open window of the railway station, looking on.

Later in the morning John Vincent called on Mrs. Grant. They seem to have had a spirited talk, almost a contention, "on North, South, slavery, and so forth," but which of the two primarily disagreed with the other does not come out in the narrative. "At last I said, 'Well, Mrs. Grant, we won't discuss this question. I hope your husband will be restored to you in safety.' She promptly and with some warmth replied, 'Dear me! I hope he'll get to be a major general or something big.' I was amused at her courage and ambition and optimism."

When he met her in Washington four years later,

under very different circumstances, he reminded her of her confidence in her husband before his war record had justified her high hopes. Her response was, "I always knew what was in him if he only had a chance along with the other fellows."

In the *Autobiography* occurs this description of the vivacious lady: "Mrs. Grant was a strong woman, refined, accustomed to the best society, outspoken, an ideal mother, a loyal wife, in every way a worthy, positive, interesting woman—a bit abrupt now and then, but always a lady. She was as faithful to her children as she was appreciative of her husband."

Among Bishop Vincent's papers only two letters from Grant were found. Neither is so terse as might have been expected. In the one written from Cairo, September 25, 1861, Grant regrets that he is not able to address his correspondent from a point much farther south. "Our victories both at Springfield and at Lexington have been great when properly viewed. They have caused great sadness, but proved that in a contest with anything like equal numbers a just cause would be half the battle. Our troops are not disheartened, but I fear from the tone of the press our citizens are; partially so at least."

The letter dated from the camp near Corinth, Mississippi, May 25, 1862, is not of enough importance to be quoted in its entirety. It shows a genuine affection for the young minister. Of himself Grant says: "I never asked for any position or rank, but—with my whole soul in the cause of the Union, willing to sacrifice everything in the cause, even my life if need be for its preservation— it has been my good fortune to render some service to the cause and my very bad luck to have attracted the attention of newspaper scribblers. It certainly never was my desire to attract public attention but *has* been my desire to do my whole duty in this just cause.

"I was truly rejoiced at receiving a letter from you and hope it will not be the last. If you make your expected trip to Palestine it would afford me the greatest pleasure to hear from you from that far-off land, and to reply punctually to all your letters. . . ."

Of John Vincent's meeting with Grant in Virginia, at the exact close of the Civil War, a brief account will be given later. It is described in letters to Mrs. Vincent— letters which, though mainly personal and private, contain some graphic touches. In a memoir such as this it seems but right to quote a few paragraphs.

His term of service at Galena having come to an end in October, 1861, he was assigned to the Court Street Church at Rockford. The following year he was able to carry out a long-cherished plan for attending the General Sunday-School Convention in London and afterwards making a trip to Palestine. Of the great value to him in his work of such a journey there could be no question. As a delegate to the Convention (he was to go in that capacity) he would have an opportunity to meet, under favorable conditions, the delegates from foreign countries —the British Isles, the Provinces, and three or four continental nations. He was already booked for an address. The time seemed not unpropitious; no one imagined that the war, serious as it was, could become so much more serious and be prolonged for years. And he could command enough money to see him through; in the early Sixties a man was not wholly debarred from travel because his income happened to be small.

Nothing can be more dreary than to wander about Europe alone, but John Vincent expected to do that very thing. His surprise and pleasure were great when a Rockford acquaintance, a young man by the name of Robert Tinker, the son of a Presbyterian minister, proposed going along with him. Born in the Sandwich Islands, educated in America, fun-loving and even-tempered, Tinker proved to be a traveling companion of the right sort. He was something of an artist; in addition to writing a clever letter he could embellish it with no less clever sketches.

On the eve of sailing, Tinker disclosed the fact that, while fully expecting his companion to choose a berth in what part of the ship he would, he himself had made arrangements to go in the steerage. The companion was properly shocked to hear this but soon recovered. The upshot of the matter was that they both went that way. The one was forced (so he thought) to economize, and the other was too chivalrous to desert a friend.

Knowing John Vincent's fastidious taste and his preference for luxurious appointments in a public conveyance, I cannot believe that he quite liked his environment. He professes to have been perfectly comfortable on the voyage. His fellow passengers, he says, were "ministers, school-teachers, students, and business men," all of whom were willing to dispense with the honor of going first class in order to save their money. The table was plain, markedly so, but not unpalatable.

A fairly good sailor, he was spared the worst of the indignities to which travelers on the high seas may be subject. One has a right to distinguish between the state known as "having slight qualms," or "not feeling so well as usual," or "being indifferent to one's meals," and that unequivocal condition when one is absolutely prostrate and knows it.

The boat—it was the *Glasgow,* of the Liverpool, New York, and Philadelphia Steamship Company—left New York on July 5, at three in the afternoon, and arrived at Queenstown in the evening of July 17. In penning the account of this voyage, John Vincent dryly remarks that he has "never widely advertised" the circumstances under which he made his first trip across the Atlantic.

CHAPTER VI

THE record of the trip was kept in five little blank books, each containing about eighty-five pages. The handwriting is exquisite, but often so fine that a reading glass is needed if one would go through the narrative with any degree of comfort.

Other entries are made in addition to the regular notes of travel—a list of addresses, tables of distances, an accurate record of money paid out and for what purpose, memoranda of the objects of interest to be seen in this town or that, a list of the sermons preached and where, prose extracts, many poetical quotations, always apropos and no doubt set down from memory. One volume contains, in a third of a page, a complete abstract of the novel of *Rob Roy*. The travelers were in Scotland at the time and had discovered that there is no better guidebook than a stirring romance.

In short, the journals are not only informing but a model of conciseness, a capital illustration of the way in which any man of sense might, if he were so minded, make the best use of his opportunities. In spite of their precision and the multitude of dates the little books are anything but pedantic or stiff. They abound in descriptions and historical references, yet are agreeably human, occasionally blunt, and always entertaining. It is evident from their frankness that they were not meant to be printed, only to serve as reminders of an interesting journey.

The travelers landed at Queenstown and went at once to Cork. Newsboys were crying, *Morning Herald,* sir —all about the American war, sir—it's only a penny, sir." They saw Blarney Castle, Killarney, and Muckross. At the Gap of Dunloe the "mountain-dew girls" followed them, expatiating on the merits of what they had to sell, whisky and goats' milk; "but failed in every attempt to get anything into or out of us." Turning eastward they went, via Mallow, to Dublin, saw all the customary sights there, made an excursion to Bray and Wicklow, and then started for the north of Ireland.

At Belfast they went over one of the great linen factories ("we were conducted by Mr. Mackie, a Wesleyan") and visited a model school. The school appeared to be well organized and well equipped, but the noise made by the pupils was deafening and the brogue used by the teachers of a most aggravated character. The journey to the Giant's Causeway involved, so says the journal, sixty-eight miles by rail and eight miles on foot; I have not verified the figures. Eight miles are not so much. The tramp that day was a mere foretaste of what was in store for them. The two Americans did, first and last, a prodigious amount of walking.

At every place to which he went John Vincent sought out the ministers of his denomination, preached in their chapels, and made brief talks in their Sunday-schools. In the south of Ireland he addressed one congregation of twenty people, probably the entire membership. Having mistaken the hour at which a certain Sunday-school was held, he arrived just as it was dismissed. It consisted of one teacher and three pupils.

Leaving Ireland, the travelers crossed to Stranraer on Loch Ryan. The three or four hours' passage was more deadly in its effects than the whole voyage across the Atlantic had been. "After tea," says the diarist, "I wrote awhile and then went to a Presbyterian Church (this being a fast day). A young, red-whiskered, deep-brogued man preached a plain sermon in a cold, affected, self-complacent way."

The journal contains many such entries, not all of them critical by any means—if by that we are to understand hypercritical. There is a pen picture of a minister of the Free Church at Inverness: "The preacher is about thirty-five. Long, stiff, grayish hair which he handles a good deal with one of the prettiest and softest looking hands I ever saw. He displays his hands too much. . . . He talks and acts like a spoiled child who has been petted a good deal but who is on the whole a very good sort of babe." An analysis of the sermon follows. It is complimentary in the extreme. The "babe" knew how to preach.

John Vincent was curious to learn what he could about the "Morisonians," and when spending a Sunday in Glasgow went to their church. Morison himself was present, but took no part in the service beyond making the prayer. The journal for that day contains a minute personal description of this able and amiable man, who has been pronounced "of all Scottish sect makers the least sectarian."

I will outline the route of the two Americans, though it differs little if at all from that of tourists in general.

From Ayr and Mauchline (where they saw everything that related in any way to Burns, including the Masonic lodge into which he was initiated) they proceeded to Glasgow, took a steamer up the lake, climbed Ben Lomond, and then went on to Inverary and Oban. A walk of twenty-five miles is chronicled on one of these days. It includes the ascent of Ben Lomond. After viewing the Pass of Glencoe they turned southward and made their way by Dunkeld, Perth, and Stirling to Edinburgh. The usual excursion through the Trossachs ("tame after what we had seen further north") and to Loch Katrine was religiously made. What most strikes one in the descriptions of these overfamiliar places is their freshness and unconventionality. If there is no absolutely new word, the hackneyed phrase and the trite reflection are at least avoided.

The four days in Edinburgh and the vicinity were spent pretty much as people do spend their time when paying a first visit to the romantic city. One day was devoted to Abbotsford and Melrose Abbey. John Vincent's admiration of Scott was great, but not so great as to exclude other admirations, as the following extract will show: "I was anxious to see Buccleuch Place, in which Sydney Smith had rooms when the *Edinburgh Review* was projected. This is a very quiet and comfortable-looking part of town. It has more the appearance of elegance and domestic retirement than any street we chanced to see in the Old Town. The houses are of stone. . . . The moss was upon the stones in the street. I was glad to stand there for Sydney Smith's sake."

They left Edinburgh for York on August 18, and

[59]

reached the cathedral city at two in the morning. Not a bed was to be had at any hotel. A policeman took them to what he called "a dramshop." There they found the proprietor, his wife and baby, and a friend sitting about a table; the friend was fortified with a mug of ale. "Every bed in this establishment was also full and the landlord permitted us to occupy the benches of his beer shop. So stretching ourselves on these hard beds we slept a little. At five I rose and walked about the town." The humor of the situation was not lost on John Vincent; a line in his expense account reads, "Bench and breakfast, one shilling and threepence."

The two friends arrived in London on August 22, having had glimpses en route of Manchester, Kenilworth, Warwick, and Stratford. Hard put to it to find a place to sleep, they at last secured one "through the influence of Clayton's Hotel." They presented themselves at the office of the Sunday-School Union, were kindly received by the officials in charge, and then began their explorations of the town.

On the Sunday following, John Vincent had an opportunity to hear Spurgeon, and thought his preliminary exposition of a psalm better than the formal discourse. He describes the sermon thus: "Plain, tedious, well delivered, and an apparently forced earnestness. Too many words. I do not think he could have gained his reputation on such sermons. He is earnest and talented, with a fine voice, and is no doubt very pious. I was better pleased than I expected to be with the man, but not so well pleased with the sermon."

In a little talk he had with Spurgeon—possibly at this very time—he asked the celebrated preacher when he expected to visit America. Spurgeon replied, with a smile, "After the Day of Judgment."

The Sunday-School Convention began on September 1, with an afternoon session, and closed on the evening of September 5. Most of the meetings were held at the building of the Sunday-School Union, 56 Old Bailey. One public gathering took place at Exeter Hall. In addition to the two hundred and seventy-eight English delegates from town and country, there were present representatives from Canada, the United States, France, Italy, Switzerland, and Australia. Of the thirteen foreign delegates, seven were Americans.

John Vincent gave his principal address at a public meeting of the Convention held on September 2 at the Mansion House, in the so-called Egyptian Hall, a room famous for the aldermanic banquets so often described by novelists and satirists. The general topic for the evening was "The State and Prospects of Sunday-Schools Abroad." His speech reads in the report as though it had been written out in full and were delivered from manuscript. He was, however, quite capable of giving, without the aid of a single note, a forty-minute address characterized by the same precision of statement, logical joining of the parts, and not unpleasing formality of the English that may be observed in this one.

In paying his tribute to Robert Raikes, he could not forbear telling his auditors that thirty years before the experiment at Gloucester was made, a Pennsylvanian of Lancaster, one Ludwig Thacker, started a Sunday-school and kept it going. "But we, with you, understand that it was Raikes who gave the first impulse to the general Sunday-school work of the present age."

He took part in one of the afternoon conferences on the training of teachers. At another sitting, he explained the theory and work of the Palestine Class. By the name itself he set no great store. Let them call it what they would; but let them have the thing, or something very like it. The report of the Convention shows that he was one of the speakers at the final meeting, a social affair in part—with mitigations in the shape of tea, coffee, and buns—the sort of affair described in the Victorian period as a *soirée*. Educational features were not wanting to the evening's entertainment. In addition to oratory and tea the committee provided an exhibit that comprised illuminated missals, rare Bibles, autograph letters, maps, prints, and models of the Tabernacle in the Wilderness and of Solomon's Temple.

From London he went to Paris, and from there to Geneva. John Vincent's method of sight-seeing in Paris was to walk to all the points that could be easily reached, and where the distances were great to take a *voiture* and practice his French on the driver. He never remitted his efforts to get some command over the language of his forefathers—a language so easy to read and so elusive when one tries to speak it.

From Geneva he made excursions to Chamounix, Martigny, and to the Hospice of St. Bernard. Rarely does he allow himself in his notes and descriptions to become florid. The account of the hospice is restrained, graphic, and distinctly "literary." It is agreeable reading, barring the passage on the charnel house. And that could not be agreeable, if faithfully done, no matter who wrote it.

Up to this point in the Swiss tour the party had consisted of some half a dozen Americans. When they broke up and went their several ways, John Vincent and Robert Tinker spent a while in rambling about that over-described part of the country of which Lucerne is the center.

The district is really beautiful, neither of the two suffered from a jaded taste, and there was no kill-joy of a globe-trotter at hand to pity them for taking pleasure in what he himself had learned to pronounce tame. So they climbed the Rigi in peace, lost their way and missed the sunset by being five minutes too late, missed the sunrise the next morning because it was cloudy, and in the main followed a course that to them was none the less agreeable for being perfectly orthodox.

One day, as they were viewing the celebrated Lion of Lucerne, a gentleman who recognized them for Americans spoke to them. It was William C. Wilkinson, lately pastor of a Baptist church at New Haven. He was John Vincent's junior by one year. The acquaintance begun then soon ripened into friendship.

They were unlike in many ways, and the unfeigned satisfaction they took in each other's society would be surprising were there not so many known instances of comradeship between opposites. In Wilkinson the critical faculty was overdeveloped and his talk revealed more than a trace of the sardonic (I speak from hearsay, not from personal knowledge). Now Vincent, being ardent, optimistic in spite of an inherited tendency to melancholy, and disposed always to praise in glowing terms that which he really admired, may have enjoyed his friend's skill in cool and cutting analysis, as well as his zeal in quenching enthusiasms, his own no less than those of other people. Wilkinson would say, when confronted by some univer-

[63]

sally acknowledged marvel of architecture or scenery,
"Well, Vincent, here's your chance; let yourself go."

The three companions agreed to make the journey
to Italy together. They set out on October 2, and walked
all the way from Fluellen to Bellinzona. The distance is
set down in their itinerary as being about seventy-six
miles. Nothing is said in the journal about their getting
footsore or exhausted. These three youngish men belonged to that "fourth estate" of which Thoreau speaks;
namely, Walkers, an estate "outside of Church and State
and People." He also remarks that Walkers are born,
not made.

The notes relating to Milan, Venice, Bologna, Flor-
ence, and the intermediate points are carefully written
and go into detail. Among other entries is an account
of a visit to Powers's studio and a talk with the sculptor.
Powers was a Unionist and an Abolitionist. "He says we
have been blistering, poulticing, bathing, compromising,
and so forth. He demands the knife now."

The journey from Leghorn to Civita Vecchia meant a
night on the Mediterranean. It was not uncomfortable;
the sea was calm and there was a moon. At the landing,
the customs officers subjected their baggage to a close
examination. "They searched chiefly for tobacco, pictures of Garibaldi, and 'ideas.' "

Not to desire, on the occasion of one's first visit to
Rome, to see the Colosseum by moonlight means that
one is either old or blasé, and possibly both. It is to the
credit of the travelers that they made their way to the
Colosseum the very night of their arrival. They found
the entrance guarded by French soldiers; no one was
admitted without a special permit. That they had reached

a principality where they were not free to do as they liked became apparent on Sunday. Desiring to worship God in their simple provincial way they discovered that they could only do so at the American consulate, and then only if the Stars and Stripes hung over the preacher's head.

The tourists spent nineteen profitable days in Rome, four days in Naples and the environs, and then took a steamer for Marseilles. John Vincent's destination was Paris; the proposed trip to the East had for the moment been given up, possibly for the lack of funds.

Neither he nor his friend Wilkinson had more than enough cash on hand to see them through the next stage of their journey. The story goes that when they went to the office of the steamship company, to engage their passage, they found that they could not afford a state-room or any sort of place among the cabin passengers. The company's circular gave three rates—the price of a cabin passage, the price of a deck passage, and the rate for the transportation of dogs. Wilkinson read it through and grimly remarked, "Vincent, we have just enough to go as dogs."

The officials, once the situation was explained to them, showed a disposition to be generous. The Americans were allowed the freedom of the deck, with the priv-ilege of going into the hold in case of a storm. John Vincent alternated between the two forms of torture. An entry in the journal reads: "To-night it is very rough and the boat rolls disagreeably. Tried to sleep on deck but could not. So into the hold again." In which place he was no less uncomfortable than he had been at a first trial of its merits. He was annoyed, too, to find that in descending he had got his gloves covered with fresh paint. Some one should explain the origin of that custom of painting exposed places in a boat just before the passengers come aboard.

The Americans had provided their own food, or the greater part of it. Only biscuits are mentioned in the narrative. "Mr. W. had polenta this morning; it was amusing to see him eat it." In Howells's account of a voyage in one of the small Mediterranean boats, "sardines and fruit pie" have a conspicuous place among the available viands. These would be costly dishes, and quite beyond the reach of the clergy.

In Paris (where he spent the next five weeks), John Vincent had time for more sight-seeing and for regular lessons in French. He did the museums and galleries thoroughly, much as a man might do them who expected never to be in Paris again, and he was vastly diverted by the shops, the people, and all the life of the streets. Having friends in the city he did not lack for companionship; but his evenings were mainly spent in study, private correspondence, and the writing of letters for the home newspapers. In consequence the weeks slipped rapidly away. His hope of making a pilgrimage to the Holy Land revived. The obstacles, whatever they may have been, now seemed likely to be overcome.

Naturally curious to obtain a glimpse of Louis Napoleon, he was so fortunate one day as to meet that enigmatic personage almost face to face. "He was walking with three other gentlemen—he leaned on the arm of one. Dressed in citizen's clothes, a plain suit of gray, the sack coat tightly buttoned, he wore lemon-colored kid gloves and carried a small cane. He is short and rather stout—has a very ungraceful walk—a sort of lameness which is scarcely lameness, yet I don't know how else to describe it. His face is very pale and seemed careworn. He is much older than I supposed. He bowed to all who lifted the hat to him and did it in a quiet, mechanical way. Quite a crowd followed him."

The tourist in his rounds encountered the Emperor a second time and had another good look at him. He thought himself well treated that day, in his quality of insatiable sight-seer, and was little prepared for a spectacle that offered itself within the next hour.

Returning to the hotel from a long walk, he halted for an instant at the corner of a street near the Arc de Triomphe. Two carriages, with outriders, rapidly approached, each drawn by six horses. In the first sat the Empress with a lady of her suite. The American promptly uncovered. His salute was acknowledged with a most gracious bow. He always insisted that this bow of Eugénie's was his private property, he being the only person at that corner when the carriages passed. His family scouted the claim when he made it, using mocking words, as is the way of families. He was not to be shaken in his conviction.

By the end of the year his plans were nearly perfected. The trip to the Levant was to be made after all, and he was buying guidebooks to Syria and Palestine, and a suit of rough, durable cloth to travel in. What a golden age was that when one could procure a complete outfit for seventeen dollars, with a hat, a necktie, and a pair of suspenders thrown in!

At the close of the journal for 1862, John Vincent counts up the number of miles he has traveled since

July 1. The sum total came to eight thousand three hundred and fifty, "of which I have *walked* nearly eight hundred and fifty." He left Paris on January 12, one of a party of four, all bound for Cairo, Jerusalem, and Damascus.

CHAPTER VII

EGYPT AND PALESTINE

THEY crossed the Alps by the Mont Cenis route, not underground in part, as is the easy modern way, but over the picturesque old road. The terminus of the railway was at, or near, Modane. Here diligences were in waiting. For the most difficult part of the ascent covered sledges were provided. These singular vehicles were well lined and well cushioned. Flat metal tanks filled with hot water lay along the bottom. By putting one's feet on the tank and giving a loose to the imagination one could be fairly comfortable. These "tin warmers," as the diarist called them, might have been seen on Italian railways as late as the year 1885.

At some points the narrow road lay between walls of snow ten or more feet in height. Again there would be a perpendicular mountain crag on one side and a black abyss on the other. "It was a long way up. . . . I shall never forget that summit of Mount Cenis amidst snows and the biting breath of January, 1863."

If the ascent was tedious the descent was exciting. With only one mule to a sledge—the animal's business was to keep the machine front-end foremost while gravity did the work—they came down at a breakneck pace. From the account in the journal, one infers that the drivers were skilled technicians and exceedingly playful;

[69]

it afforded them infinite pleasure to display their art in negotiating sharp turns.

The playfulness and the zigzagging continued after the change back to the diligence; but the road was more open and the tourists had reason to believe that the bottom of the pass must be somewhere in the near distance. They now began to meet other diligences laboring up the steep incline; every vehicle was drawn by fourteen horses or mules, a veritable circus parade. At three o'clock in the morning the party arrived at the railway station on the Italian side and at once took a train for Turin.

Wishing to visit one of the Waldensian valleys, and to learn by personal observation something of the people and of the work done in their schools, John Vincent went by rail from Turin to Pinerolo, and thence by coach to La Torre. There was a heavy fall of snow all that afternoon and it continued during the night. In the morning workmen were clearing the snow from the roofs of the houses, and incidentally talking of the possibility of avalanches farther up the valley.

The American breakfasted with the village pastor and afterwards made the round of the schools—the College founded some thirty years since by William Stephen Gilly (an Anglican clergyman), the Normal School, the school for girls, and the orphanage. One large recitation room was in an old convent, in the erection of which, so the visitor was told, the Waldenses had worked under duress, like the Israelites in Egypt. In the library were framed engravings of Cromwell and Milton, and a portrait of Colonel Beckwith, who had spent thirty-five years of his life in this district of Piedmont in an entirely successful effort to better the condition of the inhabitants. Beckwith's death occurred only six or seven months before the American made the pilgrimage to La Torre.

The journal is extremely copious at this point, as it never fails to be when the subject is one that has engaged the writer's sympathies or is familiar to him through much previous reading.

On January 17, he left Turin for Genoa. Six days later he arrived at Naples; during this second visit he climbed the cone of Vesuvius. The party, now increased to six, sailed for Malta; they were in the harbor of Valetta by February 11. Several pages of the journal are devoted to a carefully written account of a trip to St. Paul's Bay. On Sunday morning John Vincent preached in the Scotch Church. He describes the building as large and neat. "It was filled with a respectable congregation, including a great many soldiers."

It was the time of carnival, and on Monday and Tuesday the streets of Valetta were crowded with maskers in grotesque costumes. One unusually clear day they had a glimpse of Ætna from the roof of the hotel. The island contained enough objects of interest to entertain the party for a month, but they were anxious to get on to Alexandria with all reasonable dispatch. In those days the tourist was at the mercy of whatever sort of craft came his way, and at the mercy of hotel proprietors if no boat at all came. If he was at Malta he possessed his soul in patience until he had a chance to leave. The particular tourist with whom this narrative is concerned writes that one steamer was so long overdue that a report circulated to the effect that she had gone down. And when finally he and his companions left Valetta it was in weather so rough that other boats were turning back rather than take any risk.

A veritable storm came on, the rudder was either unshipped or broken, and while the damage was being repaired the boat rolled in the trough of the sea for an entire day. Here is an extract from the journal:

"It was the first time in my life that I ever faced death as a near possibility. I did not expect to escape it. As I lay in my berth—the whistling winds shrieking through the rigging like ghosts of the damned—the dashing of the waves on the ship's side and occasionally the breaking of a wave over our decks—the thundering of the cargo as it moved with every motion of the boat—the breaking of crockery—altogether made one of the most dismal days of my life." It was February 22, Washington's Birthday, but neither he nor his stateroom companion (Graydon) was in a mood for the expression of patriotic sentiments.

The storm lasted two days. How a man could make notes of his various experiences, mental, spiritual, and bodily, in such a hubbub it is difficult to see. The notes exist, however, and the handwriting is in some sort an index of the progress and subsidence of the tempest. Forty-eight hours later he was playing shuffleboard on deck, and was also being initiated by the captain into the mysteries of the ancient game of "squails," the latter "not very entertaining." Between whiles he read *The Last Days of Pompeii,* a volume of *Tales from Blackwood,* and a historical work on Alexandria.

On February 27, about noon, land was in sight. "The low, sandy shores of Africa lay against the horizon and looked like mounds of ashes, with low chalky ridges rising here and there like walls. . . . As we approached the coast we saw the white fortifications of Alexandria, with houses and palaces rising against the sky."

The boat was in the harbor by six o'clock, but the passengers were not allowed to go on shore until the next morning. The account of the landing is brief, graphic, humorous, and contains substance enough for a dozen printed pages. There is a deal of color in it, for the actual scene was filled with color. Had the native boatmen and stevedores chosen their costume with an eye to the effect it would make on Westerners they could have done no better than they did. Everything was delightfully Oriental.

To John Vincent the best part of the whole tour was that which lay in the Near East. For the purpose of seeing Egypt and Palestine he had expressly come abroad. His journals (two volumes are devoted to this period) are crowded to the margin with suggestive facts. On going through them one is again surprised to find how much he could pack into a small space. There is no waste of words, no running off into passages of dithyrambic prose. He at no time betrays the orator, is always the acute, keen-eyed citizen of the world.

His notes (capital reading just as they stand!) should have been invaluable for his own purposes afterwards. By their aid he could recall a hundred or so of points that he had not the time to put down on paper. They range from neatly executed vignettes of the scenery to fragments of a dialogue with the natives. "Where did you learn English?" he asked an Egyptian donkey driver. "In missionary school at Cairo," was the reply. "How long were you there?" "Quarter of an hour." Another time he questioned a boy as to the name of the beast he was driving. "This donkey Mrs. G—d d—n," said the boy.

Frequently a pen-and-ink sketch is introduced into the journal, the outline of a range of hills or the perspective of a building. The account of a visit to some historic structure is accompanied by a plan; it is invariably well drawn and, what is of most importance, shows an eye for proportion.

Of his stay in Egypt little need be said. We know what one expects to see, and is expected to see, at Alexandria and Cairo. At the former place, while riding through one of the broad, shaded avenues, he heard the murmur of childish voices and learned from his guide that an Arab school was in session. He dismounted and went to the door. In an unceiled, unplastered chamber, possibly twelve feet square, were gathered some eighteen or twenty youngsters. Seated on the ground they rocked to and fro, and conned from wooden tablets their lesson (passage of the Koran); their profesor, a young man of twenty-five, lay stretched at ease on the floor. They stopped their monotonous chant and stared at the caller. He told them, through the guide, that he was an American and that he wanted to hear them recite. They at once resumed the lesson and the professor asked for baksheesh.

John Vincent records dispassionately one small adventure at Alexandria: "To-day I was thrown from my donkey in the public square." He could not boast of the experience on the ground of its being singular; his friends Hartley and Graydon were thrown from *their* donkeys the same day. Thus did the gentlemen divert themselves when not performing their set tasks, such as going to see Pompey's Pillar and Cleopatra's Needle and the palace of the Pasha. Half the joy of foreign travel consists in beholding sights not prescribed by the guidebook, and in performing successfully evolutions for which one has not been trained.

The ascent of the Pyramids was made in the customary way. Two Arabs went ahead and pulled the victim by the arms, a third followed on behind and pushed; the formula seems never to vary. John Vincent's mechanicians sang at their work. The refrain was: "Allah, Allah! Goot gentleman, very goot Ameliken! Baksheesh!" the final word delivered *sforzando*.

On their return, the dragoman advised against their camping out in a ruined temple and hinted darkly of callers in the shape of hyenas. They spent the night in an Arab village, at the house of the sheik. The account of the experience is realistic; it makes one earnestly hope never to enjoy entertainment of a similar sort.

On March 10, after a tedious passage in a Russian steamer, the tourists had their first glimpse of Palestine. Seen from the deck of the boat it was no more than a long, low line of lead-colored mountains, falling away gradually to the south. The uproar and wrangling attendant on disembarkation at Joppa were irritating in the extreme. Says the diarist: "I resolved not to forget as I made my first step on shore that this was the Holy Land." But when he found himself (along with his companions) the center of a screaming, gesticulating mob of dirty Arabs, flanked by loaded camels wearing the supercilious expression that camels always wear, and the landing stage simply muck and mud, he forgot.

The pilgrims made the Latin convent their stopping place. Dinner was served at night: "Soup strong with mutton, eggs, mutton boiled, mutton roasted, beets prepared with olive oil, and then cheese and coffee." They did not always fare so well as on this occasion. Between two and three the next afternoon they set out for Jerusalem.

In 1863 there were no public conveyances. Horses had to be hired or bought, officials propitiated, and a dragoman engaged. One night must be spent on the road. The sights by the way were novel. As the party were taking their midday meal under a fig tree an old sheik came down from a neighboring hilltop and had coffee with them. "He was well dressed and rode a fine charger." The sheik was a collector, not of books or curios or purses but of visiting cards, surely an innocent hobby. Jerusalem came in sight about four o'clock of the second day. "The first view of the Holy City is not imposing from the Jaffa side."

True to his habit of taking a panoramic view of either a place or a subject John Vincent climbed to the top of a building that afforded such a prospect. Satisfied with this he proceeded, day by day, to examine every spot that rightly or wrongly was identified as the scene of some episode in Biblical history. He had all the names at tongue's end and the topography was as familiar to him as that of his own county. The descriptions in the journal are precise, even to the number of steps one must descend in entering a tomb or a cave—precise yet flowing; they might be inserted in a guidebook and are free from the dryness of that species of literature.

Of naïveté there is not a trace. Take for example

this sentence: "A single cutting in the rock toward the foot of the hill is shown as the place where St. Stephen was stoned." No further comment is made. One does not become eloquent over a single cutting in the rock if one has doubts as to whether it marks what it is said to mark. The phrasing of the sentence indicates the attitude of mind in which this observer viewed many of the objects he had come so far to see. He was to some degree a historical skeptic, though stopping short of iconoclasm. The absurdity of the multiplication of so-called Holy Places—a new shrine to meet every new demand—would be as evident to him as to a professional archæologist. He is never satirical; at all events, not in his notes. How he may have expressed himself to his companions there is no way of finding out.

Of descriptive passages the most detailed and elaborate are those of the Mosque of Omar, of Bethlehem, and of a journey to the Dead Sea and the Pilgrims' Ford of the Jordan. The notes are usually short and condensed, though little is omitted that there was time to set down. Of personal impressions there is a multitude; also of touches that throw light on the cosmopolitan civilization of Jerusalem. We learn how and where the traveler spent his time, whom he met, and what he saw. I dare say he was not blind to the seamy side of the life about him—he had the seeing eyes and nerves of peculiar sensitiveness. But there can be no doubt as to the character of the impressions resulting from his stay in the Holy Land; they were deep and lasting. He was profoundly moved as he gazed on scenes that were to him of the highest significance in that they formed the background and setting of a great drama—a drama the essential truth of which, historical or religious, he never questioned.

The journey northward was deliberate—it could not well have been otherwise. The party was now large and the sections kept close together. They slept under canvas; twelve tents were pitched nightly. Once, after riding all day in the rain, they stopped at a khan and dried out their clothes by a charcoal fire. Sunday was rigidly observed. One of their number preached and a prayer meeting was held. A surprising variation in the order of exercises occurred at Safed; the Jews and their dragoman had a fight. The fact is recorded without comment, as is the incident of their being stoned by natives as they were passing by Dothan. As a rule they were well treated. One horse was stolen, but that might have happened in America.

At Hasbeya they saw the castle where a massacre of Christians had taken place. The event was so recent that the horror of it could be realized. It was said that fourteen thousand Christians had been murdered at Damascus and in the Lebanon. The travelers met a few of those who had contrived to escape. Later, at Damascus, they walked through the Christian quarter, still in ruins.

After a week at Damascus, a profitable week, John Vincent went to Beirut and embarked for Athens. The steamer was small and crowded with pilgrims. Calls were made at Cyprus, Rhodes, and Smyrna. The city was illuminated in honor of the Sultan. His Majesty rode by the hotel in a closed carriage, to the annoyance of those who wanted to see what a Turkish potentate would look like. Later he appeared in state, mounted on a gaily caparisoned white horse and followed by a brilliant retinue. Three close-written pages of the journal are given to the account of an excursion to Ephesus. Of the journey to Athens, the sights there, and the voyage to Ancona, nothing need be said. The last word in the journal is "Outrageous!" It refers to an overcharge made by the Italian customs officer.

Fragments of two lectures on Palestine were found among John Vincent's papers. Incidents that are told in a few words in the journal will sometimes be elaborated, in the lecture manuscript, into a page. The first form is the more striking, the other better adapted for public delivery. In the matter of telling epithets and plain expression of opinion there is little to choose between the two. Of the effect of the lectures when delivered we can get an approximate idea. It is interesting to observe how admirable some of the descriptive passages are when read aloud.

CHAPTER VIII

THE SPECIALIST IN SUNDAY-SCHOOLS

On his return to America John Vincent at once resumed his pastoral duties at the Court Street Church, Rockford. By some arrangement with the bishop, the intricacies of which are doubtless quite clear to the learned, the pulpit had remained legally his during the months of his absence.

The Palestine Class gave him a warm welcome. The members felt that it was a distinct gain to have as teacher one who had seen the Nile, the Dead Sea, and the Jordan, and who had made the journey from Jerusalem to Damascus. He himself was well aware how much his class lectures had gained in variety and precision by reason of this foreign tour. One's first trip abroad is an event, whether made in the day of sailing packets or of fourteen-day steamships or of modern liners. But a first trip that included the Holy Land was an affair of moment in 1862-3. The novelty of it was great, almost as great as was the discomfort.

If, as we have seen, John Vincent had good reason to remember Joliet as the place where he first met his wife, he had good reason to remember Rockford as the place where he first met his son. The latter meeting took place, presumably, on March 21, 1864. The boy was christened George Edgar. As he began to grow up his sayings and doings proved an endless source of amusement to the father—no unusual circumstance in the history of fathers in general.

Early the following October, his term of pastoral service at Rockford having expired, John Vincent was assigned to Trinity Church, Chicago. The building stood at the corner of Indiana Avenue and Twenty-first Street. A somewhat uncomfortable parsonage adjoined it. The membership though not large was made up of well-to-do people. They are said to have been a trifle self-satisfied. To be in easy circumstances is to have grounds for complacency. Urbane and easy-going, cordial enough in their attitude towards the new pastor, they were nevertheless conservative. They displayed "little enthusiasm about anything." For such innovations as a Palestine Class or a Normal Class they professed to have no time.

The material for classes was not abundant; there were few children and young people in the congregation. Those who might perhaps have been counted on appeared disinclined to give up Saturday afternoons to study of any kind. The distractions of life in a city that was fast approaching the date when it could claim three hundred thousand inhabitants were manifold.

In a situation unlike any he had hitherto known, John Vincent found an outlet for his superabundant energy by joining a group of progressive workers (not all of his denomination) who, like himself, were zealous for the betterment of Sunday-schools. They, no less than he, held that this department of the Church ought to be something more than "a society for pious appeals to little children." They welcomed the new ally. His enthusiasm, force, geniality, and inventiveness soon made him conspicuous among them.

[81]

To these men he was much indebted, and always frankly acknowledged the obligation. What he contributed to the common stock had been independently acquired. Besides turning over the subject in his mind he had made experiments. In presenting his ideas he had concrete facts to show; he was not a mere theorizer with an engaging gift for speechmaking. Naturally the gift stood him in good stead when it came his turn to take the platform.

John Vincent was early convinced of the necessity of applying to Sunday-schools "all the most advanced methods of the public school." Though not a pedagogical expert—not even in the sense in which the phrase would have been used in the early Sixties—he had a quick apprehension of the problems involved in an attempt to bring about a reform of the old ways, and he knew by instinct how to begin such a reform.

He had himself taught school, and it may be said of him that to have been a teacher once meant always being a teacher. Among his favorite figures of speech was that of the Church as a school with many departments, each well equipped and well officered, all working in harmony. From the pastor in the pulpit to the parents in the home the adults were nothing less than members of a faculty. Their business was to instruct, and they should know the best way of going about that business.

The man liked system, in part for its own sake but chiefly as a means to an end. He was never impatient of routine, only of a dull and uninterested performance of regular duties. Of all manners he most despised the listless. The service, consultation, or business meeting under his control began on time, and, what is still better, ended on time. It was animated. Of the art of tiring out an audience or a committee he knew nothing. His genius for organization and dispatch made itself felt the moment he had taken hold of a Sunday-school. One was conscious of a breath of new life.

The introduction of a stricter way of doing things meant in his case no stiffness, like that of a military drillmaster, and therefore no hardening of attitude on the part of teachers and pupils. His gracious manner, his keen intelligence, and his surprising adroitness made service under him a pleasure. Along with all this should be taken into account his genuine interest in children and young people.

With boys he dealt as man to man, not by condescending to them. His attitude was reassuring where a natural suspicion existed as to what the minister, being a minister, might say. He said the right thing. To talk with a boy as if he were an inferior animal is not only dangerous but argues a lack of humor. John Vincent had humor in various kinds. One cannot believe that a boy would run from him after having made his acquaintance; he would be more likely to run after him.

Besides being friendly he had a love of the picturesque as embodied in suggestive names, mottoes, symbols, and banners. Whether he was the first to introduce features of this sort into the Sunday-school is a point not to be settled offhand. That he made an extensive use of them is certain. Their object was to promote the feeling of solidarity—no undue emphasis was laid on what is the costume or trappings of an organized body.

Of prime importance in his conception of a Sunday-school was the subject taught; hardly second to it was the method by which the teaching was done. He insisted on having a definite subject and on having the subject handled in a definite way.

In secular schools it was never left to the individual teacher to decide whether he would give a lesson in arithmetic or one in elementary physics. He had his textbook and was bound to cover the ground that the textbook covered. The teaching might be well or ill done, but it at least aimed at something. And the instructor could be called to account if he failed in doing what he was hired to do.

The Sunday-school, too, had its textbook, the Bible in the King James version, a composite work in any number of pages. What was most needed was an intelligent way of using this textbook. To take out passages and verses at random, and interpret them with no regard for the context and very little for the historical background, was hardly less than absurd.

To bring order out of a chaotic state of affairs was one of John Vincent's great aims, yet subordinate to the greatest of his aims—that of being a pastor. At the outset he had made a resolution to care equally for all departments of the Church. He honestly tried, he says, to secure "that even balance of administrative policy" that he felt to be all important. No one of the responsibilities that lay on him as a pastor would then be overlooked. The sentence is followed by an expression of regret that he had never so much as approximated his ideal.

He evidently gave an unusual amount of time to the children, and in consequence ran the risk of being called "the children's preacher," a term he deprecated. He is a rare man who can adapt a discourse to the infant mind, and that with so sure a touch that it becomes perfectly simple—even to the extent of being within the grasp of adults—yet stops short of puerility.

He would reach the children best through the Sunday-school—directly by his familiar talks to them, indirectly through his teachers. Besides drawing up a plan of study for the year he held what may be called faculty meetings (not his term, by the way). They were the germ of the Sunday-School Teachers' Institute. By their means another step was taken in the direction of concerted effort and an accredited system of instruction. It only remained to unite the teachers of several churches and a genuine Institute would be created. Give it official sanction, that of the Conference, and it would have a standing. The sanction might consist of a mere blessing and a recommendation to the body to do as it liked, but it had a value.

All of this is simply an adaptation of secular school practices to a department of the Church where individualism had hitherto reigned supreme, and to the satisfaction of everybody. The teachers in the public schools have their Institutes, and the county not only authorizes them but provides in part for their maintenance. Educators are booked for addresses. As a rule they are, or have been, practical men whose acquaintance with the schoolroom and its needs makes their talks of peculiar import to young teachers.

If, prior to 1860, the County Institute existed in about the form in which we now have it, it must have been the model after which the Sunday-School Institute was

[85]

shaped. To be sure, attendance on the one was enforced, while in the case of the other it was voluntary. In many respects the two were not unlike.

The question of Institutes was brought up at the annual session of the Rock River Conference in 1860. The committee appointed to deal with the business advised the holding of such a meeting. A group of teachers assembled at Freeport, Illinois, on April 17, 1861. This may have been the first, in a historical sense, of all Sunday-School Institutes. John Vincent conducted it. One feels sure that under his leadership it could have been no tame affair.

The presumption is that other Institutes soon followed this one, and that he took a hand in their management. They would be denominational by reason of their origin, but not denominational in spirit. The idea of a concerted effort on the part of all Sunday-school workers, irrespective of creed, was in the air; it had yet to be made a fact. Not until 1864 did the Union Sunday-School Institute for the Northwest come into being.

John Vincent, now a pastor in Chicago, proposed its establishment and urged the starting of a Sunday-school magazine for the Northwest. He was chairman of the committee that handled the details of the union and of the one that had to do with its literature. When the first number of the magazine came out (in January, 1865) his name appeared on the cover along with those of E. A. Pierce and W. W. Evarts. The three men, all ministers, were designated as the "publishing committee." John Vincent was generally spoken of as the editor, but all three had a hand in the affair.

[86]

The name of the magazine was *The Northwestern Sunday School Teachers' Quarterly*. Strictly speaking it had no publisher, and the initial number does not so much as mention who the printer was. On the other three numbers will be found the name of a well-known firm of printers and stationers. The committee financed the undertaking throughout. Possibly they did not even approach a publishing house with a view to having their magazine brought out in the customary fashion. They might have been unsuccessful. Publishers are peculiar in that they love not to work without the prospect of pay.

The January number of the *Quarterly* contained only thirty-two pages, but the April number was more than double that size. In July the subscribers were given one hundred and twenty-four pages, and in October one hundred and fifty-six.

Four lesson lists were printed, one arranged from that of the London Sunday-School Union, one that was used at Christ Church in Chicago, the third a plan of study, somewhat modified, that had been taken up by the Bishopsgate Chapel Young Men's Bible Class (in London), and the fourth a plan prepared expressly for the *Quarterly*. This was a liberal way of dealing by the subscribers; the committee might have presented only their own course. Of miscellaneous articles bearing on the cause for which the magazine had been founded there was an abundance. They are of varying degrees of merit, though alike in their open-minded tone.

"The *Quarterly* had but a limited circulation, but it met a want and kindled a fire." The sentence comes from a manuscript account of the steps that led to the adoption of an international lesson scheme, found among John Vincent's papers after his death. It may or may not have been printed in its entirety. He probably jotted down the points for the purpose of making clear to himself his part in a remarkably popular movement.

Briefly stated, his contention is that the present system, a thing of gradual growth, began with the issue of a periodical lesson leaf, with notes, et cetera, and fostered the idea of uniformity among the various schools of a given denomination. Out of this came the idea of a series of lessons so compiled that all denominations could and would use them. Such lessons were actually compiled, but their use was confined to a limited territory, to what was generally spoken of as the Northwest, an indefinite region of which Chicago was assumed to be the center.

The third step was taken when the whole country had come round to the idea of uniform Sunday-school lessons, the denominations having consented to study the same passages and provide their own notes. Once nationalized, the plan readily became internationalized. The system then devised still exists. Besides being a convenience it is believed to make for unity.

Now *The Northwestern Sunday School Teacher's Quarterly* was succeeded by *The Chicago Sunday School Teacher,* a monthly, edited during the first third of the first year of its life by John Vincent.[1] The initial number contained a specimen lesson leaf. In that leaf might be found the Golden Text, a topical outline, home

[1] He was followed by H. L. Hammond, and he in turn by C. R. Blackall. John Vincent, however, supplied the lessons for the entire year. When Edward Eggleston became the editor he drew up his own scheme of lessons.

[88]

readings and graded questions, illustrations, and notes. As a matter of fact it was not merely a forerunner of the present leaf but the thing itself. The editor had planned and written it, and was then using it in his own Sunday-school at Trinity Church.

Of the true source of the International Lesson Leaf he felt reasonably certain. "It remains," he says, "to settle the question as to whom credit is due for having suggested the several steps in the movement."

It must have occurred to more than one of the men who were active in the Chicago Sunday-School Union that it would be possible so to draw up a scheme of lessons that its convenience and worth must be apparent to representatives of all denominations. Carried thus far the plan could be easily worked out in detail. This idea of nationalizing whatever system might be agreed on was the one to which B. F. Jacobs gave himself whole-heartedly, and he is credited with the invention of it. John Vincent's doubts as to its feasibility were raised by the prospect of entanglements with publishers. He was in favor of the plan and gave it energetic support.

Obviously the reform in Sunday-school methods was due to no one man. Many ministers and many laymen had a hand in bringing it about. At the outset each worked in his own way. Then they began to act in concert. To distinguish each reformer's contribution from that of his fellow is difficult, perhaps impossible. John Vincent was as fertile in devising new methods as the next man, but he at no time assumed that the best of these was wholly due to himself.

Being willing that each should take his own, he merely hoped that no one would be so careless as to take more than his own. He was distinctly annoyed when, as late as 1891, a former colleague (in a reminiscent mood) appropriated rather too much, and was somewhat loose in the statement of what had long been accepted as historical facts. I believe he made no reply over his own name. The documents in the case were turned over to an expert, an article based on them appeared in a Sunday-school weekly, and there the matter rested.

The Palestine Class was the earliest of a series of reforms that John Vincent effected. In a little circular that he once issued, without date, it is described as "a new department of Sunday-school instruction." He maintains that the outlines of Bible history, chronology, and geography should be better known than they are. Because of unfamiliarity with these simple facts the force and beauty of many an allusion are quite lost. The hour devoted each week to the Sunday-school class is not the best or even a proper time for the study of purely historical and topographical subjects; other hours must be found for lessons that are of high importance, though they happen not to deal with ethics and religion.

He insists that what is generally taught in detail only in theological schools ought to be taught, in outline at least, in all church societies. The children and young people should be drilled until they are perfectly familiar with Scriptural places and personages and modes of life.

The circular gives full and explicit directions for organizing and conducting Palestine Classes. There is a list of books of reference, a list of maps, a scheme for grading and examining the pupils, and a set of rules that every teacher would do well to follow. Two of the rules are just what a man might be expected to lay down who hated to be bored himself, and who had determined never to bore others if he could possibly avoid it. The first reads: "Let each session be short, and introduce as much variety as possible." It is followed by this: "Take short lessons from the textbook, and secure prompt and spirited responses."

It is well to note that in proposing this new department in the Sunday-school proper, John Vincent was unconsciously feeling his way toward what in time grew into the Chautauqua Assembly, with its public platform, its schools, its Reading Circle, and its clubs. One might almost say that the first meeting at Fair Point on Chautauqua Lake in 1874, was no other than a gigantic Palestine Class.

His energy in promoting Institutes for the training of teachers, and in devising methodical lessons to take the place of the haphazard lessons so long in general use, showed him to be the man his Church needed to take hold of its Sunday-school affairs. While still at Trinity he was made a Sunday-school agent, with how extensive a jurisdiction the notes at hand do not make clear. In 1866 he was asked to take the office of General Agent for the Union, presumably under Daniel Wise. He therefore, on May 1, left Illinois for the East.

Not only was his position subordinate, but the exact limits of his work had yet to be defined by the General Conference. The office that he would ultimately hold was still to be created. It was well known what its functions were likely to be, and equally well known that he had no political rivals. How secure he felt as to his immediate future is evident from the fact of his buying a house almost at once. His frien. ' Whitney, then a pastor at Plainfield, New Jersey, always claimed the credit of having persuaded him that it would be to his advantage to settle in that pleasant town.

It was understood that, as General Agent, he would travel far and wide, hold Institutes, make speeches before conventions, and in all possible ways awaken a greater interest in the department of Sunday-school work. He was now to do officially the very thing he had hitherto done voluntarily whenever he stepped outside the pastoral charge. He is believed to have been from the first pretty much his own master, to have made his own program, to have decided what journeys ought to be taken and what topics it was needful to discuss.

He had little idea when he left Chicago that he would never again resume pastoral work. He was out of it for the next five or six years at the least reckoning. Although no longer under the necessity of making a hundred and more new sermons every twelve-month, he resolved not to intermit his theological studies.

At this point in the narrative we must go back a little and give a few biographical facts that were passed over for the moment because unrelated to the work of the Sunday-school specialist. They are grouped under the next chapter heading.

CHAPTER IX

WITH THE CHRISTIAN COMMISSION

In 1865, while still the pastor of Trinity Church, Jchn Vincent went to the front as a delegate of the Christian Commission. Ministers and laymen of all denominations took part in this work, and for longer or shorter periods of time as circumstances required. They received no pay; merely their expenses.

Men who could effectively address an out-of-door meeting of the rank and file were in great demand. The Commission regarded this gift as one of prime importance; for meetings of an informal character it was not difficult to provide leaders.

The delegates also visited the wounded in the hospitals, wrote letters from dictation or at their own instance, and made a record of what was needed in the way of common comforts. Their duties were often trying, and in so brief a term of service as theirs it was not always possible to become hardened to the ugliest aspect of war. Scenes like those described in Walt Whitman's *The Wound-Dresser* had sometimes to be witnessed, and the effect on the nerves was racking in the extreme. Nevertheless, men who, having been bred to scholastic pursuits, seemed ill fitted for any kind of hospital service, proved invaluable when it came to the test.

[93]

Their assignments might even take them to the battle-field, during or immediately after an engagement. As to this part of the work the manual of instructions is explicit and imperative: "No difficulty, however great, no obstacle, however formidable, short of impossibles and impassables, should stop any delegate of the commission on this side of the ground where the wounded may die for want of the aid he can render them." Then follow directions as to the delegate's equipment—the dress he is to wear, the supplies he is to carry, the means he is to employ for getting from place to place, and so on.

John Vincent was at the front in late March and early April. The record of his experience—a meager record at best—is to be found in such letters to his wife as happen not to have been destroyed, and in the note-book that he carried while making the round of the hospitals. The letters, written with a lead pencil on whatever scrap of paper came to hand, are dated from City Point, Virginia, and from Petersburg. He went by steamer from Baltimore to Fortress Monroe, and had a wild night in the Chesapeake Bay; the storm reminded him of the one on the Mediterranean two years before. When he heard the man at the wheel tell the captain that the heavy sea might "sweep off our deck cabins" he felt disinclined to get into his berth.

The boat from Fortress Monroe left at ten the following morning and reached City Point at eight in the evening. To the traveler the most interesting sight on the passage up the James River was the wreck of the *Congress,* one of the frigates that fell a victim to the *Merrimac.* The day after his arrival in camp he was the unwilling witness of a military execution; two young men were shot as deserters.

Having presented his credentials and been assigned a lodging in one of the tents of the Christian Commission, the delegate went to headquarters and called on Grant. The meeting is briefly described in one of the letters to Mrs. Vincent: "He gave me a cordial welcome. . . . He thinks we shall be in Richmond soon. He has word from there every day. Recently a lady in Richmond sent him a beautiful silk flag (Union). He thinks there will be but little more fighting." Within a short time the newly arrived volunteer had taken up the duties that his colleagues appointed him to do. These duties were painful and useful, and, he says, "I want to be useful."

The stained and shabby notebook contains many names and addresses. Beneath each is a memorandum, either some word relating to the case or an abstract of what is to be written to the soldier's wife or mother.

One man—from whose left breast a ball had just been extracted—is most unhappy because he cannot learn whether the fifty dollars he sent his wife some time since has been received. The next, a young Confederate, wants this word sent to his people: "Went forward to the charge *bravely*. Fell into hands of enemy. They have been kind. Tell mother to return ring to Lizzie and she to keep mine." The writer evidently expected to die. The touching little message makes one hope that he was disappointed in that particular.

Only in a single instance does an entry like this occur, "indifferent and trifling"—a proof, seemingly, that the consolation offered was not wanted. Not all of the wounded were chiefly concerned about themselves. One dictates a letter to the wife of a comrade who had fallen at Dinwiddie Courthouse. Now and then occurs a note so pathetic that it is painful to read; as in the case of a boy of sixteen whose agonized cry for his mother must have been heartrending. The phrasing of the note shows how deeply affected was the man who stood by that bedside.

Some roughness and bluntness and brutality the delegate expected to meet with. At the conclusion of one of the services a drunken soldier said to him, "I've had delirium tremens. If you Christians can do anything for me, do it." Whether this was a half-serious expression of a willingness to be reformed or merely a challenge cannot be made out. He to whom the remark was addressed reminded himself that such men had been saved. That the present case required a special handling was only too apparent.

The name of every man is followed by a succinct description of the nature of the wound from which he suffers and a word as to his state of mind; these two facts are to be reported to his family. One message reads: "Right hand off. Getting along well. Home in a few weeks." His neighbor dictates these three sentences: "Wounded in right arm above elbow. Good spirits. Not so painful as I expected it to be." And again: "Wound little above left knee, bone little fractured. Getting along right." Yet another was having his second experience: "Wounded in thigh. Flesh wound. Good spirits. Well cared for. In hospital with same boys I was before." In one of the wards John Vincent found a former Sunday-school pupil of his from North Belleville, his first pastorate. The man was in a bad way.

On almost every page of the book is a note relating
to the personal needs of the soldiers. Among the things
they wanted were the commonest of articles—shirts,
underclothes, handkerchiefs, stockings, writing paper,
crutches, comfort bags, and, in one case, merely a lemon.
It was the business of the delegates (so one gathers
from similar records) to go to the depot of supplies,
seek out what was required, and carry the articles to
the hospital. The practical nature of the service would
alone have recommended it to John Vincent. The cure
of souls was his province, but he was emphatically a
brother man. No one could have been quicker than he
to perceive the absurdity of talking religion to a sufferer
at a moment when the crying need was for ministrations
similar to those of the good Samaritan.

There is no reason to think that he overestimated
what he had been able to do during the short time that
he spent at the front. It was an average man's work,
part and parcel of a concerted effort that was being made
by hundreds of ministers, all as disinterested as himself,
to help those who were sorely in need of help. He
would regard his share as below what he ought to have
contributed. His standards were high, and he was slow
to admit that he had at any time succeeded in measuring
up to them. Yet he was quite free from the trick of
self-depreciation, that artificial humbling of oneself for
the sake of being contradicted. A man of his benignity
would do a world of good to a wounded soldier by the
mere manner of his approach. If he gave advice it
would be seasoned by manly optimism and plain common sense.

The stained memorandum book from which the above

extracts are taken is not a "document" in the sense of
throwing any new light on what occurred during the
last weeks of the war; it is simply corroborative of what
may be found in many books of a like sort. What it
certainly does is to reveal the man himself as he jotted
down these vivid records of hospital life. He made
little or no use of them afterward; in the *Autobiography*
he barely alludes to the fact that he served for a time on
the Christian Commission.

His letters to his wife are, as they would naturally be,
a mingling of what is strictly personal with what might
possibly interest the general reader. Here are two or
three short extracts.

"This A.M.," so runs a paragraph in the letter of
March 27, "I called on President Lincoln at Grant's
headquarters. Took with me Mr. Coffin of the Boston
Journal (the correspondent 'Carleton,' who writes so
much and so well). Gen'l Grant introduced me to Lincoln and we had a pleasant interview."

In the course of the talk the President made a good-
natured reference to the fact of his having gone on an
excursion up the James River the day before (Sunday).
He said he "supposed it was wrong," but it was war
time now "and we get ourselves into it." Lincoln knew
that John Vincent had been invited to go along on that
same excursion. Having to preach twice and to conduct
a Sunday-school for the soldiers, the delegate was not
in a position to accept the invitation, or even to regard
himself as seriously tempted to break his custom of rather
strict Sunday observance.

Here Grant remarked that "he had not attended
church three or four times since he got into the war, and

that then he was followed by an orderly with clanking spurs, bearing dispatches that required an immediate answer. He said that when he was in Galena he used to hear me regularly . . . he thought he never missed a morning sermon while I was there."

That same day the delegate saw a large part of Sheridan's force cross the pontoon bridge at Point of Rocks. "Eight or ten thousand must have crossed. It was a glorious sight. These fellows are war-worn and weary, dusty and shabby—but brave, tried, and true men are they all." Rawlins introduced him to Sheridan, "who is preparing for a bold movement south of Petersburg. He is a small, stout, spirited little fellow." There had been some severe fighting within the past twenty-four hours. "The wounded have been brought down to our Hospital. Eighteen carloads arrived yesterday."

In making his way to the next field of labor (Petersburg and the vicinity) John Vincent had to walk from Meade Station, on the military railway, to the town. The footpath lay across the recent battlefield, where might be seen many a poor victim of the war stretched out in death. They were mostly Confederates. "One was holding his canteen as near his mouth as possible, as if trying to get a drink. The scene was horrible."

He found Petersburg perfectly quiet. The stores were closed; not a civilian appeared in the streets. He was struck by the look of the private residences, their air of distinction and elegance. The town was absolutely unharmed. Apprehensive of rudeness on the part of the victorious soldiers, a number of families who were without adequate masculine protection had asked that members of the Christian Commission be sent to their homes.

John Vincent, with another delegate, was quartered for the night at the house of a Mrs. Mertens. He met there a charming young lady, a Miss Boisseau, "who," he writes, "is bristling with secession quills." She would have been lacking in spirit had she not darted her quills right and left, and he in his usual good-humored imperturbability had he not enjoyed the exhibition. His comment is, "We told our friends some things they did not know. On the whole the interview was pleasant."

Lincoln and Grant had passed through Petersburg the day before. "They made a fine impression on the citizens. To-day Lincoln has gone to Richmond, I think to issue a proclamation to the South. It will breathe love, good will, and forgiveness. Before two years Lincoln will be respected all over the South." A few days after these lines were written the President was shot.

John Vincent was in Richmond directly after its evacuation, and preached in Libby Prison to a body of Confederate soldiers who were being held there. Their principal need was food, as he well knew. In giving out the hymn he did not notice, until it was too late to change, that one stanza contained the line, "Dear Lord, and shall we ever live at this poor, dying rate?" But the men sang it, nevertheless, for they knew that an order for rations had been issued. When in Washington, on the return journey, he had one more glimpse of Lincoln; he heard him make an address (his note says "from an open window") on the Tuesday night before that fatal April 14.

The following anecdote has already appeared in print but will bear repetition. One moonlight evening in Washington, as Grant and his former pastor were strolling about the town, the latter "remarked on a peculiarity of the dispatches which the General had sent from the field: 'It has been noticed that you never speak of God or invoke the divine aid, and uncharitable critics have commented unfavorably on the fact.' "

" 'That's true,' replied Grant in his quiet way. 'The other side were always calling on God, but I thought it better to trust more and say less. At the same time I always had the most implicit faith in superior wisdom, and none of my plans ever miscarried without a better result than if they had been fulfilled.' "

A few months after this talk Grant surprised John Vincent by appearing at Trinity Church one Sunday morning. At the close of the service the entire congregation showed its gratitude and affection by the one method that Americans have perfectly mastered. The news of what was going on spread through the neighborhood and the whole body of worshipers at another church poured out and poured over; they were determined not to lose so good a chance of shaking hands with a celebrity.

The pastor of Trinity had seen Captain Grant leave Galena when the war broke out. He had the great pleasure of seeing Lieutenant General Grant return to Galena after the war had ended. A special train conveyed the party from Chicago to its destination. The rear coach was set apart for the use of the national hero, his family, and his friends.

If we may believe the papers, this coach—which had been converted into a sort of mid-Victorian parlor—was a miracle of elegance and good taste. The furnishings were luxurious. They included not only sofas and easy

[101]

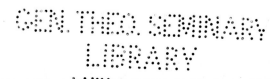

chairs but also a marble-top table. To the eye of the reporter they made "a charming picture." With praiseworthy exactness he gives the names of the furniture-dealer and the upholsterer who had parted (temporarily) with their best to do honor to the occasion. When Grant was asked, by his clerical friend, whether he did not find all this a striking contrast to his situation in the Wilderness, he promptly replied, "Yes, it is very fine; and, but for the sufferings of the men, I greatly prefer the Wilderness."

John Vincent was Grant's personal guest at this time and had been duly warned as to what would be expected of him when the speechmaking at Galena should begin. It is to be hoped that he had the warning before he boarded the train, but there is some doubt as to that. The presumption is that on the way down he had to spend a part of the time in going through the process known as "collecting one's thoughts."

The formal address of welcome was made by E. B. Washburne. Grant's reply fills exactly four and a third lines of newspaper print—six lines, if we include the preliminary "Friends and Fellow Citizens of the City of Galena." It runs thus: "I am truly glad to meet you at this time, and I have requested Mr. Vincent, who came with me on the train, to return you my very sincere thanks for this demonstration."

The thanks were then returned, in phrases that were well chosen, heartfelt, and entirely free from any touch of grandiloquence. The speaker regarded himself as simply one who was privileged to convey to the audience what Grant himself would have said had he been in the habit of making public addresses. "To sustain his well-

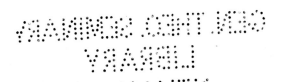

known reputation I must be very brief, and secure your commendation by uttering only the wise words he has suggested to me." What follows is in keeping with the exordium. The speech is not too long to be reproduced in a biographical sketch such as this. To quote it in full would be to lay more stress on it than did John Vincent himself. He had no copy of it—he spoke extemporaneously—and one must go to old newspapers to learn what was said on the occasion.

From those same newspapers one may gather no end of details relating to the affair. There were decorations of the customary sort, bands of music, and triumphal arches. The principal arch was "crowned with thirty-six of the loveliest young ladies that ever graced the earth or broke a heart. These ladies were dressed in white, fleecy as the silver lining of a summer cloud." They sang divinely, too, and almost smothered the General with floral offerings. In a word, nothing was wanting that might be supposed to give brilliancy and charm to a public reception.

As every American town contains a certain number of citizens with a taste for waggery, it follows that Galena must in that respect have resembled all its neighbors. Possibly it excelled them. For on one of the arches was displayed in bold letters the legend, "General, the Sidewalk is Built." The story is an old one, and amusing, of how Grant said that he had no mind to the Presidency, that the only office he would accept was the mayoralty of Galena; and that if he ever got it he would have a sidewalk built from his house to the railway station. "General, the Sidewalk is Built." This was a stroke of genuine American humor, as pleasing as bouquets and oratory.

CHAPTER X

EDITOR AND CORRESPONDING SECRETARY

At the General Conference of 1868, held in Chicago, certain departments of the Church were reorganized. It was decided that in future the editor of *The Sunday-School Journal* should be Corresponding Secretary of the Sunday-School Union, and Superintendent of the Department of Sunday-School Instruction. When it came to the balloting, John H. Vincent received all but twenty of the two hundred and one votes cast. His predecessor, Daniel Wise, was provided for, if not magnificently, at all events respectably.

On May 31 the new incumbent learned through the newspapers of his election, and the office was turned over to him on June 5. His temporary quarters in New York, at 200 Mulberry Street, were in the library. A year later, or thereabouts, the Book Room was moved uptown, to 805 Broadway. One remembers the office there as a rather dingy apartment, somewhat narrow for its length, with one corner set off by glass partitions for the editor's sanctum. The whole place was crowded to suffocation with books, pamphlets, and periodicals. Editorial offices are not picturesque, though their denizens fondly describe them as such.

The windows of this same room, giving upon Eleventh Street, commanded a prospect not without a certain charm for a man of urban tastes. The spire of Grace

Church could be seen at the left. Directly across the way was the St. Denis Hotel, not architecturally beautiful, to be sure, but a popular caravansary and, because of the excellence of its cuisine, a source of expense to anyone troubled with a discriminating palate. The whole district up to Twenty-third Street was lively and enlivening. Besides being as gay as fashionable shops and crowds of shoppers could make it, it was brighter and more open than at the present time. Buildings of ungainly proportions, towering to a preposterous height and crowned with huge barrels, were as yet unknown. The day was far distant when a city street might be converted into a cañon or cave of the winds, and often sunless throughout its lower depths.

The new editor took charge of a magazine that had hitherto appeared as an eight-page quarto; the authorities recommended its being turned into a sixteen-page large octavo. The first number was dated October, 1868. The title-page, or cover, reads, "The Sunday School Journal for Teachers and Young People." Rev. J. H. Vincent, Editor." Then follows a table of contents without the names of contributors. The matter was uniformly set up in double columns unless an article happened to be of such a nature as to require a different arrangement. The subscription price was low, forty cents a year. A group of subscribers (six or more) might obtain the twelve numbers for thirty-five cents by having their copies sent to one address. No teacher could plead poverty as an excuse for not taking the *Journal*.

In the November number was printed a leader on one of John Vincent's favorite themes—education. Sunday-school teachers whose boys might, perhaps, be debating the question of going or not going to college were urged to influence them in the right way. In the fifth number appeared a long article on Pestalozzi, not by the editor but written at his instance. One may take for granted that the *Journal* had not been narrowly denominational under its former editor; that it would not be so during the new régime soon became evident. The October number of 1869 contained articles by W. C. Wilkinson and H. Clay Trumbull, the one a Baptist, the other a Presbyterian.

At the close of the first year of the new series the editor was able to report substantial progress. When he took charge of the *Journal* it had eighteen thousand subscribers; it now had thirty-seven thousand. Some changes were announced for the near future. Instead of sixteen pages of text there would be twenty-four. And the price would be raised, though not to a perilous height. Hereafter one must pay sixty cents a year. The person most averse to giving money in exchange for Biblical literature, and at the same time convinced that he ought to do so, could calm himself with the thought that after all he would be out of pocket only five cents a month.

With the second volume began the regular issue of book notices, brief reviews of current literature. Always carefully written, they were of necessity somewhat limited in scope. Not every good new book could be mentioned in a magazine that aimed to reach a special type of readers. The editor proposed to make the *Sunday School Journal* so useful that no teacher would feel inclined to do without it, and this ambition of his largely determined what books were to be reviewed.

The new series was barely under way when specimen lessons began to be printed in its columns. In the second number, November, 1868, were given four versions of a lesson, each of the four adapted to one of the grades of a well-classified school. The lesson had originally been printed in the *Sunday School Teacher,* the monthly conducted by John Vincent in Chicago. The well-known "Berean Lessons" began in January, 1870. This issue of the magazine contained the first four of the series entitled "Twelve Lessons about Jesus." The series was continued. When printed in a leaflet, so that every pupil might have a copy, it attained such popularity that editions of nearly half a million copies had to be struck off to meet the demand. And this within the space of two years.

Much was required of the .editor besides compiling lessons, writing notes thereon, and looking over the manuscripts of would-be contributors; he was not expected to be a diligent office drudge merely. From one of his date books it is possible to get an approximate idea of the amount of work done in a given period. For example, in 1871 he preached sixty-five times and delivered ninety addresses, making a total of a hundred and fifty-five pulpit or platform talks. I mention the exact number, not because it is extraordinary—many a professional revivalist does as much or more during the heart of the season—but simply to give the facts.

Within the same twelvemonth he held twenty-nine Institutes, the total number of morning and afternoon sessions coming to one hundred and eight. A prodigious amount of teaching was involved. Of this very little would take the form of question and answer. John Vincent lectured to his classes, and teaching by lecture means carrying the whole burden oneself. Discussions of certain points might take place, but the leader was the life of almost every Institute, the promising and the unpromising alike.

And lastly, there were nine Annual Conferences to which official visits must be paid and the claims of the Sunday-School Union presented. For the year in question the journeys made for one purpose or another were frequent and some of them were long. The notebook shows that the editor must have covered in his travels a little more than seventeen thousand miles. The record for 1872 is less striking; fewer addresses were made and fewer towns visited. It was the year of the General Conference, which alone would account for the falling off. But to reach the several points where Institutes were to be held required almost as much travel as did the itinerary mapped out for 1871.

In the meantime the office in New York must be kept supplied with copy. Every year saw an increase in the circulation of the *Journal*. By 1872 sixty thousand copies were being regularly printed and distributed. The figure was surprising and gratifying; but the man who was chiefly responsible for it had the burden of keeping the magazine up to the standard that had produced such results. He seems to have done it rather easily. John Vincent could write as well on the road as in his own study at home. Oddly enough the roar of Broadway often disturbed him, though the roar of a railway train did not. If his articles were frequently journalistic (in the sense attaching to anything written in haste and for immediate publication) they betrayed no sign of loose thinking. When he advocated some policy he gave his reasons; he was logically precise, though his style might be colloquial and, now and then, redundant in the matter of phrasing.

His official reports make good reading. One would not affirm that he could draw up a report in such a way as to interest an outsider. But were he himself to read from manuscript a report like the one he submitted to the General Conference of 1872 it would be found engrossing. Yet it is strictly a report, the essential dryness unrelieved by a single anecdote or one pardonable touch of pleasantry.

The noteworthy characteristics are clarity, orderliness, common sense, and an entire freedom from gush. One learns what has already been done, and what (in the opinion of the editor) ought still to be done. Plain speech is not lacking. Of one of his schemes he says, "I name this feature of the plan with firm faith in its advantages, but with little expectation of its adoption." The plan itself might possibly have been adopted at once had it not included the launching of a weekly paper for Sunday-school children who had outgrown the juvenile literature that was current, but who were as yet too young to care for the *Journal*. The number of these pupils ran into the hundreds of thousands.

To Sunday-school enthusiasts the year 1872 was notable because of the adoption of a National Lesson System. The desire for uniformity had for several years been growing stronger and stronger. So well convinced was John Vincent that the denominations were on the point of agreeing on one series that in June, 1870, he postponed the announcement of the "Berean Lesson" list for the coming year and called a meeting of editors and publishers to discuss the subject.

Lyon (of the firm of Adams, Blackmer & Lyon, publishers of the *National Sunday School Teacher*) wrote John Vincent that if uniformity was so very desirable it could be secured by adopting the series published in his monthly. The tone of his letter was high and mighty. There was an excuse for it; the *Teacher* had done remarkably well under Edward Eggleston. By some good judges Eggleston's lessons were thought to be an improvement on those of his predecessor. And the Chicago monthly had a capital subscription list. The publisher was not disposed to make concessions that might injure a good business.

Lyon's communication was dated July 22. The representatives of the numerous Sunday-school magazines met in New York on July 26. They regretted their inability to accept the Chicago publisher's plan for achieving their object. Some of them proposed making a series that should take no account of the *National*. There were many objections to this; for example, it would show that Sunday-school men were divided in spirit rather than united. Even though they agreed on their list it would not result in a uniform lesson; the publisher of one of the most successful of all systems would be left out.

Nothing resulted from the meeting. The gentlemen came together, talked over the question of uniform lessons for an hour and a half, agreed that they could not without loss of self-respect submit to dictation, and then took leave of one another. The account of their informal proceedings is given in J. M. Freeman's report, July 27, 1870.

By July, 1871, Lyon had been won over to the cause of uniformity, in what way is not apparent. After a few hitches a committee was appointed to make out a tentative list, August, 1871.

The International Sunday-School Convention (the fifth) met in April, 1872, at Indianapolis. The account of the proceedings resembles in a way the account of what goes on at any political convention. But all this excitement had nothing to do with the naming of candidates for office; it came about through the zeal of certain progressive men for the systematic study of the Bible. And they wanted above all to persuade the great army of teachers and pupils to study the same lessons at the same time.

The supporters of uniformity easily carried their point under the leadership of B. F. Jacobs. Of him Edward Eggleston afterward wrote: "He is the original Jacobs, to whose tireless persistency, vehement urging, unruffled and imperturbable good nature, and general faculty for having his own way, we are indebted for the present consummation." A committee, composed of five ministers and five laymen, was appointed to draw up the outline of the course. John Vincent was the chairman. The lessons were to run through a period of seven years, and were "to embrace a general study of the whole Bible, alternating between the Old and New Testaments semiannually or quarterly, as they (the committee) shall deem best." The lessons for the first two years were to be made ready at once.

Whatever obstacles stood in the way of agreement as

to the exact form of the lessons were finally overcome. There was a deal of rivalry between the publishing houses; with them the question was one of dollars and cents. Such rivalry as existed between the authors of the systems already in use was of a friendly sort. Amiable men, though authors, they were disposed to let live as well as live. One expert says that in their final form the lessons were a blend of the *National* (Edward Eggleston's), the *Berean* (John Vincent's), and that of the committee itself.

Eggleston had always been skeptical as to the worth of uniform lessons and took the side of the minority at the convention. It is said that he doubted their usefulness after the plan was generally adopted. To internationalizing the system, he was out and out opposed. Yet he contributed an important share to a scheme of Bible study that within the next three years was accepted by the Sunday-schools of nineteen nations.

Two years or more before the adoption of uniform lessons by the United States and Canada, John Vincent was exchanging letters with English Sunday-school workers on the question of a system that would admit of being internationalized. One correspondent (James Gray, of Halifax, Yorkshire) wrote: "I do not think the scheme is at all practicable; and if it could be carried out I do not think that the advantages would repay for the toil." It was the writer's opinion that the Sunday-School Union of London would not be inclined to give its support, and outside the Union parties were too much divided to agree upon any one system. Denominationalism stood in the way of their uniting for the common good.

The letter was written early in 1870. John Vincent must have been agitating the subject some little time before that date. He approved of denominationalism, provided the sects would let one another alone, and at the same time was in favor of uniform Sunday-school lessons. And he saw no reason why the lessons should not be drawn up in a way that would be as acceptable to Great Britain as to the United States. In his book entitled *The Modern Sunday School* he says that he proposed and strenuously advocated the international system on both sides of the Atlantic. In spite of James Gray's doubts the Sunday-School Union of London did, after all, give its support, and that "with royal magnanimity and zeal."

The international system had been in existence through two periods of seven years each and was beginning its third period when *The Modern Sunday School* was published. The author sums up the advantages of the new method under eight heads. Briefly stated, they are these: The International Lessons have advertised the Bible; Unity in the study of the Word has promoted a spirit of unity among the people; True educational methods and philosophy have been introduced; The International System has proved to be a convenience; A common interest in specific lessons has led to profitable conversation among Christian people; The fact that so many different minds are engaged in preparing lesson helps has been an incitement to healthful emulation; The union conventions and institutes have been made doubly interesting.

He then comes to his eighth and last point, that denominational interests cannot suffer under this plan. The lessons are selected from the Bible, but the committee provides no comments. Each branch of the Church is free to interpret the passages in its own way. It was quite like the writer to emphasize that freedom of thought that has resulted in the multiplication of sects.

As he had been eager almost from the beginning for union of some sort in the matter of Sunday-school lessons, so was John Vincent no less eager for the extension of the system finally adopted. In 1878, when a guest of the Sunday-School Union in London, he had an opportunity of meeting the committee of the Church of England Sunday-School Institute and laying before them the international plan. The conference took place at Westminster School, at the house of one of the masters. He was followed with close attention as so engaging a speaker would be. We have no reason to think that his Anglican hearers were convinced of the expediency of joining forces with a heterogeneous non-Anglican body.

CHAPTER XI

IN June, 1862, when John Vincent was on his way eastward to take the steamer for Europe, he spent a day or two with friends at Westfield, New York. While there he took walks and drives about the country, and was duly appreciative of the beauties of that really charming district. In his journal he speaks with regret of having had no time to cross the range of hills and see what was represented to him as "the highest navigable lake in the world, Chautauque"—for so the name was spelled in that day. He little suspected how familiar both the lake and the name were to become to him.

If not so high in the world as the natives fondly believed it to be, Chautauqua Lake had (and still has) the distinction of beauty, and in 1862 must have been a lovelier sheet of water than it is now. No lake is improved by a railway, trolley lines, hotels, and densely populated summer resorts.

A few historical associations Chautauqua enjoys. Céleron de Bienville, with his party of Canadians and Indians, crossed it in July, 1749, on his way to the valley of the Ohio. He represented the governor of Canada. His mission was to warn the English away from lands on which they were encroaching, and to reassert the claims of the French to territory they considered their own.

The party, in twenty-three birch-bark canoes, had left

[115]

La Chine in the middle of June. By the middle of July they had reached the point on Lake Erie where the village of Portland now stands. There they shouldered canoes and luggage, and made their way over the ridge to the upper end of Chautauqua. Having launched their canoes they paddled down the lake and through the outlet. On arriving at the Allegheny they went through the ceremony of taking possession. A sheet of tin bearing the arms of France was nailed to a tree, and an inscribed leaden plate buried in the earth beneath it; a notary made an official record of the affair. Other leaden plates were buried in the course of the journey; a few of these have been recovered.

In the later days of the Chautauqua Assembly this voyage of Céleron's was commemorated by a pageant. The chevalier was made to land at Fair Point. Very possibly the real Céleron may have done so.

John Vincent was always fascinated by the pictorial side of history, but it was not the memory of something he had read about the Frenchman's voyage that drew his attention to this pretty body of water. For so much— and a good deal more—he was indebted to a friend. While conducting Institutes in various parts of the country he had met, and become intimate with, Lewis Miller, Esq., of Akron, Ohio, a man well known for business acumen and for enthusiasm in church work; the Sunday-school that he superintended had a reputation that was more than parochial.

When the question was raised of holding an Institute on a large scale—of making it national as well as interdenominational—Lewis Miller suggested Fair Point on Chautauqua Lake as a very proper place for the session.

As president of the Camp-Meeting Association he had only to say the word and the grounds were at his disposal for the object in view. My understanding is that at first John Vincent was strongly opposed to going to Fair Point. For many reasons he preferred a city. He admired trees but had no passion for living in the woods. And being out of sympathy with camp meetings in general, he feared that the Institute would suffer not a little if held in such a place—its purpose would be misunderstood.

By amiable insistence and cogent argument Lewis Miller was able to bring his friend around to his own point of view. It was agreed between the two that the plan was worth trying. Fair Point was not ill adapted for an Institute. There was a roofed platform for the speakers, seats for the audience, and a ring of primitive cottages round about in which the visitors could be housed. Tents were to be had in case more people came than were expected.

The first out-of-door Institute was held in August, 1874. The session lasted for two weeks only. The projectors divided the responsibilities of the undertaking between them. Lewis Miller, as was fitting, he being a man of affairs, took charge of the business side and was known as President; his colleague assumed the unpretentious though adequate title of Superintendent of Instruction. We may disregard for the moment the changes subsequently made in the form of address. It is only needful to bear in mind that Lewis Miller was perpetual President of Chautauqua, and John H. Vincent perpetual Superintendent of Instruction.

The official relations of the two men never changed.

Their respective functions somewhat overlapped; the man of business had progressive ideas about educational and Sunday-school matters, and the minister was not wholly unversed in affairs. But they kept in step.[1] Matter enough for discussion there must have been. Chautauqua soon became a complicated piece of machinery, and its management a deal of a problem.

Speaking of that first session, John Vincent says: "I gave it the name of Assembly to distinguish it from ordinary Sunday School institutes and conventions." For many years it was known as The Chautauqua Assembly. Its official name has been changed at least twice. The older generation still clings to the old form.

The compiler of this memoir has no intention of trying to sketch the history of Chautauqua. It will be only needful to point out its salient characteristics, and to show how that which at first was strictly limited to the study of one subject—an engrossing and many-sided subject, to be sure—became in time broadly educational. The growth of the Assembly was rapid, and while its original scope was by no means lost sight of, the innovations obscured it. Those very innovations, for which John Vincent was mainly responsible, made Chautauqua popular. Hundreds of people who took but a languid interest in Sunday-school matters were attracted by the miscellaneous lectures and entertainments, the academic

[1] How well they kept in step, and how bent they were on continuing to do so, may be learned from a little paper that they drew up and signed in 1899. The pith of it lies in these two sentences touching the origin of the Assembly: "The question of personal pre-eminence or priority as to the original elements and plans is forever dismissed. The two claim joint ownership and fellowship; and no recognition of the one shall by our permission be acknowledged without recognition of the other. . . ."

classes, the athletics, and the social life. The lake was of course a powerful magnet; fish were plentiful and eager to be caught, and the boating was none of the worst.

Regular annual meetings followed the initial one. Each year some new feature was added. The Superintendent of Instruction knew the value of a map, a plan, a model, a cast, or a costume in clarifying one's ideas of Biblical places, people, and modes of life. A tourist of average intelligence will spend an entire day at Waterloo, with the most voluble of Belgian guides, and not learn as much as may be learned in half an hour by staring at the model of the battlefield in the Royal United Service Museum. One easily grasps a thing seen in miniature, yet finds confusing that same thing in the large. The little model of Jerusalem that was exhibited at Chautauqua gave real pleasure to the people who had never been to that ancient city; they learned something from it. Traveled folk were at liberty to pass it by if they chose.

Of great value to those interested in Biblical geography was a park in which the topographical features of Palestine were depicted with reasonable accuracy, and the towns and villages set down each in its proper place. The original park (of 1874) was only a hundred and twenty-five feet long. As must be the case in all contour maps, the mountain peaks and ranges had to be exaggerated in respect to the height, otherwise they would have been almost invisible. Built of perishable materials, this out-of-door map soon lost its freshness. In successive rebuildings its size was trebled and concrete was used at certain points to insure permanency.

The park was laid out by the shore of the lake, which,

in the eye of the imaginative student, became the Mediterranean Sea. As the Assembly grounds are on the western side of the lake, it was necessary to reverse the points of the compass. Whence the following witty comment: "Chautauqua has always been under a despotic though paternal government. But the sun persists in its independence, rises over Chautauqua's Mediterranean Sea where it should set, and continues its sunset over the mountains of Gilead, where it should rise."[1]

One might also mention the reproduction of a typical Oriental house, large enough to serve as a museum; a sectional model of the Great Pyramid, made thus to show the chambers and passages in the interior; and a model of the Tabernacle and its furnishings. Lecturers lectured on these various objects. A peripatetic audience followed their speaker from Joppa to Capernaum, or gathered around him while he expounded the domestic economy of the Orientals. The properties, though sometimes crude, were effective. The men who used them knew their subject and were enough in love with it to put up with the simple apparatus that came to hand.

The Oriental house and its contents formed the nucleus of a museum of respectable size in which might be seen a good collection of casts—sculptured figures, obelisks, the Rosetta stone, and so forth—photographs in great profusion, costumes, maps, and a few books of reference. It was the projectors' idea to admit to the museum only what threw light on Biblical antiquities. A generous public, however, insisted on bringing gifts of a most incongruous character. Both the givers and their offerings were hard to dispose of.

[1] Hurlbut: *The Story of Chautauqua*, 48.

The heart of the Assembly was the Normal Class, at which was pursued a systematic course of Bible study and of modern methods of conducting a Sunday-school. To this, in the early years, all else was made subordinate. At the second session (1875) the class numbered one hundred and ninety; two lessons were given daily, with an examination to mark the close.

The presence at Chautauqua of an always increasing number of children led to the formation of a Children's Class. It was a lively and popular exercise. The daily meeting lasted exactly one hour. Thirty minutes were devoted to Biblical lessons cleverly adapted to the infant mind and thirty minutes to entertainment. At the end of the season the youngsters took an examination with a gravity only surpassed by that of their parents in the normal department.

At the second session of the Assembly a class in Hebrew was organized. It may be taken for granted that of its forty members the larger part would be ministers or theological students. This little class has been pronounced by a high authority the germ of the Chautauqua School of Languages.

Fully organized by 1879, the School of Languages proved to be one of the best features of the Assembly. At that time hardly a college in the United States offered summer courses. At Chautauqua, in exchange for a trifling fee, one might have lessons in French, German, Anglo-Saxon, Latin, Greek, and Hebrew. The teachers were experts, men accustomed to handle large groups. The classes in the modern languages were naturally the ones the best attended. It was a droll sight, the spectacle of one of these classes in action, so good-humored

were the pupils, so vociferous, and in such deadly earnest.
They recited in concert—no other method was possible.
Without doubt they picked up a good deal, and were
set on the right track in the matter of pronunciation.
Best of all, they learned how to use their textbooks.
One had to watch them only a few minutes to discover
that they heartily enjoyed going to school at an age
when school was supposed to be over and done with.

The academic department of Chautauqua has always
flourished. At the College, as we may venture to call
it, many subjects are now taught besides language and
literature. There is a school of pedagogy, of expression, of art, and of music. The work done is of the
sort described by educational writers as "intensive." That
is to say, given a period of six weeks in which to do what
would ordinarily be done in three months, it follows that
the student must bend all his energies to the task in hand.
There is also a school of athletics—very popular, as
such a department is bound to be. Its annual exhibition
is one of the spectacular sights of the Assembly.

From the very beginning of the schools the management has aimed to secure a competent faculty. In the
course of fifty years some queer cattle have turned up.
But queer cattle turn up in universities now and then
and are allowed to remain until they die. In the case
of Chautauqua, with its shifting summer staff, they go
before they die.

At the third session of the Assembly (1876) a three-
day Scientific Conference was held. This was not the
first time that men of science and clergymen occupied
the same platform and made an honest effort to come to
an understanding, rather than wrangle over the meaning

of the first two chapters of Genesis. Nevertheless enlightenment of any sort had been gradual and was still far from widespread. Yet forty-six years had elapsed since Milman (aiming at a scientific treatment of Jewish history) made the orthodox shudder by speaking of Abraham as a sheik, and thirty-two years since Robert Chambers caused a panic in their ranks by hinting that the doctrine of evolution was not necessarily irreligious. *The Vestiges of Creation* was published anonymously; Chambers had too much sense to imperil his social position and injure the cause by a premature acknowledgment of the authorship of a seemingly dangerous book.

Much remained to do. A few lectures by men of standing in the scientific world could not be expected to work a miracle. The lectures at Chautauqua were mainly significant as a proof that the Assembly stood for a free expression of opinion.

The discussions by men of science were immediately followed by a Temperance Congress. Then for the first time—so it is said—John Vincent became convinced that women were not out of place on the public platform; he had heard Frances Willard. He still doubted the right of more than an elect few to be heard on any platform. No woman, however, was at any time denied the privilege of speaking at Chautauqua merely because she happened to be a woman.

Other bodies followed the example of the two just mentioned and held conventions, congresses, and what not at the Assembly grounds. Their meetings might, or might not, form a part of the regular program. That depended on circumstances—the number of delegates, for example, and the nature of the discussions. The National

Education Association met there in 1880; the place was absolutely theirs and the program of their own making.

The institution of public lectures on strictly Biblical themes (talks aside from, but related to, the work of the Normal Class) led to the giving of addresses on all manner of subjects. Two or three lectures of a popular sort were delivered at the first session. The number of these increased from year to year as the need for them became apparent. In this way the platform was rightly and pleasantly secularized. History, biography, science, politics (when not outrageously partisan), literature, travel, and exploration were among the themes presented. The lectures were supplemented with readings, impersonations, concerts, and an evening of pure fun-making now and then, often in the form of a travesty on the faculty's mannerisms and methods.

The platform standard at Chautauqua has been high, indeed remarkably so. No one rostrum of a purely popular character has been graced by so many men whose addresses had both substance and art. It was necessary to have speakers who really knew how to speak. To bring out before the audience a man with a weak voice, or an involved style, or a lackadaisical manner was to insure disappointment. Neither his learning nor his reputation would save him. And strange to say, the orator pure and simple, a compound of voice, frock coat, and efflorescence, could not always be depended on to make a hit.

It may be observed in passing that the platform at Chautauqua is no place for a timid man. The auditorium appalls one by its mere size. To face a thousand auditors is sometimes dismaying. But to face five times that number, and expect to hold them, is a strain on the nerves of any but the most adroit and hardened of speakers. Fortunately, through the wisdom of the management, a smaller hall was provided for lecturers whose subjects could by no possibility be termed popular. If one wanted to hear the man who had a message for the world relating to Hegelian philosophy, or edible fungi, or lizards, or the minor characters in *Sordello* one could go to that smaller hall and be satisfied.

For a long time the public lectures were reported in full. A daily paper was published throughout the season. It began in June, 1876. In its files are to be found many a striking discourse that has never been reprinted, though doubtless the substance has appeared in some treatise or collection of essays. Sticklers for orthography will be glad to know that when this daily paper was in its prime it gave evidence that a serious attempt was being made to spell correctly; the grotesque forms invented by a subsidized board of simplifiers had been to some degree anticipated, but the columns of the press were made cheery by other means.

In 1880 a monthly magazine was founded, *The Chautauquan,* and had a long and prosperous career. It was so well edited that it might easily have lived by reason of intrinsic worth. As the starting of a new periodical is always a dangerous venture, the circulation of this magazine was made certain by printing in its pages from month to month the required readings of the Chautauqua Literary and Scientific Circle.

Admirers of George Borrow—a rather numerous body at the present day—will bear being reminded that an article first printed in *The Chautauquan,* and afterwards issued as a pamphlet, was the kernel of Knapp's monumental life of Borrow. Other articles might be mentioned that in addition to being timely had virtues that made them worth a reading when, presumably, their little day was past.

One would not for a moment wish to convey the impression that John Vincent was the sole inventor of every device employed to stimulate interest in the educational side of Chautauqua. He had able coadjutors, some of whom were scholarly in the strict sense of that word, and all of whom were alert and creative. They had full credit, both popular and official, for what they did, and were more likely to be put forward than kept in the background. What the Superintendent of Instruction did, besides setting on foot a multitude of projects of his own, was to furnish the motive force and develop an esprit de corps. His was a compelling personality. To work with or under him was reckoned a privilege. His firmness, his winning address, his tact and humor, his liberality, and his gift for organization made him an ideal leader.

Chautauqua was not sectarian. The teachers of Bible history, antiquities, and geography, and of Sunday-school methods were chosen from various denominations. This was politic on the part of the Superintendent of Instruction; but I am convinced that had it been represented to him as impolitic he would have followed the same course. He could be tenacious in respect to a stand he had once taken, and he was for toleration if not over-solicitous about union.

Consequently one met, at the Assembly, Presbyterians, Congregationalists, Baptists, and Episcopalians (to name but four of the divisions of the Church). A man was invited to come, not because he held this creed or that, but because he was an adept and knew how to interpret his subject. One recalls the apparition of an Orthodox Jewish pundit, brought to the Assembly to teach Hebrew. Picturesque and venerable (he had never marred the corners of his beard) he was said to cook his own meals; the now familiar legend on many New York restaurant signs, "strictly kosher," was unknown to the Gentiles who frequented Chautauqua.

The presence of these various instructors had a marked effect in making no less various the body of students and the popular audience. In time denominational houses began to spring up, and to be used as centers for conferences, religious meetings, and social affairs. The author of *The Story of Chautauqua* mentions nine such houses. Their existence is a witness to the catholicity of the Assembly.

It will have been guessed that while the educational side of Chautauqua, both Biblical and secular, was taking shape many problems arose that taxed the ingenuity of the President, Lewis Miller. An Institute of only a fortnight's duration was not so difficult to finance, merely because it was held in a grove. When, however, the original period was augmented by putting a week before it as well as a week after it, and then by adding yet more weeks, the President had to look to ways and means. Men of distinction were brought to lecture or to preach or to hold daily classes; no one supposed that they ought to give the Assembly their services.

A gate fee was charged. One could take a ticket for the day, for a week, or for the season. To the holder of such a ticket all the public affairs were open. If he attended but a half of them he got his money's worth. Now there are people in this world who are opposed to paying for anything if they can avoid it, and who intensely dislike the idea of parting with hard cash to the end that they may be uplifted; all the uplift must be at another's cost. The American people are trained to think that education ought to be free—and much of it is. All our great universities are eleemosynary institutions; no undergraduate pays for what he gets.

The Chautauqua Assembly could not subsist on kind words and loving thoughts, so it was decided that a modest tax, extremely modest in the beginning, should be imposed on whoever attended the sessions. The arrangement was accepted with good grace by a majority of the visitors. Only that peculiar remnant who wanted a dole, in the shape of lessons in Biblical history and so forth, stood out. Their subterfuges to escape paying forty cents a day, on high moral grounds no doubt, were ingenious.

A merry war sometimes raged between a firm and adroit management on the one side and the advocates of the everything-educational-for-nothing theory on the other. Had large fees been at stake the authorities must have bewailed the depravity of mankind. As it was they could only marvel that certain worthy good souls should go through so much to save so very little. In the end the delinquents saved nothing—the system devised for collection was exact. Possibly they had a change of heart and sought to impress on others the wholesome truth that in general anything worth having is worth paying for. Other problems than that of financing the platform arose, a multitude of them. The one cited above is singular in that it brought out in bold relief a droll side of human nature.

John Vincent had a strong prejudice in favor of the commandment that forbids worldly activities on the Sabbath. Among these activities he classed picnics and excursions. In the case of Chautauqua they were eliminated by the simple plan of closing the gates, to the general public, and keeping them closed from Saturday night to Monday morning. The rule was not enforced with absurd and tyrannical strictness. Exceptions were made. The right of entrance and egress at will was merely suspended for about twenty-four hours. No boats were allowed to land and consequently no horde of trippers, bent on pleasure-making, settled down long enough to satisfy their curiosity, and then noisily departed, leaving fragments of their lunch scattered over the grass plots.

Regular patrons of Chautauqua soon inured themselves to the quiet and serenity of the day as it was observed there and were quick to make a protest when the rule seemed in danger of being relaxed. They understood that this was one of the few places in America where they could see the old-fashioned day of rest kept in a modern way; that is, untouched by the acerbity that formerly marked it. The time passed almost too rapidly. The morning service was impressive. It bore the stamp of John Vincent's personality. It showed his love of order, dignity, seemliness, and grace in churchly offices. The ritual was, I believe, drawn up by himself. In his hands it would not be over-elaborate. He valued such aids to devotion, but he valued the sermon more.

JOHN HEYL VINCENT

The Chautauqua Assembly had cost its projectors so much in the way of time, physical strength, and ingenuity of all sorts, to say nothing of the sums of money the President had spent out of his own pocket, that they were decidedly averse to having their field encroached on. To John Vincent's annoyance a rival institution was started across the lake, in plain view of the original. He had no objection to its existence, only to its location. He doubted the purity of the motive that led to its establishment in that exact spot.

That it did not flourish to the extent he feared was no sign that it might not, under favorable conditions, draw off patronage that rightfully belonged to the older of the two assemblies. He said to his son, "The Baptists will find some bright, aggressive young minister of their denomination, put him in charge over there, and give him a free hand." He perhaps recalled Frederick the Great's remark, that "of two Frenchmen at the same court one must perish," and applied it to the case of two Chautauquas within half a mile of each other.

With this thought at the back of his mind, he was prepared to act as soon as he heard of W. R. Harper, a young professor at a well-known Baptist theological school, the sort of man an enterprising board of directors, with their wits about them, would be likely to choose as the head of their enterprise at Lake Chautauqua. He wired the professor from St. Louis, where he happened then to be, to meet him at a point midway between St. Louis and Chicago; this in order to save time. The two came to an understanding. Harper accepted an instructorship in the School of Languages. In 1885 he became the principal of the Chautauqua College of Liberal Arts.

He did not drop the work he had undertaken there after becoming the president of the University of Chicago, though the major part of it had to be delegated to subordinates.

His affection for the founder, the people, and the place was great—as great as were his services. For some years he regularly spent the week-end at Chautauqua, taking a night train out of Chicago on Friday and returning so as to be at his post on Monday morning. The incident of how, at the age of twenty-seven, he came to attract the notice of John Vincent is not generally known. I have heard it cited as a capital illustration of John Vincent's talents in the rôle of impresario. A conspicuously bright man was needed for the School of Languages, and it was needful that he be a Baptist as well as a bright man, the very person whom the people across the lake might pitch on to make a success of their venture.

CHAPTER XII

THE READING CIRCLE

It was never John Vincent's way to arrogate anything to himself. He preferred to extol, in his fluent and emphatic manner, the achievements of other men. If he claimed, as he did, the invention of "The Chautauqua Literary and Scientific Circle" he undoubtedly had a right to do so. It was founded in 1878.

Familiarly known as the C. L. S. C., it has numbered readers by the hundred thousand. By some virtue peculiar to itself it caught the public fancy, yet was nothing more than a course of reading designed for the use of a mature and busy people who could give but a few minutes of each day to a serious book.

The popularity of the C. L. S. C. was in a measure due to certain beguiling features. The readers were divided into "classes," after the custom of every American college. The course of reading extended through four years. A class that began in 1878 would naturally be "graduated" in 1882. The consciousness of belonging to a little army of students, all aiming at the same goal, proved to be inspiring. Habitual loiterers made an effort, for once, not to fall behind.

The classes were distinguished from one another not only by the date of the year in which their prescribed reading came to an end; they were given (or gave themselves) picturesque names, such as "The Pioneers"—an appropriate designation for the first class of all. Every reader looked forward to the day of his graduation; that is, to "Recognition Day." Special ceremonies of an impressive nature marked the occasion.

Great stress was laid on these ceremonies at the outset. Their value was patent to the inventor of the Reading Circle; it only remained to find out by actual trial whether the readers as a body would take his point of view.

John Vincent maintained that sentiment has always played a large part in fostering what is commonly known as college spirit. No one would be so paradoxical as to dispute this. Class reunions during the week of commencement are, as everybody knows, decidedly sentimental affairs. An affection for Alma Mater, and for one another, that barely existed in the undergraduate years now blossoms out in a surprising manner. The alumni —strong men for the most part, and not easily melted— enjoy their own tenderness. Their purse strings are relaxed in the genial warmth and the college profits thereby.

Any one can see how a feeling of solidarity would first be created and then intensified by the ordinary associations of the club, the dormitory, and even the lecture hall. As for that greatest of all unifying forces, the stadium, what words are adequate to describe its power! Certainly there is no congregation quite so maudlin as the one that collects to watch a football game. The ties are exceedingly strong.

When sketching (in a chapter on the origin of the C. L. S. C.) the invariable effect of college associations, John Vincent had in mind a force other than that emanating from the arena or the recitation room. There is, for example, that sense of the continuity of academic life. Moments will come in which the most callous of undergraduates is impressed by the fact that the college had a prodigiously long career before he honored it with his presence, and that it will continue to live, as best it can, after he departs. He discovers that there is something rather fine in making one of the large company that has marched through its main portal, lingered a while, and then marched out again. He falls into the ways of the place, learns and respects its traditions while affecting to scoff at them, picks up scraps of its history, and becomes a staunch supporter of old customs as well as a raucous singer of time-honored ditties. And the basis of it all, to a greater or less degree, is sentiment.

Convinced of the worth of the class spirit in keeping people together, and of the songs, the emblems, the set forms—of everything, in short, that goes to make up the pageantry of academic life—John Vincent determined to bring to the Reading Circle as much of this element as the conditions would allow. It had been found profitable elsewhere and should be no less so here.

He admits that he had his misgivings. "The appeal to sentiment was an experiment." It might not meet with a response from the mature men and women of whom the Circle was almost sure to be mainly composed. In that case "it would prove both ridiculous and disastrous." On trial it was found that the members not only had no objection to processions and memorial days, but that they took to them with avidity. The idea was a happy one, it was presented in a felicitous way, and the people were receptive.

A class widely scattered over the country, doing its prescribed work at home, its members seldom or never meeting unless they live in the same town, cannot have an academic center in the common usage of the phrase. In another sense they may claim to have one—the white-columned building that stood for years in that part of Chautauqua known as St. Paul's Grove, and since supplanted by a more substantial edifice. It is called "The Hall of Philosophy." The name, if fanciful, is not wholly a misnomer; some genuine philosophers have instructed their audiences from that platform, not a few of whom had the gift of making themselves intelligible.

The Hall is a scene of notable activity on Recognition Day. The order of exercises is about as follows—I give the main points without going into details:

A procession is formed in several divisions. These unite in St. Paul's Grove. The graduating class assembles before the so-called Golden Gate. At a given signal the gate is opened to admit them, and immediately closed and locked, only to be opened again when the graduates of the next year take their stand before it. A set ritual is observed. It never varies; no change that might be made would be in the nature of an improvement. And the service is endeared to Chautauquans from having been in use for forty-two consecutive years. It has become a tradition, along with other customs and usages, as the man who drew it up hoped it might be.

The members obtain their diplomas at the Hall. The address to the class is given in the Amphitheater. The ceremony as a whole is fully as impressive as that to be witnessed at a college commencement, perhaps more so. It is surprising to see what a large number of not alone

middle-aged but of elderly people have had the courage
to follow out the course. Octogenarian readers have
by no means been a rarity. The appearance of one
such in circumstances where she can be recognized—the
heroic octogenarian is invariably a woman—is certain to
call out a round or two of applause.

In the speech in which he first laid his plan of the
Reading Circle before a Chautauqua audience (August
10, 1878) John Vincent said, "I have already the names
of a few candidates. I do not know how many. If we
have ten to begin with I shall think it quite a success."

"Ten to begin with!" He had at least two hundred
within an hour. The local bookstall was stripped bare
in a short time, and the publishers of one of the prescribed volumes found it difficult to supply as many copies
as were wanted. It was assumed that the first class
would be small, and that each succeeding class would
be a little larger. At some undetermined point of time
the limit of growth would be attained, and from then
on, as other educational novelties took the fancy of
the public, there would be a gradual falling away. The
event turned out much as predicted; the capital error
lay in the assumption that only a few hundreds would
enroll in the first class.

Admitting, as we must, that the argument from numbers is not the one most conclusive of merit, we may
find amusement in glancing at some of the figures. The
total enrollment for the first year was over eight thousand four hundred. Had the entire body of readers
followed the course to the very end, the Superintendent
of Instruction would have been justified in announcing
his belief in modern miracles. Many dropped out after

doing the work for a year or two. The entering classes were large and enthusiastic. In 1891, thirteen years from the date of its foundation, the Circle numbered a hundred thousand readers; this would be inclusive of those who were doing supplementary work. The three undergraduate classes had at that time twenty thousand members each. The class about to be formed promised to be as large or larger.

The first class to be "recognized" numbered about eighteen hundred. Of these some eight hundred came to Chautauqua to receive their diplomas in person. The one thousand graduates who were unable to be present contented themselves with recognition through the post.

Needless to say that no academic degrees were conferred. The diploma may be described as merely a certificate, the purport of which is that the candidate declares, on his word of honor, that he has done the required reading and that the officials believe him. Credit for the supplementary readings is given in the form of seals attached to the original diploma.

The address to the graduating class is sure to be notable. In the list of speakers one finds the names of Lyman Abbott, Edward E. Hale, David Swing, Alice Freeman Palmer, Mary A. Livermore, Hamilton Mabie, Charles W. Eliot, and C. H. Brent. The full list is too long to be quoted here. John Vincent's name appears but once. His theme, an eminently appropriate one, was "The Chautauqua Idea."

Readers living in the same town found it to their advantage to meet at stated intervals and discuss the books. Hundreds of these local circles were formed, and their members went through the course together. The well-known head of a theatrical company organized a circle among his people and conducted the class himself. He played the schoolmaster in a way to convince one and all that he possessed gifts other than the histrionic. Circles sprang up in Japan, in Russia, and in South Africa. The Russian readers were attracted to the C. L. S. C. through articles on Chautauqua written by a Russian woman, a journalist, who lived in America. Some of them, when applying for membership, enclosed the fees in the postage stamps of their own country. Such exhibitions of naïveté are confined to no one nation or race.

An education that is limited to the reading of a few good books every twelvemonth for four consecutive years can hardly escape the epithet of "superficial." It was not supposed that the course would do more than quicken the reader intellectually and give him an outlook that he had not enjoyed before. One reads certain works at the instance of one's college professor; the members of the C. L. S. C. were guided by the recommendation of an advisory board, composed for the most part of college men. The books selected in the earlier years of the Circle were anything but superficial, were possibly a little stiff for the reader of average attainments. It was found expedient to lighten the task somewhat.

John Vincent believed that Chautauqua, through the C. L. S. C., if no substitute for the college, at all events did an effective work in building up the college and the university; it educated the parents.

This particular Reading Circle, though not the first of its kind, was the largest and the most distinctive; and it became the parent of a host of others, all modeled more or less closely upon it. If there be any virtue in a device that has had the effect of leading a vast number of people to read systematically, and to read books that are worth while, then the C. L. S. C. should have whatever credit is its due. It is believed to have had a fructifying influence in several directions; that is to say, as a part of the Chautauqua Movement taken in its entirety. Only two summers ago (1923) a lecturer at Oxford was heard to say that while the idea of University Extension is of English origin, dating from 1850, the idea of the Extension Summer Meeting ("the bringing people together into a Vacation University") is due to Chautauqua.

A word about some of the books. One finds in the list of required readings for the first year Green's *Short History of the English People,* Mahaffy's *Old Greek Life,* and Stopford Brooke's *Primer of English Literature,* notable books all three. In addition to these (not counting the little manuals compiled to serve as guides) four other books were required, one on astronomy, one on physiology, and two on the Bible. The course was somewhat miscellaneous; the advisory board was feeling its way, or *his* way, if, as I suspect, one man drew up that first of all the lists.

Among the required books of the second year were Merivale's *General History of Rome,* a history of the United States, a primer of Latin literature, one of American literature, a treatise on biology, another on theology, a third on bodily health and how to secure it, and four or five specially compiled handbooks. Again the course seems to embrace almost too many subjects.

Fewer books appear in the third year's course—*Hy-*

patia is the one piece of literature among them—and the collection is not so heterogeneous. Neither science nor theology is omitted—"required readings" on both subjects were printed in the magazine. In the fourth and fifth years greater emphasis is laid on Greek history and literature. This was a step in the right direction. The earlier courses had covered too much ground. That, indeed, may have been one cause of their popularity. Every one found something to his taste.

Another word about certain books; those designated as "preparatory" and "collegiate" courses in Greek and Latin.[1] Inasmuch as the idea of the series was John Vincent's, and the four volumes were made at his suggestion, a short account of their form and contents will not be out of place.

Each volume consists of passages from approved translations of classical authors, with a running commentary, historical and critical. By reason of the arrangement of the material, the books are fairly entitled to the designation of histories of literature. The question of their absolute intrinsic merit does not concern us. They were well done and served their purpose. Had they been compiled with less care their usefulness would not have been much impaired. What the directors of the C. L. S. C. aimed to do was to put a body of classical literature into the hands of their readers, and to give it such a form as would admit of their taking it in.

The first of the two Greek books is a survey of all the ground that must be covered by a student who is preparing for college. There are preliminary sections on Greece, its people and its literature, together with a

[1] By William C. Wilkinson.

list of the grammars and other textbooks in common use
in preparatory schools. Then follows a chapter on the
"Greek Reader." On running through it one finds that
it contains extracts from Æsop, Plutarch, Lucian, and
Xenophon (the *Memorabilia*). To the *Anabasis* something over fifty pages are given, to the *Iliad* and *Odyssey*
about a hundred and twenty-five pages. The metrical
illustrations are not all from one hand. Sometimes a
passage will be quoted in the forms in which Pope, Tennyson, and Bryant respectively saw fit to render it. The
three versions are placed side by side so that they may
be compared. In gathering his illustrations the author
has not forgotten Worsley's remarkable performance in
turning the *Odyssey* into faultless English verse. The
commentary is halted at one point for the introduction
of a few pertinent and helpful remarks on the subject
of meter.

The second of the two Greek courses begins with
Herodotus and Thucydides. A chapter on Plato follows. To each of the four great dramatists a chapter
is given. The extracts are copious. The lyrical poets
receive due attention. Eloquence is represented by passages from Demosthenes and Æschines, and the historical
commentary is ample; any reader would be able to understand the circumstances under which the celebrated
speeches were delivered.

To be sure the Reading Circle was encouraging the
use of translations, a most unscholarly proceeding. The
majority of us must use them or be counted among the
wholly unlettered. We spend years in acquiring enough
Greek to construe a few books of the *Iliad* or a play of
Aristophanes. Having nothing to show for it, we ex-

plain that it has been a good discipline. "I wouldn't give up what little Greek I have," says one—meaning the almost invisible modicum that he brought away with him when he left college. He is quite in the right, but if he really wants to know the *Iliad* he takes down the prose translation by Lang, Leaf, and Myers, and goes through its five hundred pages from cover to cover much as he would go through a novel. The Reading Circle may have incited not a few people to do this very thing. There is no telling to what lengths the public will go once it becomes enamored of books.

In the earlier days of the C. L. S. C. a number of the books prescribed proved formidable from their mere size. Every line of Green's *Short History* is interesting, but after all there is a good deal of it. Merivale's *Rome* (the stout one-volume textbook once much used in colleges and now supplanted) was thought to be a little heavy and the matter capable of compression. The experiment was tried of having books made especially for the course. Every volume was executed by an academic, and was therefore accorded both the respect due to the quality of the workmanship and something more—the reverence properly felt for any piece of writing that drops from the pen of a professor.

If in some instances the books were written by men who had to get up the subject assigned them they were none the worse on that account. They may even have been the better for being all but improvised. Naturally a zoölogist would not be asked to write on literature or a theologian on chemistry. What the counselors had to guard against was the failure that is sometimes made when a man deeply versed in a given subject attempts to present that subject in its broad outlines; he knows all there is to know, but does not know what to leave out. An amateur will make a better book than he.

We have seen that the collection of required readings was at first decidedly miscellaneous. Each volume was chosen for its own sake, and with no reference to its neighbor. A sensible change was made when all the readings for a given twelvemonth were so arranged as to give unity to the course. There was a "European Year," for example. One of the books dealt with contemporary European rulers (a number of whom have since disappeared), another with social progress, yet others with art, scientific achievement, home life, and with the study of some important capital. During the "Roman Year" the emphasis was laid on Latin literature and Roman history. The convenience of the arrangement is obvious. Diverse as were the topics, there was a genuine unity in the course.

Nothing gave John Vincent more satisfaction than to meet with proofs that the C. L. S. C. was a help to people who had hitherto read aimlessly, or in some cases had given up reading in any proper sense of the word. Some one wrote to him of finding a set of the books in the caboose of a freight train in Missouri. The conductor was going through them. The brakeman read with him. We knew that Bret Harte's miners liked Homer, and conceived an immense respect for Ash-heels. Brakemen would be no less receptive.

In the volume entitled *The Chautauqua Movement* are printed some twenty pages of extracts from letters testifying to the value of this system of self-instruction. Coming as they do from people of all sorts and conditions, the letters make a striking little sheaf of documents. All the writers were engaged in the pursuit of knowledge under difficulties.

We have seen that not one quarter of the first class was graduated. But nearly two thousand were, and all of the original body had learned something by undertaking the work. How one of those who had dropped out of the course felt about it we know from an incident told in *The Story of Chautauqua*. Edward Everett Hale, on one of his journeys, fell into conversation with a fellow passenger and soon gathered that the chance acquaintance knew something about the Reading Circle, that he might even be a member. On being questioned, the man admitted that he had begun the course but had never finished it; as a matter of fact he had read only one book. He then added, "But any institution that can lead a man to read Green's *Short History of the English People* has done considerable for that man."

CHAPTER XIII

THE popular platform at Chautauqua (in distinction from the academic, the professedly educational) had to be maintained through the presence of speakers who understood how to attract and hold a vast audience. They were in general men and women who had made their reputation, and whom everybody was eager to hear. They might talk on any subject they liked provided they talked their best. What the people wanted was the sort of performance commonly described as "a brilliant effort." The speaker must delight, astonish, inspire, or even antagonize his hearers; if he also convulsed them with merriment at frequent intervals he was none the less well thought of.

The so-called popular lecture has a character all its own. It is often stuffed with anecdote, though not always. It abounds in passages that are decidedly rhetorical, in examples of genuine eloquence, and in quick transitions from the sentimental to the broadly humorous. It will sometimes create the impression of being rough-hewn, yet in reality it is a consummate piece of art.

One of its peculiarities is that it seldom reads well. What was so captivating when heard is robbed of its magic in the process of reporting it. The flavor evaporates in print. The popular lecture may be anything

we choose to call it—so long as we do not call it literature.

The Superintendent of Instruction knew perfectly
what a miscellaneous audience required. He gave his
people an opportunity of hearing Gough, Talmage, Mc-
Cabe, Cook, Conwell, Henson, Willetts, Gunsaulus, Mrs.
Livermore, Miss Willard, and a host of other speakers
of recognized standing. In describing them as "popular"
one does not mean to imply that they were merely that;
every one of them came bearing what earnest folk char-
acterize as "a message." The auditor was at liberty to
receive it or not, but hear the message delivered he must
because of the skill with which the presentation was
made.

For years together one might depend on John Vincent's
being in charge of the platform at each of the three
daily public lectures in the Amphitheater. He was a
masterly presiding officer. It was a profitable study to
watch his mode of procedure. What he did there might
have been done differently and with equal skill—it were
hard to say wherein it might have been better done.

Naturally his main business, as Superintendent of Instruction, was to introduce the various speakers to their
respective audiences. How important from his point of
view was this apparently simple function may be known
from the fact that he rarely deputed it, and then only
to the most trustworthy of his lieutenants. The task
must have been burdensome. The meetings lasted about
one and a half hours. On red-letter days they often
ran to two hours. This included the announcements and
the introduction. The presiding officer aimed to keep
every meeting within reasonable bounds. But orators

must have their way and entertainers their fling. It was not his duty to curb a celebrated man who had fallen into the vice of prolixity, or arbitrarily to strike out features essential to a given program.

His introductions were models in the *genre*. One exaggerates no more than is pardonable when one says that he never made a mistake. He had facility in the shaping of happy phrases, unrivaled quickness in seizing on points that would tell—especially such points as showed him to be conversant with what was uppermost in the public mind—and a wit as keen as it was unfailing. A number of his introductions are current, one hears them quoted (or misquoted) from time to time. They are not the best because the most popular. The greater number are now irrecoverable.

The theory that an introduction should bear to the discourse that follows it a relation not unlike that of the title-page of a book to the text is not unsound. It ought, therefore, to be accurate, emphatic, attractive, and brief. John Vincent's introductions possessed these four virtues, and many besides. He was urbane. The speaker had good reason to be thankful who found himself recommended to an audience with so much courtliness and generosity. If a sensitive man, he was encouraged; if confident and disposed to think well of himself, he was put on his mettle.

The presiding officer of Chautauqua had a threefold duty to perform; in addition to presenting the speakers he must make the announcements, and also advise the people on matters touching their daily life in a community that had grown so fast as to have taken on the aspect of a good-sized town.

In general the announcements that precede the event of a given session are dull enough, and as necessary as they are dull. By some knack, of which he almost alone possessed the secret, John Vincent contrived to give these dry details a charm that somehow was not out of keeping with their practical character. His touch was light, his humor never misplaced. A visitor at Chautauqua was once overheard to say that he "would as soon hear the Doctor read from his program book as to listen to a lecture by So-and-So," mentioning a then popular but now forgotten spellbinder.

The miscellaneous talks from the platform were many and varied. When of a hortatory character they might involve an amiable chiding of the audience for misconduct—such misconduct, that is to say, as so mature, sedate, and intelligent an audience could be capable of.

Now there is a tradition that at Chautauqua during the Golden Age—an indefinite period the chronological limits of which are hard to define—nobody ever left the Amphitheater, or for that matter any assembly hall, in the middle of a lecture. The tradition rests on a substantial basis. A state of affairs so nearly perfect could not last. A few people would slip out on one pretext or another and go their several ways. They aimed to be as self-effacing as possible, and were the more conspicuous by reason of their patent efforts not to disturb.

This defection on the part of the few rather annoyed the presiding officer. Always willing to sit out any speech or discussion or entertainment himself, he could see no reason why others should not do the same. At last that which had been merely sporadic threatened to become a habit. He began to admonish his people. His strictures were cleverly put, they were often little masterpieces of restrained irony; it was a pleasure to hear them. The audience would laugh and applaud and be thankful that they had not missed one of the best features of the hour by going out prematurely.

Chautauqua is not the only place where the solid mass of auditors that greets the speaker at the beginning of his discourse begins to melt a little towards the close. Everybody remembers J. R. Lowell's account of his anxiety as the time approached for his first course of lectures at the Lowell Institute. He had been told that he could not hope to keep his group of listeners intact beyond an hour, and he evidently doubted whether he would be able to say all he wanted to say in the period allowed him. Americans are receptive and responsive and patient, but they know when they are bored. They can be depended on at church or at the theater or at a political meeting, but not always in the lecture hall.

Over against those who would leave the Amphitheater when common politeness required them to stay may be set the very few who, for the comfort of all, should have gone before they did. Invariably mothers, they brought the proofs of their good fortune with them.

John Vincent approved of mothers and maintained a sincerely benevolent attitude towards children. He sympathized with those women at Chautauqua who were so situated that they could not enjoy the privileges of the Amphitheater unless they were accompanied by their offspring. They came and trouble ensued.

Babies have been known to lift up their voice in the congregation, if not, as some believe, to bewail the fact that they were ever born, then as an expression of re-

[149]

sentment because at so tender an age they are forced
to attend lectures. Indeed it seems unreasonable to ask
infants in arms to hear Joseph Cook discuss "The Rise
of Rationalism in German Universities."

Odd as the statement may sound, it is quite true that
the wailing of a healthy child is distinctly audible to
everybody except its own parents, who at such times wear
the look of inane rapture given by the Old Masters to
the committees of saints stationed at the bottom or on
the right and left wings of ecclesiastical paintings. That
an entire audience (to say nothing of the speaker, who,
being an immortal soul, has responsibilities and anxieties
of his own) should be disturbed by one crying child
seemed to John Vincent an intolerable state of affairs.
He must and did speak his mind on the subject. His
appeals were suave, ingeniously worded, and firm. He
was so reasonable that you would have said it must be
a pleasure to follow his suggestions.

But no; there was always one mother who held, seemingly, that any lecture was the better for being provided
with an obbligato accompaniment of the sort her child
was qualified to supply. Deeply hurt, perhaps angry,
she would seek out this champion of the greatest good
of the greatest number and reproach him for heartless-
ness. As the man had too much heart, and was in con-
stant danger of being victimized through his sympathies,
the attitude of the mother in question filled him with
astonishment.

He held his ground; it became an unwritten law of
the Amphitheater that three thousand listeners had rights
that even mothers were bound to respect. Once at least,
so they say, the unwelcome truth had to be administered

by a process akin to forcible feeding, as when, the evil being flagrant, he remarked that the building in which they were gathered together had many exits. Pointed though the observation was we are not to conclude therefrom that he had lost his temper. *That* he never lost, notwithstanding the many occasions for it during the years that he played the rôle of benevolent platform despot.

They who were daily witnesses of his skill in managing crowds—and under conditions that varied from the serene to the exasperating—quite forgot how the exhibition might strike a newcomer. The uniform adroitness and frequent brilliancy of his tactics made the novice at Chautauqua stare. Methods such as he employed, though invariably dignified and in keeping with the time and the place, had a strange flavor; they smacked of genius. Visitors accounted for the man's gifts in various ways. Geography was once made to play a part in the analysis. An enthusiastic Southern lady, extolling him in terms that if florid were not undeserved, exclaimed, "Yes, I have seen Doctor Vincent at Chautauqua, and it was wonderful, perfectly wonderful, the way he made those Yankees behave; they would do anything he told them to do." She remembered that he was born at Tuscaloosa and there was little doubt in her mind as to the origin of his skill in leadership.

Of lecturers who were brought to Chautauqua to give each a distinctively educational course there was never any lack. The Superintendent of Instruction held that if the Assembly was to succeed in providing non-collegians with what he described as "the college outlook" the end was best reached by inviting to the platform university-trained men. The majority of those who came held chairs in one or other of the numerous colleges scattered over the face of the land. A few were clergymen, editors, men of letters, or publicists who had specialized in some department, and who therefore spoke ex cathedra.

The names here given are meant to be illustrative merely; there is no point in loading the text with a catalogue from the annual program.

Among the favorite lecturers on historical subjects were Von Holst, Fiske, McMaster, and Herbert B. Adams. All were heard with deep attention. John Fiske was singularly attractive, and that without the help of those graces and flourishes that are supposed to be legitimate in public discourse. He read his lectures from manuscript. Yet he was once heard to give an hour's talk that involved the precise statement of a multitude of facts (names and dates in profusion) without the sign of a memorandum before him. He afterwards remarked that the principal advantage gained by using a manuscript was this: With the manuscript before his eyes a speaker was kept from expanding unduly matter that for the sake of proportion should be confined within strict limits.

Courses on literature were given by Mitchell ("Ik Marvell"), Moulton, Winchester, McClintock, Richardson, Perry, Griggs, and Burton. Popular for the simple reason that literature is attractive in itself, these courses had each a large hearing because of the agreeable way in which they were given. None the less were they academic, an ordered presentation of a theme, only more condensed than would be necessary in the classroom.

One has seen the Amphitheater all but filled on the occasion of a literary lecture, as when Sprague or Moulton spoke. Both these men had, in addition to solid scholarship, the oratorical gift. Sprague would build cloud-capped towers of fine rhetoric that were truly astonishing.

Among the men who discussed social, economic, religious, or strictly philosophical themes were Bowne, Gladden, Lyman Abbott, Fairbairn, F. G. Peabody, George Adam Smith, G. W. Cooke, and Henry Drummond. Among those who dealt with education in its more or less technical aspects were Stanley Hall and W. T. Harris.

Of visitors from abroad no one was heard with more interest and curiosity than Drummond. He was at Chautauqua in 1893, just ten years after the publication of *Natural Law in the Spiritual World*. His course of lectures was afterwards brought out under its original title of *The Ascent of Man*. A respectable encyclopedia dismisses these two attempts to reconcile evangelical Christianity and evolution as "more remarkable for rhetoric than logic." The Lowell Institute brought Drummond to America for the course of 1893, and the lectures were repeated at Chautauqua.

Mahaffy of Dublin, noted both as a scholar and a breezy personality, amused his audiences fully as much as he instructed them. He had not been warned that Americans love flattery above all things else, and that the surest way to their favor was to tell them, *imprimis*, that they were the greatest people on God's earth. After that he might say what he liked, provided he did not flatly contradict his introductory statement. Mahaffy lectured on "Old Greek Life," and incidentally picked to pieces the Constitution of the United States. His strictures were regarded as the natural product of an ebullient fancy.

Owen Seaman, who came later than he, lectured on Greek art and made no attempt to disturb American equanimity. If I am not mistaken, Seaman (who is now Sir Owen, and the editor of *Punch*) was the first to wear, at Chautauqua, an academic gown while giving his lectures. One had seen these gowns often enough at our own college commencements, and had never failed to notice how ill at case the professors looked in them; one now saw that they might be worn gracefully, even in the woods.

The colleges were represented at the Assembly not only by members of their respective faculties but also by their official heads. It will be enough to mention the presidents of Harvard, Brown, Columbia, Cornell, Michigan, Minnesota, Chicago, Williams, Leland Stanford, Vassar, Smith, and Wellesley. The author of *The Story of Chautauqua* affirms that he has seen on the grounds at one time no less than ten college presidents. It is impossible that all ten should have been lecturing there simultaneously. Curiosity may have drawn them to the Assembly, or philosophic interest. One of the ten may have been booked for an address, and the other nine have come to see how he would do it.

Addresses by these dignitaries usually fell on the great days of the Assembly, such as Recognition Day or a Sunday in August when the season was at its height.

The word "president" reminds one that six Presidents of the United States have been the guests of Chautauqua. The statement must be qualified; not every one of the six was in office at the time of his visit.

Only one came for the purpose of making a set speech. The first of the six, Grant, was not expected to say anything. Consequently no one was disappointed when he took his leave without having uttered a word in public. Garfield made a ten-minute impromptu talk in which there was no reference to politics. Hayes and McKinley came simply as guests; Taft as one of the participants in a platform meeting. Roosevelt was at Chautauqua on four different occasions; in 1890 for a series of historical lectures, afterwards for single addresses.

The presence of these political celebrities was enjoyed. Americans everywhere like to stare at their President, to crowd open-mouthed around him, and, if permitted, to make him physically uncomfortable by shaking his hand until it is ready to drop off. Perhaps the day will come when, owing to the gradual spread of civilization among us, the unsanitary custom of miscellaneous hand-shaking will be given up. A humorist suggests that at the White House receptions each guest have *his* hand shaken by a muscular deputy. The President is merely to look on and smile. If grotesque, the plan has at least the merit of being humane.

Of the men named in the above paragraphs Roosevelt alone ranks with the academic lecturers, whether great or small, with those who have come on a specified date to discuss a specified topic. But when he gave his course on "The Winning of the West" he was obliged to speak from the Amphitheater platform, so great was the number of people who desired to hear him. He was "popular" in the sense attached to the word by managers of bureaus and their agents. Besides being a forceful orator, with an engaging theme, he was a celebrity.

Of aspirants to the Presidency, at least three were heard at Chautauqua. Their drawing power was enormous, and there could be no question of their ability to hold a vast crowd. It is not to be inferred that they made political—that is to say, partisan—speeches. For many years the rule was strictly enforced that forbade speeches of this character. Once, however, an exception was made, in 1911. A lively campaign was in progress, and the representatives of four parties (among them a candidate) were invited to state their views. They stated them freely. If success is to be measured by gate receipts the experiment was a success. The affair was certainly a radical departure from old ways and customs.

No platform can exist without occasional spectacular displays, but the real strength of Chautauqua has lain in its distinctively educational features. It is only right to emphasize what John Vincent had most at heart when he set on foot the Reading Circle and organized, little by little, one of the first (as it is still one of the most active) of summer schools.

The work that he did in the world was various. Every one knows how he revolutionized Sunday-school methods. Few would deny, however, that Chautauqua is his monument, though not exclusively his, and one that bids fair to last. At no time given to self-gratulation, he had some excuse for the indulgence when he reflected on Chautauqua, what it had become, and what it had achieved. Over against criticisms on the institution that have the air of being almost willfully perverse may be placed the estimates of men who try to see things as they really are.

Some years ago the writer of these lines was taken by a friend to call on Charles Eliot Norton. In the course of the visit Norton made some inquiries about John Vincent and his work. He then said, in his quietly positive way, "I regard Chautauqua as the most significant and hopeful fact in American life at the present time." A year later the same two callers spent an hour with him at "Shady Hill," his home in Cambridge. Again he spoke of Chautauqua, and repeated the opinion given above in almost the same words; he seemed perfectly to comprehend what the place stood for, what it had aimed to do, the means employed, and the results.

Other tributes might be quoted, from sources quite as high. All are in the same vein. The long letter from William Cullen Bryant is so well known as to make extracts almost superfluous. It was written at the time the Reading Circle was founded. Bryant was especially taken by the liberal character of the proposed course of study. He believed, he said, that there was no branch of human knowledge so important as that which teaches the duties we owe to God and to one another. "Yet is a knowledge of the results of science, and such of its processes as lie most open to the popular mind, important for the purpose of showing the different spheres occupied by science and religion, and preventing the inquirer from mistaking their divergence from each other for opposition."

CHAPTER XIV

THE ORATOR

ALL who had the pleasure of hearing John Vincent in his prime, and on occasions that called out the best that was in him, agree in pronouncing him a speaker of rare distinction. But the number of these has greatly diminished. Accounts at first hand of his manner and method have become infrequent, and already hearsay begins to take the place of positive testimony. Though his fame, like that of most orators and actors, rests largely on tradition, we must believe him to have been what people said he was.

He had all the physical qualifications that go to the making of the accomplished orator. I refer now to the externals, or, if I may put it in so homely a way, to the machinery for the conveying of the subject matter to the audience. Take for example his voice, of which so much has been said in newspaper reports of his public work.

There are speakers whose voice is so good that it is impossible not to remark upon it; and they themselves are so well aware of the fortunate possession that they cannot hide their complacency. You would not say of them that they were "voice and nothing besides," but you would, at a first hearing, be as much impressed by the tone of the instrument as by the tune that was played.

[158]

John Vincent was not one of these. During all my long acquaintanceship with him I never heard him utter a word that led me to suspect that he prided himself on his voice; I doubt whether he thought much about it. Yet it was a very remarkable voice, characteristic without being peculiar, flexible, sympathetic, penetrating, and always under perfect control. The way in which he managed it gave one the idea of a deal of power in reserve; one felt that even in trying circumstances he would not use himself up, and be in a state of partial exhaustion when he left the platform.

His command of the technical side of his art appears to have been more or less instinctively acquired. The majority of young men consult professors of elocution—they are supposed to hold the key that unlocks the mystery of successful public discourse—and he himself once sat at the feet of one of these pundits.

When a student at Newark he heard, through his friend Whitney, of a man who had actually taught senators how to speak, and among them Webster and Clay. Mainly at his instance the man was brought to the Wesleyan Institute. He stayed two weeks. Faculty and students formed one large class and listened to his instructions. No doubt he had many things to impart. An elocutionist who allowed himself to be advertised as the mentor of Webster and Clay would speak with authority. One cannot fancy a skeptical student coming out with the blunt question that Doctor Johnson put to the elder Sheridan, "Sir, what do you mean to teach?" But the professor stayed only two weeks, and "eloquence" is a subject so vast and vague that the time hardly sufficed for going deeply into it.

As for seeking out other professors, I have never heard that John Vincent did so. He let slip no opportunity for hearing men of established reputation, such as Wendell Phillips, Edward Everett, Henry Ward Beecher, and the then celebrated E. H. Chapin. In 1852 all these men were in their prime. Any youthful enthusiast would learn much from them, and the brighter he was the more exactly would he distinguish between what was idiosyncratic in their mode of speaking and what they held in common. He would know that the one element was to be as carefully avoided as the other was to be cultivated.

John Vincent, then, resembled hundreds of able speakers in that he was mainly self-taught. A natural orator, rarely florid or rhetorical, exact in the details of preparation, fastidious in his choice of words, holding in respect all legitimate means for the achievement of the principal end of public discourse, he was at the same time so well balanced as to be incapable of putting more stress on the manner than on the matter of any given speech. He began by speaking well, and having begun thus it was easy to improve. In the matter of technique he at no time dropped below the high level he attained before he was thirty years of age.

Doubtless he held that the least any man can do is to enunciate distinctly, and in a tone proportionate to the size of the audience room; whether he formulated a little body of maxims and theories beyond this must be learned from those with whom he may have talked on the subject. No small part of the satisfaction one had in listening to him was due to the fact that one could listen without effort; he was a most comfortable

person to sit under. And one's satisfaction was increased
by the trait already alluded to; namely, that in the presence of the largest of audiences he made no visible effort
beyond what was fitting and agreeable.

He was practically free from one of the minor faults
to which many speakers are prone, that of lowering the
voice at the end of a period, whereby the last two or
three words become almost inaudible. When, as is sometimes the case, those very words are needed to complete
the sense, the habit can only be described as exasperating.
It is like being told all of a witty story except the point.

John Vincent's fondness for the conversational manner and tone did betray him now and then into talking
too intimately with the front benches, though with no
thought of depriving remoter parts of the house of the
benefit of what he was saying. This once happened at
Mountain Lake Park, Maryland. The auditorium was
small, and looked smaller than it really was; it was the
pleasant *old* structure in general use before the mammoth
pavilion was built, and he simply underestimated its size.
Rarely did he miscalculate as to the amount of voice
needed for reaching the auditor who sat farthest from
the platform.

As to his manner and appearance on the platform, it
may be said that the one was as commanding as the
other was agreeable. Somewhat above medium height,
well built, with a fine head, an expressive mouth, and
piercing gray-blue eyes, he made a capital figure. His
gestures were easy, appropriate, neither too few nor
too many in number, and characterized by what may be
called an unstudied grace. Often extremely forceful in
emphasizing a thought, he was never violent. In gesticu-

lation as in the choice of words he showed consummate good taste.

There was something of quiet elegance in his dress. He wore clerical attire and it became him. He believed in a public man's conforming to a certain sartorial standard and then dismissing the whole subject. He was not one of those who maintain that clothes are an affair of minor importance and at the same time look well to the quality and cut of their own garments. Having a sharp eye for inexcusable failings he once, at Chautauqua, reproved a colleague for gross negligence in some point or other. The man said, in a hurt tone, "You really have a *great* many things on your mind, Doctor Vincent, haven't you?" The Doctor admitted it, with a laugh, and went on his way. Possibly he regretted having spoken when and where he did, even though it effected a partial reform.

I am inclined to lay no little stress on the attractive features of John Vincent's platform presence; his personality was winning in the extreme. It is a deep-rooted conviction of mine that a man's looks and bearing have, at the outset, much to do in winning the attention of the audience. When the thought begins to take hold the orator himself is forgotten, but not till then.

And lastly, he was a fluent speaker. Yet it would be difficult to name a man less eager than he to go on and on because it cost him little effort to do so. He knew the virtue of brevity and was never long-winded. He advised preaching short sermons, and thought that an hour was, as a rule, long enough for a lecture or an address.

He made effective use of that rhetorical device which

the summer session. Attendance was voluntary. But nothing could have kept them away, so extraordinary was the hold the man had over them. The age limit was set by the speaker for his own convenience; he had only adolescents in mind when preparing each talk. The society took a pride in the thought that this was *their* hour, and that adults would not be admitted. It has been said of these addresses that had they been collected and put into print they would have made an invaluable little manual on the building up of true character. My object in speaking of them here is to call attention to their form and to the manner of delivery, not to their content.

Almost equally felicitous were the talks given, year after year, at a service held to mark the formal close of the Chautauqua session. They deserve a passing mention because the chroniclers have somewhat neglected them. The service was brief, consisting of a hymn, an invocation, and a valedictory of not more than twenty minutes' duration.

The Superintendent of Instruction was in excellent form at such a time. One heard him to advantage. Yet the hour was unseasonable—nine o'clock in the morning —and the day one on which a majority of the people were distracted by the confusion due to the breaking up of the Assembly. In the circumstances the audience would be small, numbering not above four or five hundred. But the speaker never failed to make the occasion memorable. He was then at his best. I can well believe that many of his friends would rather hear this short and graceful valedictory than the most spectacular flight of eloquence that the season had to offer.

JOHN HEYL VINCENT

In the same class, and no less distinctive, were his talks at the regular Sunday vesper service at Chautauqua. However emotional they might be—though always in a restrained way—they were also practical. When the hearer left the hall he carried with him a good deal more than that elevation of soul and that mental quickening produced by rhetoric. He had indeed enjoyed a most excellent example of what spoken discourse could be, but he was also a better man.

CHAPTER XV

AMONG John H. Vincent's numerous lectures and set addresses, there were at least three which he was disposed to regard as fairly representative of his method, style, and teaching. Their titles are well known: *That Boy, That Boy's Sister* and *The Church of the Future.* The first two are related by virtue of the subject and the treatment. All three were striking, the first popular to an extraordinary degree. How many times the lecture on *That Boy* was delivered there is no way of finding out. The speaker himself loses count of the number of repetitions of a given address for which there are many calls each year.

Like all discourses of a similar character this lecture was a thing of slow growth. Whatever may have been its earlier form—it was always effective, by the way— it changed materially as time went on. No doubt the outline persisted; in the matter of phrasing and illustrative anecdotes it must have been subjected to endless revision.

A happier way of saying a thing than that he expected to use will come to a man in the very act of speaking. He not only betters the original text but betters it to a degree he can hardly account for. These inspirations of the moment—often so slight as to consist in the change of a single word—are difficult to recall afterwards. What it was that caused a look of surprise on the faces of the auditors, or awakened laughter, or produced a marked heightening of the general interest, the speaker will cudgel his brain in vain to recall. Yet at the very next delivery of the speech the lost phrase may turn up.

Many anecdotes must in course of time have been taken out and others substituted. The speaker had a wide field from which to choose. The newspapers abound in tales of the sayings and doings of children. What cannot be learned there may be learned from one's friends. Proud parents are sure to come to one with numerous and overwhelming proofs of the cleverness of their offspring. An observant man profits most by what is directly under his eye. It is suspected that this particular lecture was much improved when John Vincent found himself so situated domestically as to be able to study a boy at close range.

The lecture was written out in full at the last, and with the manuscript in hand it is possible to get some idea of its distinctive quality. But only an imperfect idea; the engaging personality of the lecturer himself is wanting. His sincerity, his tact, his force, and his singular gift for stating a thing positively without leaving the impression of cocksureness and arrogance can only be guessed at with the text before one. He had an artful way of making a friend of the auditor who wholly disagreed with his position on this point or that.

Wanting above all (in the manuscript) is the clue to the man's inimitable way of telling an anecdote, whether pathetic or humorous or merely elucidative. The flavor cannot be conveyed by print. Dashes and exclamation points are of little avail; one must hear the voice if one would know how effective the anecdote was in the delivery. In the copy as it stands (partly written and partly typed) punctuation marks are made to do their customarily imperfect work. If the gist of a story lies in a single word, and that the last of the sentence, a dash is placed before it. The dash of course represents the pause that a speaker will naturally make before disclosing the droll turn that he means to give to the phrasing of an idea. The pause may be so prolonged on occasion that the audience begins to think out an ending for itself, often the right one, but lacking the color that a happily chosen word gives. Were the anecdote printed in a book the dash would be necessary—and also inadequate.

The lecture is a plea for a better understanding of boy nature, and for a course of training at once more liberal and more rigorous than is commonly given. It pictures the ordinary human boy at various stages of his career, the petted darling in infancy, then the bona-fide boy ("a colt and not a lamb, a young elephant and not a kitten"), and so on.

The boy's appalling frankness is brought out by stories that must have convulsed any audience. He is pictured at the age of twelve, when he has become an irritating problem and in consequence "hears more growling, scolding, protesting, expostulating, and all that sort of thing than he ever hears in all his life—until he gets married!" (This thrust is enjoyed by the husbands because of the queer nature of husbands; the wives forgive it because it is so winningly put and so absolutely untrue).

The principal needs of the ordinary human boy are

pointed out—authority and tenderness. "Not authority that becomes severity, not tenderness that degenerates into indulgence, but an authority firm and uncompromising, exercised with a tenderness born of ability and abounding love." What may be expected in the case of a boy who is not subjected to discipline on the part of firm, fair-minded, and affectionate parents is dwelt on at length.

Then follows an amusingly satirical picture of the boy at the age of sixteen, when he has become conscious of his personal attractions, finical in the matter of cravats, and fully satisfied, notwithstanding the lack of down on his upper lip, that it is his duty to begin to shave. He has opinions, too, about things, and utters them in a tone of finality. Nothing is more formidable than the opinions of a young fellow of sixteen. One may well tremble when such an oracle as he deigns to speak. But there is no great harm in all this. "I love to watch a boy trying to be a man. I would not give much for a boy of sixteen who does not enter into the life, the spirit, the habit, the bearing of a man. But I am anxious that he should have the right idea of what constitutes true manhood. . . ."

At this point in the lecture the claims of three great institutions are presented in behalf of the boy. They are the Church, the Public School, and the Family. What excuses a boy will make to escape going to church, what sudden attacks of indisposition he will have, always on the same day of the week, all the world knows. "I am ready to acknowledge that the boy may not be able always to understand the sermon. There are some sermons that nobody can understand. But I am not ready to acknowledge that he does not understand what is going on." The service is an object lesson. "The spirit of reverence promoted by the average service is perhaps its greatest benefit to the boy."

The habit of churchgoing is not to be fixed without the exercise of will on somebody's part. In short the "rose-water" method of bringing up one's offspring is silly, and the result may be disastrous. And with a sarcasm that is none the less effective for being temperate, this method is analyzed. Every auditor could enjoy it because it would make him think of the way the neighbors were bringing up *their* boys.

In the passage on the public schools, there is a plea for a liberal expenditure of public money to one of the greatest of ends. "No cheap teachers but the best that can be had, and no wailing over increased taxes if better schools result therefrom."

But the school of schools after all is the home, the family. And during this important part of the lecture it were well if such boys as had strayed into the hall were first dismissed lest they should take an unholy glee in what might be said to and of their parents; for parents are now to be castigated wittily and lovingly. The punishment will resemble in character that described by a certain modern novelist in one of the best episodes of his best book; it was administered, he says, "not so as to hurt, but to awaken the moral sense."

Among the failings of fathers, so the lecturer held, is stand-offishness. The man and the boy never really meet on common ground, and the blame rests not on the younger but on the older one of the pair. They should be friends and companions. "Why don't you consult

your father?" said his teacher to a boy who had come
to ask for what, in the way of a trade or profession,
he had better prepare himself. "Well," replied the
boy, with a frown of perplexity, "I'm not very well
acquainted with the old gentleman." Among the occasional failings of mothers is a disposition to regard the
furnishings of a home as of more value than the home
itself. "Are both you boys on that lounge again?" she
cries. "You'll break it down. Only last week I paid
three dollars and seventy-five cents to have that lounge
repaired." And so this feminine worshiper of furniture
and sofa cushions drives the boys out of the parlor.
The picture here drawn with considerable detail is exaggerated. But, then, the soul of effective public speech
is adroit exaggeration controlled by common sense.

Lectures of this sort must of necessity contain much
that is trite and commonplace. The public not only
needs advice but the indications are that it rather craves
it, only stipulating that it be cleverly put. It must be
varied to suit the type of reader or hearer it aims to
reach. And it is so varied. When Thackeray penned
Mr. Brown's Letters to His Nephew what did he other
than make a lecture on "That Boy"?

It would be impossible for the compiler of this memoir
to count up the number of times he has heard John
Vincent preach, lecture, give formal addresses on state
occasions, and informal talks on occasions of minor importance. But it so happens that he never heard him
speak on "That Boy." Curious to know what impression of the lecture remained in the mind of an acute
observer, he wrote to inquire. This friend, the late
Frederick E. Partington of Washington, was for a num-

ber of years the principal of the New Paltz Academy, New York. It was his custom during the period of his incumbency to bring men of distinction to the school, to speak to the townspeople and students. Here is an extract from his letter:

"Among all the lecturers we had in those courses I recall no one who so quickly captured his audience, and as I always felt a personal responsibility in the matter I can even now bring back the sense of comfort and satisfaction I enjoyed when Doctor Vincent began to speak. He spoke straight on— with ease and swiftness and that happy authority which always wins an audience. I think his subject had much to do with the success of that particular lecture. The people saw that it was no pleasant theory he was talking about, but a real boy, and they listened rapturously to this study of a type they understood well enough but had never seen presented in so amusing a manner and with such fidelity to the facts.

"I well recall Doctor Vincent's fluency, his independence of notes, and all the charm of a practiced speaker. He talked for an hour and a half, sometimes at an incredible rate of speed, never hesitated for a word, and, as I have said, had not so much as a scrap of paper to which he might occasionally refer."

At the close of his letter the writer again emphasizes the point that the audience was won over at the very beginning, by almost the first sentence that came from the speaker's lips. Other men had a way of engaging the attention little by little. A perceptible amount of time elapsed before the body of hearers was captured and carried away.

The lecture entitled "That Boy's Sister" is the complement of its predecessor. Its keynote is that "as each sex is most true to itself it is of most value to the opposite sex." Admit if we will that it may be of advantage to some women to possess masculine traits; nevertheless, "for the highest good of the soul, and for the present good of society, it is well that man be manly and woman be womanly." Then follows an episodical passage, a description of the ideal woman. No one who knew the lecturer personally would take for a mere fanciful sketch what was clearly meant for a realistic study. Those who knew the model—and many people knew her—could easily supply what was missing in the swiftly drawn but exact outline.

In tracing the history of the average girl, discretion is needed. A boy will stand a good deal of banging—in a lecture. His sister's foibles must be dealt with in another way, through raillery chiefly, and that of an amiable sort. What so many American girls of to-day are, and what they might and should become, form the substance of the discourse. The materials are handled much as were those in the companion piece. The girl is pictured as she might be at this or that stage of her development, her mode of speech is reproduced in fairly long quotations (fragments of dialogue actually overheard if not participated in), and her vanities are satirized.

The type of American girl has changed since this lecture was prepared. A somewhat different mode of treat-

ment would be needed at the present time. The frivolous
young lady of one period is sobriety itself in comparison
with her analogue in the next. Gissing must have written
very differently had he produced *The Emancipated* in
1925 rather than in 1890.

Various matters are touched on in the lecture, among
them woman's mission. One might suppose that John
Vincent's well-known predilection for the home-keeping
woman would have led him to affirm that home was the
only place for her. What he really says is this: "Some
of you think that woman has more power for the highest
usefulness without the ballot than with it. . . . Let us
give women the ballot to decide that question for themselves." He was a suffragist then, after all, though often
set down as one who was opposed to granting women the
right to vote. No doubt his view of the subject under-
went a gradual change. He did not, like his brother,
hold that womankind would be the worse for the extension of the suffrage.

Other lectures he had, such as *Tom and His Teachers,
The After-Boy and His Friends,* and *The Model Husband.* The first would be a comparison of old and
modern ways of training youth; the second would take
the typical boy whose earlier growth had already
been described and show what it was possible for him
to become. The third—a fearsome topic—may have
served principally as a vehicle for good-natured satire,
the kind of satire in which this speaker excelled. That
such a *lusus naturæ* as a model husband existed he would
have been slow to admit.

One finds on his list the following titles: *To-morrow,
a Study in the Church Life of the Future; Among the*

[177]

Heights, a Study in Travel and Biography; On Deck, A Plea for Broader Horizons in Church and State, and in Social Life; An Everyday Parliament, or the Power of the Parlor; The Receding House Mother; School Out of School; The Value of the Unit. At least six lectures on travel figure in the list. Not all would be purely descriptive, certainly not the one entitled *From Eisleben to Eisleben,* a study that was repeatedly given.

Having acquired great facility in the outlining of a discourse, John Vincent found it a simple matter to make lectures for special occasions. I recall his speaking of a lecture on Sydney Smith, and of the pleasure he had in delivering it. Not a point was lost. The audience was in a receptive mood and laughed immoderately over the stories. If the notes could be recovered one might learn what examples of Smith's humor most appealed to the speaker's sense of the comic.

In marked contrast to this lecture would be the study of Sidney Lanier, whose life and character and verse greatly appealed to John Vincent. Though prepared for a particular group—a woman's club in Indianapolis, I think—the study was often repeated. That he should have once given a talk on Hannah More is not surprising; the lady's history contains much to entertain and instruct. This address, as well as the one on John Paul Jones, must have been written for a commemorative exercise.

The preparation of a discourse of any sort is no great mystery to the initiated. One is sometimes puzzled, however, to find, as the only visible sign of the preparation, a half dozen barely legible headings no one of which is remarkably suggestive *as it stands.* The really striking part of the speech was improvised, and therefore not to be recovered. Yet again, in the case of a speech written out in full, the written text will disappoint us because it seems incapable of producing such an effect as we ourselves witnessed; we fancy that interpolations were made, and that through them the audience was electrified. We are apt to be mistaken, and to attribute to impromptu passages what was only due to the orator's way of delivering the text that possibly lay before him in manuscript.

The text is our only guide; it is not always inadequate, and it may be so written as to give an approximately just idea of the speaker's powers. Of such sort was John Vincent's discourse entitled *Lincoln as a Student.* It ranks among his greater occasional addresses. An elaborately wrought character study, it is both a tribute to the patriot and a glorification of the type of schooling that produced him. The orator who was forever sounding the praises of systematic education on traditional lines now spends a few moments in showing that colleges and professors, curricula and diplomas, are not after all so necessary as we supposed them to be; that they may often be a hindrance rather than a help. "The secret of success is hidden in the student and not in the school. . . . Nature made Abraham Lincoln a student before he opened a schoolhouse door. . . . The boy's native power guaranteed success." Then follow an enumeration of the books he read, an account of his manner of reading them, and a hint that he was on the whole fortunate in not having too much literature at his command.

The address given at the dedication of a hall in the

School of Oratory, at Northwestern University, reads well in the printed text. Here is one of the passages: "Back of the art of oratory, at the very basis of it, in fact, is personal character. To hold the truth and to love it; to have the power of expressing it; to delight in this expression for truth's sake and for the joy of it and for the sake of humanity—this is the beginning of oratorical power. The man who would awaken and control an audience must himself be a reality, and the truth he uses must be to him a reality. Character is everything."

The speaker recognizes the fact that schools of oratory have a peculiarly difficult task because they must take hold of men who have become hardened by years of bad or indifferent training. The habits of such men are fixed. "Therefore men should be trained from early childhood to express their thoughts with distinctness, directness, naturalness, and force. Training in elocution must begin very early. The nursery is the first school of speech, of vocal culture, of self-control, of accuracy in pronunciation, tone, emphasis. The mother is the first teacher of elocution." The speaker takes for granted the existence of what is rare enough—a household where the parents prefer good English to bad, and where the children are tractable.

The discourse on *The Church of the Future* was not, as its title might lead one to think, a sermon. It might have been given in a church, and perhaps was so given. Yet it was, strictly speaking, a lecture, secular in that it was meant for the platform rather than the pulpit.

Three characteristics of this Church of the Future are prophetically set forth. It is to be a militant Church, vigorous in combating sin, superstition, and worldliness. It will be unchanged in its fundamental elements. "God will be the same, Jesus Christ the same, the Holy Spirit the same, and human nature the same." And, in the third place, its central thought will not be that of systematic theology, or of ceremonies, or of government—"the seeing to it that every member believes exactly this or exactly that"—but Christ.

True to his theory that the service should be of a sort that would admit of every one's taking part in it—not an exhibition of the musical ability of four persons and the rhetorical art of one—the lecturer insists that the Church of the Future will have congregational singing.

This Church, he says, will appreciate the following truths: "The sanctity of all secular things; the legitimacy on religious lines of all secular occupations; the divinity of all improvement, whether physical, mental, social, or spiritual, and that all duty faithfully performed, whether in shop or kitchen or elsewhere, is, in the very truest sense, worship."

In a vivacious passage is contrasted the state of affairs when the Church was a tyrant and the no less questionable state of affairs when every man took it on himself to be his own pope. Another and better period might be looked for; was, indeed, at hand. At this point occurs the ensuing passage; I quote it because it gives a fair idea of the speaker's manner at times. The repetition of a thought with no marked change in the diction and none whatever in the cadence is apt to become wearisome in literature. When it occurs the reader grows impatient and turns the page. He is not impatient, however, when exactly the same device is used in address. Iteration skillfully employed is a source of power. It makes for clarity though the delivery be rapid. The passage in question runs thus:

"The accepted doctrine of the American citizen is that every man has a right to be all that he can be, to know all that he can know, and to do all that he can do, so long as he does not interfere with another man's being all that he can be, and knowing all that he can know, and doing all that he can do. The new and higher doctrine of the American citizen will be that it is the duty of every man to help his fellow man to be all he can be, and know all that he can know, and do all that he can do. When you feel that you want praying for yourself, pray for others—for somebody you don't like—and good will come to your own soul."

The lecture was a plea for catholicity, charity, tolerance, and all other virtues related thereto. The Church of the Future was to stand for these things. How the organization of such a Church might be brought about hardly concerned the speaker. His immediate aim was to inspire, not to direct. As the existing sects grew in tolerance and charity they would little by little become a part of the Ideal Church.

The only available report of this address (other reports must be in existence somewhere) is the one printed in an English weekly paper; merely the outline and a few striking paragraphs are given. At the bottom of the column the heading and a part of the text of the next article appears, an account of the activities of the sect known as Bible Christians. At the time this article was written these people were on the point of building a new chapel at Iddesleigh, in Devonshire. The Earl of Iddesleigh had given them a site and provided them with building stone. They wanted to hold a "tea." The rector of the parish refused them the loan of the school-room on the ground that "it would be inconsistent to pray against schism every Sunday, and lend it encouragement during the week."

Without presuming to criticize the rector so long after the incident took place—it was in 1889—one may remark on the oddity of the juxtaposition of the news item and the concluding sentences of the address. In the Church of the Future we shall expect to see Bible Christians tolerated to the extent of being allowed to hold their teas wherever they like.

Any pertinent comment on John H. Vincent's sermons is made doubly difficult by the fact that they were never printed in a collection large enough to admit of one's generalizing about them. He seldom wrote a sermon out in full. If his pulpit discourses can be said to exist at all they must do so in the form of notes. But even the notes seem to have disappeared. His manner in the pulpit differed hardly at all from his manner on the platform. Always dignified he had no need to put on a sacerdotal air because he was about to deliver a sermon. His inborn sense of reverence made quite impossible the introduction of an anecdote or an allusion not in keeping with the time and the place.

CHAPTER XVI

BOOKS AND PAMPHLETS

ALTHOUGH an indefatigable writer John Vincent was not, strictly speaking, a man of letters. Any estimate of his books that failed to take note of their temporary character would be unfair. All, with possibly one notable exception, were written for an immediate purpose. Of two or three it might be said that they were not only hurriedly composed but that the manuscript was sent to the printer before the ink had had time to dry.

Therefore to expect them to have in a marked degree the virtues described as "literary" is idle. A piece of literature—the word is here used colloquially, not in its exalted sense—implies craftsmanship. To produce it one need not indeed linger lovingly over one's paragraphs (assuming for the moment that it were possible to do so naïve a thing), but one must, at all events, linger patiently and while doing so marvel at the intractability of language.

Patient enough this man was in one way—he never tired of making corrections of a certain sort. They were mostly verbal, and in many cases were limited to the change of an epithet or a noun; rarely did they involve the recasting of the form of a sentence. His notes for lectures and addresses, whether abbreviated or written out in full, abound in examples of the thing. He had a way of copying the word of his second choice on a bit of paper and pasting it over the rejected word. The mucilage he used was superior to that supplied the American people on postage stamps. No one of these tiny pieces has failed to adhere to the spot where it was originally placed. Yet a number of the manuscripts are upwards of forty years old, and not a little battered through frequent handling.

The *raison d'être* of these patches is quite clear. When speaking from notes a man often finds that a long passage will be suggested by a single word, and also that the presence of a word he had determined *not* to use is distracting. If the objectionable word cannot be obliterated by drawing a line through it he must have recourse to a more drastic method.

I should say, however, that in a majority of cases the corrections were made with a view to bettering the text. The manner of making them was odd. It became a habit, and even extended, now and then, to the writer's letters to his family. No complete manuscripts of his books have been preserved; it is impossible to learn how radical were the changes made in the galley proof. In general he seemed disposed to leave well enough alone. If a volume were made up of reprinted magazine and newspaper articles, he would not care to subject each article to a wholesale revision.

Of John Vincent's first book, *Little Footprints in Bible Lands* (1860), only a word need be said. It was a manual for the use of Palestine Classes. It contained all the apparatus that a teacher might need—the questions, the bibliographical references, the maps, and the songs. Whoever cared to do so could, by following the plan indicated in this small volume, get up and lead a class very much in the author's manner, a class that would be a fair copy of the ones he himself had organized.

His hand is visible on many a page of *Our Sunday School Scrap Book* (1866), compiled by Daniel Wise and himself, a *vade mecum* of practical suggestions, illustrative anecdotes, historical or topographical essays, and so on. The ironical paper entitled *How to Have a Small Class* is exactly in his manner. He gives five rules for attaining this end: "Be tedious. Bore your class with long talks until the bell rings, and they will cease to bore you with their presence." The other four are in the same tone.

In 1872 was published his *Sunday School Institutes and Normal Classes.* A volume of less than two hundred pages, it was the natural outcome of his early experiments in reforming the department of the Church in which for years he had been deeply interested. The author's aim is to show what teachers principally stand in need of, and how that need may be supplied. Explicit directions are given for conducting either an Institute or a Normal Class. Programs of meetings of this character that have actually been held are printed in full. For Normal students a course of study is outlined under ten heads.

The volume is historical as well as practical. One finds, in the Appendix, among other matters, the program of a course of training in the theory and practice of teaching that was planned and carried out in 1859, by the London Sunday-School Union. Also a résumé, quoted from a current journal of education, of the growth of the idea of teacher training from 1684 to 1823. In spite of its technical character as a whole, the book contains passages that, if not precisely "literary," come near to being so. They read well, and they sound well when read aloud.

The same theme is treated in *The Modern Sunday School* (1887), but in greater detail and with the addition of much new matter.

There is a chapter on "The Superintendent"; how he should be chosen, what his duties are, what qualities he must have if he is to succeed, and through what defects of temper or maladroitness he may insure failure. The chapters entitled "The Teacher," "The Teacher at Work," "The Lessons," "The Senior Classes," "The Country Sunday-School," abound in shrewd suggestions that are always earnestly and often cleverly put.

Of examples of temperate sarcasm the book contains not a few. One of the best of these will be found in a paragraph on what the author described as that "semblance of spirituality which is merely sentimentality." He believes it a form of religious æstheticism, and as such to be guarded against. The paragraph may have offended some readers by reason of its pungency; yet it is perfectly fair. When passages of this sort occurred in John Vincent's lectures and addresses, as they often did, the speaker's manner relieved them of any touch of severity, and that without impairing their strength.

In 1886 he published the volume entitled *The Chautauqua Movement* (the "Introduction" was written by the President, Lewis Miller), an authoritative account of the origin of the Assembly, its growth, the development of the schools, the Reading Circle, the official pub-

lications, and the numerous clubs that had sprung up in
the course of years. One chapter answers such criticisms
as have been made on the institution; the last chapter
of all is a confident prophecy as to Chautauqua's future.
In the supplementary pages are given condensed programs. From these one can get a clear idea of what
was done at each session of the Assembly from 1874 to
1885.

Portions of the book were written for *The Chautauquan.* Other portions were first used in the form of
lectures. The material may have been recast and ampli-
fied before being set up in type anew, but it probably
stands as first written; the author says in the preface
that much new matter has been added. Whoever cares
for a first-hand account of a singularly attractive educational undertaking will consult this volume. The Superintendent of Instruction tells the story, and tells it well.

He promised himself, and his friends, to bring out
later a volume of "Chautauqua Memorials," a more extended report of the work of each year, "and with the
memoranda of things proposed from time to time, but
never yet accomplished." The latter touch is characteristic. His head teemed with ideas and it was impossible
to give material shape to more than a very few. The
"Chautauqua Memorials" was never written, possibly
never begun. He became absorbed in ecclesiastical affairs after 1888, and the leisure for the deliberate making of a book was wanting even though he had had the
inclination.

In 1892 and 1898 respectively he brought out two
little books of a strictly personal nature. The first was
entitled *My Mother.* A touching tribute to Mary Raser

Vincent it shows how admirably this man could write when moved by a theme that lay close to his heart. It is a small book, almost too intimate and too heavily charged with sentiment, but it is at the same time profoundly sincere and in point of style a little masterpiece. It is not to be read in an idle mood, and the subject alone places it outside the range of ordinary criticism.

The second of the two was a privately printed pamphlet made to commemorate his father. It bears the title *John Himrod Vincent, A Centennial Souvenir*. Admirable so far as it goes, the sketch (considered merely as a sketch) is altogether too brief. With the abundance of material at hand he might have made a small volume —and he chose to limit himself to ten pages!

He has contrived to pack into that space a deal of interesting matter. The souvenir contains a genealogical outline, the chief facts of his father's life, a few tributes from old friends, and several extracts from Himrod Vincent's letters to his two older boys. A typical passage occurs in a letter dated May 17, 1852. John Vincent was then engaged with the Newark City Mission. While ministering to the poor he was probably rather poor himself. Well aware of the state of his finances the father writes: "And although you may not have everything to make you happy, if you but do your duty faithfully, all things needful will be supplied. And should you be in particular need *let me know.*" The son's comment is: "How like an affectionate father was this added sentence!" Himrod Vincent had at that time no surplusage to speak of. Nevertheless, "let me know."

In respect to the brochure entitled *Better Not*, which will be discussed briefly in a later chapter, it is needful

[189]

to bear in mind that it was made up of editorial articles printed in *Our Youth*. Papers of this sort are written *currente calamo* and seldom reconstructed. The marks of their origin persist. The subject may be of perennial interest, but the treatment is more or less journalistic.

Of similar origin is *Studies in Young Life* (1890), described in the subtitle as "A Series of Word Pictures and Practical Papers." It is a collection of forty-one essays, generally brief, the majority of them thrown into the form of a character sketch. Every figure in the group stands for a dominant trait—a weakness of some sort, a prepossession, a palpable vice, and, occasionally, a virtue.

One is a spendthrift, another is a bore, the third a laggard, the fourth a plain unmitigated nuisance, the fifth the personification of youthful irreverence (especially in the attitude towards religion). As for the sixth he is an example of the pseudo-gentleman. The seventh, an American by ancestry, birth, and breeding, has become Frenchified through living a while in Paris; he is now more Gallic than the Gauls themselves.

In contrast with these we have sketches of "the indispensable boy," of the boy who realizes that he has a weakness to overcome and so far masters it as to be able to make real progress towards self-control, and of a young railway employee who smooths his own path, and that of other people, by square dealing with the officials and a considerate manner towards the public. The author had met a paragon of this last sort in his travels and was moved to celebrate his virtues in a character sketch.

Studies of girls are interspersed with the others. There is a study of the pretty simpleton, of the girl with one talent, of the girl who has made the curriculum her idol —first at school and then at college—to the neglect of those virtues that grace the home. She is no fool, this *demoiselle savante,* but she needs a postgraduate course "in kitchen work and nursery sympathy and drawing-room manners." Yet another paper deals with the obstinate girl, the opinionated miss on whom argument and expostulation produce no effect, and who can only be reformed, so the reader concludes, by the simple method known among the English as "smacking"; for this she is probably too old. Of these sketches of girls the longest takes the form of an anti-Romanist tract; it may be a composite, but has the air of having been studied from life. Possibly it is a portrait of some one the author had known.

Not carelessly composed, these forty-one essays plainly show that they were meant for periodical publication. The sentences are crisp and pointed. The author is not afraid of the obvious. He wants to be understood at a first reading, and he writes accordingly. Subtlety, allusiveness, and a too-delicate satire would have been wasted on the audience he hoped to reach. Yet these finer qualities are the salvation of many a book. They do not, it is true, make for popularity. In the present case the draughtsman contented himself with firm outlines and a minimum of shading. The original of the volume might be Overbury's *Characteristics,* though numerous sketches in this style have been tossed off by writers who never studied Overbury.

Three of John Vincent's more significant books are

JOHN HEYL VINCENT

The Revival and After the Revival (1882), *Our Own Church* (1890), and *A Study in Pedagogy* (1890).

The first is a comparison of the old-time mode of persuading the unregenerate to mend their ways with the newer mode, a mode that does not set at naught the apostolic law of decency and order. The author had never been able to admit that raising a hullabaloo was the best of ways in which to promote religion. If in favor of revivals, as he professed to be, he was also in favor of their being controlled with a firm hand. At the time he wrote these chapters many worthy souls might still be met with who held that a revival without extravagant manifestations was no revival at all. There had been a temporary falling away from the quiet methods that generally prevailed. John Vincent criticized in a denominational paper one spectacle that he witnessed. Rejoinders were printed. The discussion prompted the making of the book.

Our Own Church is a series of familiar talks on "The Antiquity of Methodism," "The Church and the World," "Broad and Narrow," "Our Settled Itinerancy," "The Holy Communion," "Church Loyalty," "The Story of a Revival," and similar topics. The book is designed for young Methodists. There are thirteen chapters all told, with an Appendix consisting mainly of quotations from authorities who have disputed the claims of extreme Ritualists, and of some not so extreme, as to Apostolic Succession.

In two of the chapters typical figures are sketched. The first delineates a youth whose æsthetic sensibilities have been so disturbed that he has left the Church of

his fathers, one particular father, his own, having left
first. He was not able to endure certain displays of
emotion that he had witnessed. The young man held
that emotion and hysteria were quite all right on the
baseball field or at a political meeting; neither was to
be tolerated at any public exercise that had to do with
the saving of souls.

Over against him, in the companion sketch, is set
the figure of a girl whose loyalty to her Church is based
on affection, common sense, and a fair amount of historical knowledge. She has some logical skill, too, and
is competent to hold her own in amicable debates with a
friend of ultra-Episcopalian upbringing. To write this
sort of thing is not the easiest of tasks. The dialogue
in the sketch is naïve, though not more so than the dialogue occasionally to be met with in *Tracts for the Times*.

John Vincent had a good-humored contempt for people who were ecclesiastically restless. It comes out in
this book. When the restlessness was prompted, as he
thought, by a desire to move into more fashionable quarters he was apt to become ironical. He did not deny
that good reasons might exist for making a change, but
he believed that the motive actuating the emigrant should
be disinterested rather than worldly.

A Study in Pedagogy is introduced with a disclaimer,
a warning to the effect that the writer has no intention
of treating the topic in a formal or scientific way. "Nor
do I aim at the instruction of those who are or expect
to be professional teachers." In a word, his book is
meant for the plain people, and especially for parents,
whose coöperation professional educators must have if

success is to be attained. The points are deftly made and the illustrations are amusing. The little volume abounds in quotable sayings. For example: "In the process by which a knowing mind becomes to another a helping mind, we find the art of education. The science begets the art."

He notes the laws that a teacher must observe. These can be mastered by any one. But we should not forget that there are pedagogues who are superior to common rules; they have, being men of genius, a sort of educational instinct. At this point he gives a paragraph to the word "pedagogue," remarks on the somewhat contemptuous meaning attached to it, how it came about, and why the word is no longer used in that sense. He lays great stress on the influence of the teachers, animate and inanimate, outside the schoolroom—mothers, associates, servants, pictures, furniture, public buildings, parks; in short, everything and everybody. Not to take heed of the smallest fact that may have a bearing on the development of the child is a mistake, possibly something worse.

Among special educating influences, the author places the Church first. Next comes the Home—in connection with the Church. "Erasmus pleaded for more private schools. That is what the home should be." The School comes third. "It must supplement the best work of the best parents, and be a substitute where parental influence is lacking." Fourth, and last, there is the Press. "Parents cannot keep their children from the knowledge of the evil that is in the world, but they can repudiate a daily paper that is filled with prurient reports of crime."

In a final word on the education of a boy occurs this

remark: "He must be let alone a great deal." The author had faith in a mode of training that was not too persistent, that would take some chances.

If John Vincent's writings were gauged solely by the number of titles in a bibliographical list he would be accounted prolific. As a matter of fact his printed books do not bulk large. The little piece of poetic prose which he called *In Old Bethlehem* (1890) fills less than twenty-five pages. *The Inner Life,* in part an exposition of transcendentalism, contains barely seventy pages. And again, the manual of family devotions ("meditations" is the word he prefers) published under the title of *At the Family Altar* (1896) has in it little that is strictly his own, though that little is written with his customary grace. He urges fidelity to the good old custom of family prayers if only as a reminder of a more reverent age than our own. So, too, in the case of *The Home Book* (1887) for which he supplied the plan, he seems to have written only the rather extended preface. It is a huge compilation, this book, seven hundred pages long, and in its day should have been a source of endless delight to the little folks. It is a *mélange* of stories, rhymes, games, pictures, and biographical sketches, along with brief articles on popular science and natural history. In getting together the material the compiler had the help of competent advisers.

John Vincent's *Autobiography* has never been re-printed from the columns of the denominational paper in which it originally appeared (1910), and one cannot think he would have cared to see it brought out as a book. It is engrossing, suggestive, often eloquent, and has touches of humor here and there. Passages of real beauty are to be met with. As a whole it lacks form. The author sets down what is uppermost in his mind at the time of writing a given chapter and is quite willing to repeat himself.

But even when he goes back on his track he varies the phraseology and adds new points. He is less copious on certain matters than one would expect him to be, more so on others. His waywardness is not without charm. All the same, an ordered and strictly chronological treatment would have been better. He had been urged times without number to write the story of his life, and above all not to delay setting about it. A man of greater self-complacency than he would have undertaken the task with pleasure. He waited a little too long before beginning.

The reason for the delay is plain. Accustomed to measure what he had done by the standard of his ideals he was not tempted to be expansive. For a long time he seems not to have supposed that any record of his life would be printed other than the brief notices in biographical dictionaries. He was greatly surprised, as I well remember, when told that somebody would have to write his life, and that he might as well do it himself.

John Vincent spoke better than he wrote. The outlining of a sermon or lecture, the dictating of an article for a magazine, and the planning of a book to be executed by one of his coadjutors gave him immense pleasure. For the slow process of building up a literary structure he had no great liking. When he had conceived an idea he wanted it formulated at once.

This eagerness to have a thing done and out of the way affected nearly all his writings. Never amateurish, invariably spontaneous and easy, his printed books give but an imperfect idea of what he might have done had he seriously devoted himself to letters for a part of his working life. The journal that he kept during his first tour of Europe and the East is a striking performance. It is breezy, good-humored, informing, and exact. Of superfluous rhetoric it contains not a trace, and though written from day to day, often in untoward circumstances, it is so finished that one cannot see wherein it might have been changed for the better. One may add that it is free from what the writer was wont to describe as his crying fault—that of too much preaching.

CHAPTER XVII

OF John Vincent's powers as a conversationalist only his younger contemporaries could give an accurate account. My impression is that when the talk lay between himself and one other he was apt to run into monologue. However instructive or entertaining this may be it is not, rightly speaking, conversation. There is no real interchange of ideas. One gives and the other receives. The relation between the two does not change. Yet in spite of this tendency the man could be one of the best of listeners. If you had a story to tell he would hear it to the bitter end.

As interlocutor he often resorted to the method of questioning his *vis-à-vis*. The manner became to some extent habitual with him. One question would follow another. Presently something might suggest a train of thought that he was interested in following out. He would then begin to elaborate the idea; in other words, to preach or lecture, always pulling himself up with a laugh when he realized that he had gone quite far enough.

He was humorous in ordinary social talk, often in a quizzical way, and appreciative of a sense of humor in others. His power of repartee was extraordinary. In rapid give-and-take he had few equals. Moreover his wit was of the polished sort; a gentleman's wit. It was perennial. At no time in his life was it safe to cross swords with him. When well past eighty, with a memory that had long been treacherous, he was amazingly quick at retort.

This gift—along with that of amusingly satirical characterization—may have been inherited. His father, Himrod Vincent, could say a thing in a way to make the hearer both laugh and wince. The aptitude, therefore, runs through three generations, for the Bishop's son possesses it in a high degree.

Clever at raillery, and meaning no more than to be playful for the moment, John Vincent sometimes gave his bantering remarks too keen an edge. When he found that he had cut to the quick he always made the handsomest apology, even going to the trouble of writing a letter. You felt ashamed (supposing you to have been the victim) of being so thin-skinned as to take offense.

His attitude towards his fellow workers was of the large-minded sort. Of jealousy or envy he never knew the meaning as the most of mankind know it. He could praise freely, and when he had paid a fine tribute to some one you might be sure that he meant it. Nothing was said for effect or because the occasion called for fair words; there were no mental reservations. As one whose praise carried weight he was constantly urged to recommend this or that person or project. Difficult situations arose. If satisfied as to the general excellence of a man or a measure, and at the same time skeptical on minor points, he showed both tactfulness and ingenuity in framing his replies. Generous though he was it cannot be said of him that he scattered compliments at random.

Of all his marked characteristics none was more notable than his fidelity to those whom he had honored with his confidence. Whoever had won his good will might count on it as a permanent possession. If at any time he had made a mistake in the choice of either friends or lieutenants it was difficult to persuade him of the fact. His tenacity in holding to his opinion—call it obstinacy if you like—may be explained thus. It was not due to a belief that his judgment of men was infallible, but to an always well-founded belief in the powers of the particular man who had been chosen for a particular piece of work.

His loyalty was appreciated and prized. Of ingratitude on the part of those who were beholden to him he knew something—it is to be hoped that the instances were few—but the memory was not allowed to rankle.

Original though he was, forceful, inventive, well acquainted with what the world calls success, this remarkable man was not only modest but strangely given, at times, to underestimating his own capacity and the amount of his achievement. He seemed to think that he had been crippled by the lack of a formal academic education. As though it were in the power of any college to give him more than a fraction of the training he had given himself! If he was not a man of culture our definition of culture needs revising.

That he had in him the making of a scholar in the narrower import of the term becomes evident on a superficial examination of his private papers. These records of his studies, though fragmentary, show him to have been at once accurate and systematic. They simply go not far enough. Any man who has the scholarly instinct, and will tie himself down to a single topic and firmly resist the temptation to run off into bypaths, may easily become erudite. A large part of so-called scholarship consists of nothing more significant than technical facility. It is dry, without cultural value, and at the same time indispensable. No one hopes to get on without it, any more than a violinist hopes to get on without the daily practice of decidedly monotonous exercises. But the work of a busy pastor, of the official head of a great department of church activity, and of the chancellor of a self-created system of popular education eats up time and strength. One can hardly ask such a man to make an edition of Horace or to edit Gibbon, even if he were so minded. A few men have combined interests as antipathetic as the executive and the rigidly scholarly, but they are very few indeed.

The mention of John Vincent's large-mindedness towards his colleagues leads naturally to a paragraph or two touching his generosity in respect to material things. He resembled in that trait a celebrated English author who often remarked that he never saw a boy without wanting to give him a sovereign. The illustration that follows is none the less characteristic because it happens to be a personal reminiscence.

I first saw John H. Vincent in 1867, at the home of my maternal grandparents near Oswego. He was then thirty-five years of age; if he looked venerable to me it was because to a small boy any grown-up person seems old. As a matter of fact he must have been rather youthful of appearance, notwithstanding incipient baldness and a full beard. Contemporary photographs show this to be true.

[201]

Summoned in haste from my play to be presented to him, I naturally felt the importance of the occasion. Although well equipped with uncles on the maternal side I had never, up to that day, seen either of my father's two brothers. The introduction being over I straightway procured pencil and paper and sat down in the visitor's presence to write my father an account of the great event. The new uncle viewed the operation with a comical eye, and no doubt remembered that reading and writing, of some sort, come by nature.

He was so flattering as to ask to see what I had written, and in spite of the laughter of the family I promptly assented. He should have been pleased with the proofs the letter gave of my holding original views on the subject of orthography. I was not, even at that tender age, what would be called a simplified speller—redundant were the better adjective. Nevertheless I had a marked prejudice in favor of certain forms and still revert to them on occasion. Taking the pencil in hand my uncle showed me how an E might be converted into an A, and vice versa, without the bother of first rubbing it out. It was an astonishing piece of legerdemain, not difficult to learn and most agreeable to practice; I can do the trick now exactly as he taught it me.

His visit was brief. The next day I received a mysterious package from him. When opened it disclosed a portable writing desk of the most approved fashion, having lids that raised, and small drawers that opened and shut, to say nothing of trays and other receptacles for all manner of small objects, as well as a key that could be lost within twenty-four hours and never found afterwards. There were bottles of red and black ink, sticks of colored sealing wax, penholders with pens in them, and whole boxes of pens besides. The body of the desk was crammed with writing paper and envelopes in various styles (much of it brightly tinted), along with stamps, a calendar, and packages of blotters. The gift was handsome at the lowest estimate that could be put on it; to a boy it seemed nothing less than princely.

Trivial as the anecdote is, it will serve its purpose in showing how open-handed the man was. It was a pleasure to him to give. His benefactions, large and small, were past counting. And the most significant of them were not always those that took the form of books, or money, or (in one notable case) of a round-trip steamer ticket to Europe, good for two passengers. One should not forget the innumerable letters that he wrote in the course of his busy life, many of them addressed to obscure persons with whom he had been thrown for a day or an hour, and penned with no motive beyond that of giving pleasure.

He never forgot these people—certainly not the humble chance acquaintance—though he was quite unable to remember the favors he had done them. I have known him to deny, with a laugh of incredulity, that he had at any time bestowed such and such a gift. He recalled the name and the circumstances of the meeting, but nothing more.

He was in the way to meet any number of people. His work for the Sunday-School Union kept him on the road for months at a time. What to another man might have been a burden was to him a pleasure. A born nomad, he liked to be in motion, to see new places and to face new audiences. No less agreeable was the meeting with old friends and the returning to old haunts. He relished a frequent change of scene.

He quickly accustomed himself to the necessity of doing his work—that part of it that involved the use of books and papers—wherever he happened to be. It was all one to him whether he was on the train, or at a hotel, or at a private house. He was always busy and had need to be. As his interests and responsibilities multiplied his correspondence grew to vast proportions. Yet nothing escaped him, no letter went unanswered, no speech unprepared.

He has described the enjoyment he had in his improvised "study" on the road. "The Pullman at full speed, with a section to myself, table, books, and documents at hand, stimulates me to the best kind of work I am able to do." He easily reconciled himself to luxurious appointments while traveling—resembling all of his tribe in that particular—but could be philosophical when forced to put up with inconveniences.

If doomed to spend several weeks in an uninteresting place, he always carried along with him an ample supply of materials wherewith to occupy his leisure. I once met him in a Western city where one would not elect to spend a month merely because of its charm. And a whole month lay before him, with a certain amount of official business to do, but with untold hours at his own disposal. Though aware that he was never idle, I was astonished, on entering his room, to see what a formidable array of papers he had. Arranged in convenient boxes, they were classified, ticketed, and ready for immediate use. His writing table, with subsidiary tables, was in perfect order. There were signs that he had taken up some one of several tasks.

My belief is that he kept his belongings so arranged that he could find what he wanted at the time the want was uppermost. His family may regard the belief as in some degree erroneous. But I have a recollection of a desk and workshop that were anything but slovenly, yet not a source of annoyance to a chance visitor because their orderliness seemed to proclaim the martinet.

That habit of mind that made him cling tenaciously to the friend or the book or the idea that he had tried and found trustworthy controlled him in matters of less moment. He had his favorite hotels and only abandoned them for the best reasons. How many years he frequented the St. Denis, on Broadway, it were difficult to say. When in London he was sure to put up at Morley's in Trafalgar Square. The older porters and waiters there remembered him for years after his visits ceased, and they were certain to ask how he was and when he might be expected to come again. From which one concludes that they not only liked the man for his unfailing courtesy, but that pecuniary transactions of a satisfactory sort had taken place between him and them.

In the *Autobiography* Bishop Vincent comments on the fact that during all his years of travel—and it must be remembered that he made his first long journey at the age of two years and the last one at, possibly, the age of eighty-seven—he never met with an accident. This may be set down in part to good luck, hardly to the unrivaled merits of American railroads. He was no less fortunate in his voyages. He does not forget the mishap to the ship's rudder during that storm on the Mediterranean; simply remembers that the affair turned out well. He regrets, however, that at the time of the accident he did not derive as much consolation as he could have wished from the knowledge that St. Paul was once in dire trouble in those same waters.

From his son I learn that John Vincent not only welcomed every modern improvement that made for speed, comfort, and safety in travel, but that he was enthusiastic over such new inventions as promised to be useful in the conduct of everyday business. One of the first telephones to be installed in a private house at Plainfield was set up in his home. It was popular with small boys. They appeared in troops, each armed with a plausible excuse for calling to see, and talk through, the wonderful new machine. One can readily believe that families unprovided with boys made up for the lack by coming in person to learn whether the telephone actually existed and whether it would work. A telephone was early installed at Chautauqua, but as a scientific toy rather than as a convenience.

He hailed with delight the advent of the fountain pen, and bought one as soon as the contrivance was put on the market. The original pen was quickly succeeded by an improved one, and that by a third and a fourth. At last he had a "battery" of fountain pens, all equally promising and equally unsatisfactory. One could not be coaxed to part with a drop of the useful fluid it contained (not even for the dotting of an i or the crossing of a t), while its neighbor spouted ink like a small geyser. The owner was always hopeful and always patient; in time he had his reward.

His fondness for coffee led to the purchase of machines

warranted to make the beverage with a degree of perfection hitherto unattained. The most elaborate of these had a huge glass top which now and then was projected half the length of the breakfast table. (The writer has seen that evolution performed at a friend's house with such neatness that hardly a drop of the liquid was spilled). A migratory coffee machine is unpleasing to a wife, however much it may gratify a scientifically minded husband. John Vincent was eloquent in expounding the merits of the apparatus, and denied, with proper spirit, that he ever said grace with one eye fixed on the machine so as to have warning in case it misbehaved.

The story of the burglar alarm was long a classic in the Plainfield family. The alarm was put in *after* the burglar had made his raid—on the principle that determines the locking of stable doors. No other burglar made an appearance. But the alarm was vigilant and, at times, vociferous. With a strong wind in the right quarter it would do its work with amazing promptitude. The owner was convinced that if the alarm lacked judgment it was at all events a piece of healthy mechanism. An alarm sensitive enough to predict the coming of housebreakers was not to be despised.

The typewriter fascinated John Vincent from the first. He procured one without delay and began pecking at the keys with the natural ardor of a neophyte who is also an enthusiast. He acquired skill and would challenge certain clerical friends to a trial of their respective powers; the test was speed with accuracy in the writing of a given passage. Though compelled in the end to dispose of the bulk of his correspondence by the aid of stenographers, he never lost his knack of handling the keys. He thought the perfected typewriter a marvel of human ingenuity, and he would have read with delight every line of the pamphlet recently issued describing the history of the machine during the half century of its existence.

When he heard, years since, that a celebrated inventor at Menlo Park had discovered a way by which the actual tones of the voice could be preserved and then reproduced he immediately drove over to the laboratory, taking his son with him, in order to verify the story. Edison allowed him to sing and talk into the instrument and then hear the result. In an interview printed in a New York paper, Edison, who was a bit of a wag, described the visit of an eminent divine "who had preached a sermon on top of a profane record and was much scandalized by the outcome." True or not the story is a good one. The instrument was afterwards sent over to Plainfield for the delectation of the junior member of the Vincent household.

The early phonograph was a droll affair. Stopford Brooke, hearing its dismal squeak for the first time, described it as "a revolting thing to listen to. . . . It is an ingenious piece of work, but the voice that came out of it was like the voice of a skeleton—a weird, vile, uncanny, monstrous thing! I hate it even more than I hate the telephone and all its ramified iniquities. . . ."

Among the notes touching John Vincent's zest for everything that belonged to the realm of applied science there is no mention of his attitude towards the automobile. Of this we may be sure—that at the earliest opportunity for testing the merits of the new vehicle he would be found testing them. No warning as to the uncertainty of the mechanism would have kept him back.

A young nephew of his once took him about Chautauqua Lake in a car which, if not more eccentric than most cars of that epoch, had little claim to be recognized as the best of all existing models. Somewhat reckless as to his own safety, the nephew was anxious that the uncle should suffer no bodily harm or mental uneasiness. He drove with great care. While bowling along at a fairly rapid pace he sought to allay the supposed fears of his guest by soothing words of the kind that youth always employs in its communications with maturity. When he had finished his speech, the Bishop witheringly inquired, "Won't the thing go any faster than *this?*"

It is said that the only game he ever played was croquet. He played it for the enjoyment it afforded him, disdaining the frivolous excuse that croquet was invaluable because it gave a sedentary man the out-of-door exercise he needed for his health. The plea would not have been specious—the game requires more activity than the uninitiated are aware of. The mention of croquet calls up the period when it was the rage, when it was spoken of as "the coming game," the most modern thing conceivable, when a young Oxford man (according to a certain novelist) wrote a poem on it in four cantos, after the manner of Pope, and when Anne Thackeray satirized it in a lively essay showing how it had become the bane of week-end parties and the death of rational conversation. At the period when he was most addicted to the sport, John Vincent handled the mallet with no little skill. Never in haste to lay down his tools, he has been known to prolong a game until lanterns had to be brought, so that the players could make out where the wickets stood.

Though an adept at no other game than this, he was disposed to be hospitable towards one that in the late Seventies was rapidly coming into vogue, and was destined to supplant its once fashionable predecessor. In the *Assembly Herald* of August 7, 1878, we read that "Doctor Vincent imported, on his last return from Europe, an interesting game called 'Lawn Tennis.' One of these games is set up near 'The Ark,' and under the genial instruction of Doctor V. many old disciples of the ancient game of croquet are deserting it for this new one."

I cannot think that he ever spent much time at it, or really learned to play; one does not take up so active a sport at the age of forty-six. That he was awake to the merits of tennis, and eager to have it introduced at Chautauqua, are facts worth recording.

He would stand a fair amount of teasing, especially from his irrepressible son, and was no doubt often reminded of a question that he once inadvertently asked. It must be premised that he disliked rural life and all that appertained thereto. All phases of it bored him. Though bred in the country his tastes were urban. Nothing depressed him more than, for example, to be shown the glories of a model farm. The owner of such a farm is always merciless; one must see and praise everything he has or means to have.

On a certain occasion John Vincent was being subjected to this form of discipline and was bearing it as well as he knew how. He tramped around with his host, and looked, and listened, and hoped that the end would soon come. At that moment his mind was dwelling on a new pattern of study lamp that he had just acquired. Electricity was not yet in use in private houses and the question of lamps was a serious one. He himself believed that he had found the perfect lamp, and he was forever chanting its praises. And so when the fancy farmer displayed the prize beast in his collection and triumphantly announced what she was able to accomplish in the giving of milk, John Vincent abstractedly inquired, "Is it an Argand cow?"

It was a long time before he heard the last of this. The "Argand cow" became a family word. He was so quick to pounce on lapses of a similar sort on the part of others that we may conclude that he made use of the first opportunity to retaliate on the tormentors of his own household.

His fastidiousness was innate. He liked refined surroundings, but the mere show of wealth impressed him not at all. Simplicity and good taste represented his ideal in a home. During his years of wandering he saw life in a variety of phases, some of them unspeakably dreary. Too considerate and high bred to betray the fact that he was uncomfortable, he would, at long intervals, relieve his mind by a droll outburst in a letter to his wife. The letter was never dated from the place where he was undergoing the form of torture known as "being entertained"—that is to say, ill entertained—but from the next place. And by the time the paragraph was written he was mortified to think that he had allowed himself to complain of "poor coffee, poor tea, poor butter, and a bad bed." He would deplore his weakness in another paragraph, one more droll if possible than its predecessor.

The truth is that he was at times greatly affected by his surroundings, and wished with all his heart that he were not. "I *am* sorry that I am so particular. I don't blame a man for poverty or ill health, but when he has no taste at all," and so on. The sentence was penned just after his escape from a house where everything ran at loose ends and with no justification, certainly not on the score of poverty or ill health.

Hardly any one outside his family knew to what an extent he suffered from the petty annoyances of a nomadic life. He rarely spoke of them. The chances are that he forgot the discipline he had undergone by the time forty-eight hours had passed over his head. In later life he was in a position to protect himself; but not until he was well inured to the worst—inured though not reconciled.

Any one who worked as hard as he did would be entitled to as many physical comforts as circumstances put within his reach. Here is an extract from one of John Vincent's letters: "I lectured last night; am to preach at the Presbyterian Church Sunday morning, speak at the opera house at three, and preach in the Protestant Episcopal Church at night—think of that! The rector is a member of the C. L. S. C." Three public discourses in one day must surely take a good deal out of a man. He is bound to look out for himself if he hopes to be at his best. At the age of fifty John Vincent began to wonder why he drove himself so continuously, and at such a terrific rate of speed. And yet, "How *can* I stop going? I seem impelled by some force *ab extra.*" The inner impulsion was as strong as that from without. When he felt no pressure from duties connected with his office he invented obligations. Of the pleasures of idleness he had no conception.

The sentence just quoted comes from a letter written in 1882. For possibly the first time in his life he had the feeling that he would like to rest, or at least not carry so heavy a load. The feeling cannot have lasted long. At all events he was to keep on at that same impetuous rate for nearly thirty years more.

A man who can write sermons, lectures, editorial articles, and letters on the train can also read any number of books on the train. The man in question kept no list of what he had read in the course of his long life and from chance references one may not hope to get an adequate idea. Of the sort of reading that is done merely to kill time his fragmentary diaries give but a single instance. He was marooned for a day at a house where he was entirely comfortable and absolutely without a thing to do. By the greatest good luck he found there a copy of Prescott's *Conquest of Peru*. By nightfall he had devoured the two volumes.

Another person might have asked, "Haven't you got a good new novel?" He himself very sensibly chose a book in comparison with which most novels seem dry and flat. He would have had no objection to the novel; he was not of those who torture themselves with the idea that they must always read improving books.

That he was capable of heroic reading is evident from the marks in his copy of Burton's *Anatomy of Melancholy*. The book is vastly entertaining, as every one knows who has dipped into it. At the same time it is

[213]

unquestionably long drawn out. Few of us get beyond the first hundred and fifty pages. In this copy the marks are more frequent at the beginning than in the middle, but they persist to the very end. The owner enjoyed his Burton. He found in the book many an opinion that he had long held expressed quaintly, to be sure, but with a captivating bluntness.

CHAPTER XVIII

MAINLY ANECDOTAL

JOHN VINCENT had a warm admiration for certain eminent contemporaries of his, and if an opportunity occurred for meeting any one of them under favorable circumstances was pretty sure to embrace it. He would not put himself out to secure an introduction that could lead to nothing beyond a formal exchange of civilities, and he often held back because he was averse to taking up other people's time, most of all that of a celebrity. Being modest, even self-effacing, he never assumed that because he himself had done a little something in the world everybody must know who he was.

Possibly a chance encounter on shipboard, such as he had with Matthew Arnold in 1886, gave him more pleasure than any other sort of meeting. He regarded Arnold highly, both for his own sake and because he was the son of his father. Thomas Arnold was one of John Vincent's *dii majores*.

Arnold was uniformly affable and communicative; he talked freely of well-known men of the time. Browning, he said, "was not properly educated in youth"; he was obscure, and it was an affectation to praise him as some people were doing. Huxley was mentioned, and he spoke of Mrs. Huxley's attempt to bring up her children "rationalists," and of her subsequent resolve to take them to church and let them decide for themselves. He

[215]

thought it "bigoted" on Herbert Spencer's part to decline to go to Darwin's funeral because it was held in a church. Spencer, he remarked, though not classically educated, was early taught "to read thoroughly." George Lewes he characterized as "a Bohemian, an unclean monkey, clever but without much moral sense." Charles Kingsley, he said (doubtless in reference to the dispute that led to the writing of the *Apologia*), was coarser than Newman but full of humanity, and for that reason alone would be popular.

As to himself, Arnold admitted that he had been pronounced "a dangerous man" by So-and-So (the name is illegible in the notes). His companion promptly quoted, or misquoted, the expression "the stream of tendency that makes for righteousness" as one likely to convey the idea that he was not safe. "Aw-a! that phrase has got hold, hasn't it?" exclaimed Arnold. He then told John Vincent how he had been invited to meet Disraeli at a certain house but was unable to go, and how the host afterwards reported to him that when his name was mentioned at the dinner table Disraeli said, "What phrases he has launched!"

Commenting on practices in teaching that obtained over here, Arnold declared that it was a mistake to divide American history from English history, or American literature from English literature. But what were we to do if not to chronicle our own literary achievements since our cousins over the water declined to do so? Until Clement Shorter, in 1897, brought out his *Victorian Literature* no English textbook took any account of American influence, potent as that influence had long been.

Arnold's opinion of our newspapers was the one that

ELIZABETH DUSENBURY VINCENT AND HER SON.

he had repeatedly uttered—that they were the worst
feature of our literary product. He seems now to have
been speaking of the way in which they were written,
rather than of their content. There was too much reading of newspapers among us anyway, he said, and too
little reading of books. When asked what authors he
would recommend to, say, a young man who wanted to
acquire "strength and style" he named Bacon, Burke,
and Butler. Of orators he pronounced O'Connell, Wendell Phillips, and Guizot the three greatest. Men ought,
he believed, to read the Scriptures more than they do.
He himself read the Greek Testament daily. (His own
copy, by the way, was well annotated with marginal
comments).

Of Arnold's personal appearance, John Vincent gives
the following description: "Tall, square double-chin,
short side whiskers (touched with grey) covering cheeks;
a rather large lower jaw, the chin slightly receding; a
good nose, inclining to the aquiline, the lower lip large
and firm, the eyes grey; he wears a single eye-glass."
There was something about his look and manner that
constantly reminded the observer of Edward Everett
Hale.

The famous man of letters seems to have made himself more than passing civil and friendly during this voyage; he actually presided at a concert in the saloon.
This should have been a mirthful spectacle. John Vincent saw him once again after landing, this time at Fox
Howe, Arnold's home in Westmorland, but records nothing touching the visit.

Chance meetings with other men of note are alluded
to in his irregularly kept diaries or in his letters. The

entries irritate one because so brief. They were, in fact, simple memoranda, made for the writer's private satisfaction but with no thought of elaborating them afterwards into articles.

He rejoiced in once having heard Gladstone speak. The occasion was a luncheon given by Joseph Parker to some twenty guests. Gladstone was presently to defend a measure to which the Dissenters had taken exception.

"I accounted it a great privilege (one of the greatest of my life) to sit for more than an hour —two hours in fact—very near to the distinguished English statesman and hear him make his earnest appeal designed to conciliate and to secure the sympathy of the Dissenting ministers of the country. Gladstone had an impressive presence, was frank, earnest, cordial; made a clear and forcible exposition of the measure he was seeking to carry through. He stated his case, skillfully elicited the opinions of the gentlemen he was anxious to win to the side of the government; and whatever may have been the final conviction of the company on the question then pending, I am sure all were delighted to have been permitted to sit for two hours in the close and instructive fellowship of this greatest of modern British statesmen."

The above version of the incident comes from the *Autobiography*. It lacks the personal strokes that give piquancy to narratives that the writer did not mean should be printed. When communicating with his family he goes into details, describes the costume, figure, lineaments, mannerisms, peculiarities of pronunciation. He is pointed, inclined a little (not too much so) to be satirical, and one can depend on his seeing the comic side of things.

In the preceding chapter I referred to John Vincent's sense of the comic. It is difficult to do justice to his wit and humor, because so few examples of either survive. His friends neglected to record the clever sayings for which, in his prime, he was justly celebrated. In the case of the few we have the enjoyment depends largely on an understanding of the situation that led to their utterance.

Many of his best things took the form of asides. They came out spontaneously in the course of public discussions, or at platform meetings, or in brief addresses of occasion, or in table talk. To explain at length the situation—the make-up of the company and the reasons for their having come together—all for the sake of quoting one flying remark, would be unfair to the man. It would be unfair even though the remark were exquisitely apposite, as many of his sayings were.

One hardly needs to add that John Vincent was not a joker any more than he was a confirmed anecdotist. He was not so much as distantly related to the rather numerous tribe of implacable story-tellers who are always being reminded of something they have read somewhere, and who persist in trotting it out in spite of the fact that it has no bearing on the topic of conversation. Yet he loved a good story and told it well. But he practiced economy. Self-restraint and a fine sense of proportion were apparent both in his sallies of wit and in his choice of anecdotes.

When in one of his bantering moods he generally kept himself well in hand. He liked to tease a friend or a relative—especially a relative. Displays of the latter kind, the verbal harrowing of relatives, always took place before a select audience; they were a form of mental gymnastics or swordplay. He himself could not be certain of coming off unscathed. As a rule the leadership was his not only by gift in the matter of ready retort but by right of primogeniture; he had a lordly way of putting his juniors down where they belonged.

One of his nephews remembers to this day a lively skirmish in which three combatants took part—John H., his brother Bethuel, and their sister, Mrs. Farovid. By his report each of the three coruscated. Each was polite, polished, and ruthless. The action lasted thirty-five minutes. That English novelist who declared that relatives are unduly handicapped in verbal duels was surely mistaken. They are, on the contrary, equipped with lethal weapons. Having been brought up together they know one another's weak points. One does well not to push a relative too hard; he has surprising resources.

The joy of bantering a blood relation is enormous, that of bantering a friend is hardly second to it. In the case of the friend it may take the form of bringing up, by just a word or two, an incident in which he had figured long since, an incident sufficiently annoying at the time but a matter for laughter afterwards; that is to say, provided it is not brought up too often.

At the time Grant visited Chautauqua, a friend of John Vincent's, a solid and highly esteemed citizen in those parts, the proud owner of a pair of superfine carriage horses, asked to be allowed to take the distinguished guest out for a drive. His invitation was accepted and off they went, a party of four.

Grant—whose standard of loquacity, like Words-worth's standard of intoxication, was "scandalously low" —said as little as possible during the course of the drive, and nothing at all on the subject of horseflesh. But after alighting he gave a final comprehensive glance at the handsome animals—they *were* handsome—and then re-marked dryly, "Too fat for speed." John Vincent heard this with inexpressible delight, though he kept a straight face. The owner of the team had to bear with him when, from time to time, he made a pointed allusion to the incident. It was certain to be adroitly put, and in so urbane a manner that to take offense was impossible. He kept in mind almost too many incidents of a not dissimilar type, but one must admit that he was consid-erate in the use he made of them.

It is thought that he enjoyed bringing together men of contrasting character, manners, accomplishments, and beliefs, and observing their efforts to understand one an-other. If not precisely fitted for the office that Carlyle said Richard Milnes ought to hold, the presidency of the Heaven-and-Hell Amalgamation Society, he was so broad-minded, suave, and resourceful, and had such a genuine appreciation of the distinctive gifts of the men he brought to Chautauqua, that the most reserved and suspicious member of the group gathered about him became communicative and friendly.

These meetings were as often fortuitous as designed. It was John Vincent's habit to ask distinguished lecturers at Chautauqua to sit at his table in the dining room of the hotel. If their engagements overlapped it follows that often men of antipathetic temperament would find themselves side by side three times a day for the space of a week. Once in juxtaposition they spoke their minds, with the result that onlookers were highly gratified. The given pair, or trio, of thinkers needed just such a moderator as was their host.

At a Church Congress held at Chautauqua many years ago, an oddly assorted pair of divines met for the first time under the conditions just described. They were John Hall, pastor of the Fifth Avenue Presbyterian Church, New York, and Sam Jones, the evangelist.

Hall was stately in his carriage, well dressed, the beau ideal of clerical dignity and self-possession; in his speech he was a little ponderous and elaborately Johnsonian. Sam Jones was small, alert, and slangy. The Georgian suspected the New Yorker of patronizing him, and Hall was completely puzzled and baffled by Jones. . . . Conversation became difficult to manage. Doctor Vincent had to use all his tact and ingenuity to bring about some sort of amicable relation between his guests. He had often to resort to asking questions.

One day he said to Doctor Hall, "What are your methods in dealing with young and immature minds?" "Ah," replied the New Yorker, "in the effort to establish relations of sympathetic receptivity with relatively crude and immature minds I try to employ language that is essentially simple, and to rely upon concrete illustrations and imagery which may establish some connection with the apperceptive capacities of those whom I am addressing." And so forth. (The narrator of the incident says that Hall ran on in this vein until he "ran down").

Doctor Vincent then turned to his other guest and said, "Mr. Jones, what are your methods?" Speaking shortly, and a bit caustically, Jones replied, "Oh, I put the fodder on the ground, where anything from a jackass to a giraffe can get at it."

At the same table occurred the following brief dialogue, one of those entertaining encounters that are forever taking place in a family where the habit of free speech prevails. The interlocutors were John Vincent and his next younger brother, known among his intimates as "Beth," an abbreviation of Bethuel. The latter was a radical prohibitionist and had been known to call his senior to account for supposed laxity. On the occasion in question there was served at dinner a pudding which under normal conditions, and at worldly resorts, would have been labeled with the phrase "tipsy parson." It was not so designated on the menu of the Chautauqua hotel. On putting the spoon into his dish the younger brother thought he scented evil. As nearly as the writer can recall it, the dialogue that ensued ran something like this:

B. T. V. "John, I'm sure there's liquor in this pudding."

J. H. V. (after taking a good-sized spoonful) "I think you're mistaken, Beth."

B. T. V. (tasting the dish again, but cautiously, as if it might be poison) "I am *not* mistaken. Don't you detect it?"

J. H. V. "Really I do not; it must be your imagination, Beth."

B. T. V. (indignantly) "Nonsense!"

J. H. V. (after sampling the dish afresh, and with evident approval) "It seems to me quite harmless."

B. T. V. (beginning to suspect that by "harmless" his

brother may mean "inadequately seasoned") "John, this sort of thing ought not to be allowed here at Chautauqua. You must put a stop to it."

J. H. V. (much amused) "If what you have in mind *is* really going on here, some one certainly ought to take it in hand. But I still think that you are mistaken. And furthermore" (making an end of the dish of pudding he had so greatly enjoyed), "the sphere of my influence is limited—I am merely the Superintendent of Instruction."

His passion for teasing anybody known to have marked prejudices in favor of this or that was under perfect control; that is to say, he knew exactly when, where, and how to give it rein. His favorite sister-in-law, who often presided at his table, had opinions of her own as to what was a proper seasoning for mince pies, and may, or may not, have ordered the cook to make them so that they would be perfect to the taste and at the same time innocuous so far as morals were concerned. With this in mind, John Vincent would say, "What an excellent mince pie! Yet I miss something, Caroline. Doesn't it lack just the one thing that no mince pie should be without?"

He was not incapable of ringing a variation on the theme by ironically professing his own indifference to, or dislike of, the one thing no mince pie should be without, and representing himself as victimized by the dissolute Presbyterian tastes of his wife and her sister.

He could be remarkably terse when introducing a speaker. Once he had occasion to present a newly returned traveler of distinction who was advertised to speak on the subject of "A Yankee in Japan." Having simply read out the announcement of the lecture as given in the program for the day, he added, "You all know where Japan is—*here* is the Yankee."

His introduction of P. S. Henson is the one most often quoted. There are doubtless happier examples of his wit hidden away in the files of old newspapers, but none to match this in popularity. Henson was brought to Chautauqua to give his very popular lecture entitled "Fools." In presenting the celebrated Baptist minister, John Vincent said, "Ladies and gentlemen, you are now to have the pleasure of listening to a lecture on 'Fools' by one"—a long pause—"of the wisest men in the United States."

Henson retaliated neatly. Coming forward, he said, "Ladies and gentlemen, I am not so great a fool as Doctor Vincent"—a very long pause—"would have you believe."

The man who had made his name familiar in business by some catchword or phrase might expect to find himself identified thereby if the Superintendent of Instruction presided. A once well-known manufacturer was presented thus: "Mr. Jones will now address the audience —Jones of Binghamton; he pays the freight." The formulæ repeated *ad nauseam* for advertising purposes are rarely clever. But any audience would smile broadly on hearing Jones mentioned in connection with freight, and would be delighted to see the very Jones who announced in all the papers how very prodigal he was disposed to be if allowed.

The story of how John Vincent lost a good new hat, and was compelled to put up with the indifferent one that was left in its place, exists in two versions. Although the incident belongs to a later period of his life, it may be set down in this chapter of anecdotes.

The hat was carried off by one of his colleagues, Bishop McCabe, a man who could sing a good song, tell a capital story, raise vast sums for the building of churches, and lecture eloquently on *The Bright Side of Life in Libby Prison.* He was no Brummel among clergymen but rather the opposite. The chances are that he did not know how much better Bishop Vincent's hat was than his own when the exchange was made.

The two men went their several ways, not to meet again until the purloiner of the hat returned from a long journey to Africa and stopped off at Zurich to visit Bishop Vincent. His property was returned to him at a reception given in his honor at the Hotel Bellevue. It had first been sent to a hatter and made to look as well as the headgear of such a devil-may-care character was capable of looking. The only handsome thing about it was the box in which it was enclosed. Bishop Vincent's presentation speech came at the end of the banquet; it was reported by A. J. Bucher.

After a tribute to the visitor's zeal and self-denying labors, the speaker said:

> "Now a personal word. Do you remember our farewell meeting in New York, dear colleague and friend McCabe, many months ago? We said good-by in a hurry, and I did not notice that some other man had walked off with my brand-new and expensive hat, leaving an old slouch in its place. It was high noon. I went down Broadway, and was greatly

surprised that I, being anything but a singer, all at once felt an impulse to sing with shouting voice right there on the crowded street of the metropolis, 'Palms of victory, crowns of glory,' and 'We're building three a day, dear John, we're building three a day.' I managed to suppress the emotion when another irresistible impulse took hold of me. I felt like pulling out my purse and distributing every last dollar I had among the passers-by. But once more I gained control of myself.

"Then, like darts from an unseen bow, fragments of other men's sermons began to shoot through my head, and it was all I could do to keep from jumping on some stepping-stone or soap box and preaching those fragments to the throngs. But when I came to take my hat off to acknowledge a lady's kindly smile I noticed, the moment that she had passed, that it was *your* hat. And now the strange impulses that kept me busy fighting against myself were all clear to me. I was wearing your hat, dear bishop. But I took good care of it, as I am sure that you did of mine. I have the pleasure to return you your property unharmed."

At this point Bishop Vincent reached under the table, brought out an elegant hatbox, and produced from it the renovated hat. In return, Bishop McCabe presented him with his own hat, "in an inexpressibly dilapidated condition." It had been to Africa and it looked it.

In the search for illustrations of John Vincent's happy way with children, and of his ingenuity in doing things for them that they were not likely ever to forget, the

[227]

following anecdote came to light. It will be recognized as typical.

A correspondent writes that sometime in 1885, when she herself was a very little girl, Doctor Vincent spent a few days at her father's house at Salem, Ohio; he preached and lectured in the town. A church bazaar was in progress. He dutifully went to it, and while there bought a doll for his host's small daughter; it was to be presented to her on Christmas Day. From the account one infers that the doll had a wardrobe that was both extensive and fashionable.

The child's parents suggested that she write to the giver and thank him for his gift. "I did so, and told him that all the dolls were *named* by the ladies who had dressed them, and that this doll's name was Ada. So I called her Ada Vincent. I have always kept the letter that he sent me in reply." The letter, by the way, was addressed to the doll itself, not to its owner. I quote it in full.

"DEAR ADA: I am told that you surprised my little friend, Helen Carr, on Christmas Day, and I am glad she gave you a name in which I am interested. And now, Ada Vincent, I write you a few lines which I wish you to remember.

"You are nothing but a doll, but even *you* may set a very good example to some little girls who live in or visit your house. You may, for example, be a very quiet doll, not making a noise when other people are trying to talk, and never crying for things your parent thinks you ought not to have. When you are told to sit down in a given place,

you can sit down and stay there till you are permitted to move. You can keep in yourself all the
temper you have, and never let it spoil your pretty
eyes and lips. There are many things that in this
negative way you can do.

"Now I want to tell you of something else you
can do: By your looks you can remind your
Mamma—Helen—and her friends of the following
important little rules:

"1. To be obedient to parents.
"2. To study diligently the lessons that are
appointed for day school and Sunday
school.
"3. To keep a clean face and a sweet face day
and night, at home and abroad.
"4. To learn how to sew, wash dishes, go on
errands, take care of baby, and do everything else that Mamma commands.

"Now, Ada Vincent, *you cannot do these things
yourself,* but you can put on that look of yours, and
whether you sit on a chair or lie in your bed you can
remind Helen, and the rest of the live dolls, how
they can observe laws about which you in your beautiful stupidity know nothing.

"I wish you a good time in the Carr mansion.
May you be saved from knocks, scratches, bruises,
and other results of carelessness and accident, and
may your face be a perpetual lesson to your little
Mamma. Give her my love.

"Truly your friend,

"J. H. Vincent."

The compiler of this volume knows nothing about children and frankly confesses to standing in wholesome fear of them; but he can see how a letter like the one just quoted would delight a little girl. It certainly pleased Ada Vincent's Mamma, who, on growing up, became a member of the Reading Circle and finally spent a summer at Chautauqua. She writes, "I wanted to speak to Doctor Vincent about the doll, but did not have the courage to do so."

Here is yet another example of his letters to children. It was addressed to a little namesake of his in Baltimore.

The date is January, 1906:

"DEAR JOHN VINCENT SCOTT: You are more than seven months old, and I am a good deal more than seventy years. Think of it! Well, you can't think of it yet. But some day you will. I am ending my life, you are beginning yours. If you live after I am dead I shall be waiting for you to come. And I hope you will live a long, strong, useful life here on earth.

"You have fine eyes to see things with. Look only on good and pure things. You have a sweet mouth. Keep it from all naughty words. You don't reach out for a handshake, but some time you will. Never use your hands for evil deeds. And fill that fine head of yours with noble and useful thoughts. And keep your heart filled with the love of whatever things are good.

"There, John Vincent Scott, I have written you a

love letter. For the present, good-by. My love to
your Mother and Father.

"Faithfully yours,

"John Heyl Vincent."

Although the boy was brought up to revere the man
whose name he bore, and by whom he had been baptized,
it so happened that he never met him until the summer
of 1917, at Chautauqua. I give the touching conclusion
of the story in the father's words.[1]

"The Bishop came to Chautauqua for a brief stay,
and the first sight my boy caught of him was on the
occasion of planting a memorial tree. The respect
and veneration every one paid him impressed the
boy. 'Mother,' he said, 'I can understand why you
named me John Vincent; everybody seems to love
him!'

"The following spring my boy was busy planning
what he would do at Chautauqua as soon as summer
came. I had been away from home for about six
weeks on war work, and had returned. One evening
when I leaned over to kiss the laddie good night I
saw a picture hanging over his head, which in the
dusk I did not recognize. 'Whose picture is that?'
I asked. 'Why, father, don't you know? It's my
great Original!' It was the good bishop, whom the
boy wanted to have near him.

"The next day he started out on an errand for

[1] From a letter from James B. Scott to George E. Vincent.

JOHN HEYL VINCENT

his mother . . . A slip of the foot, a fall, and the
light faded out of those sparkling brown eyes. The
little John Vincent and his great Original are now
fast friends in the larger world."

The bishop's letters to his grandchildren were playful,
affectionate, and often ingeniously phrased. Being his
they would not fail to abound in good advice. In a bright
little missive to the younger of the two granddaughters,
this paragraph occurs:

"I am growing hungry to see you. It seems to me
that we ought to have a new kind of electric system by
the aid of which a grandpa might look into a little box
or something, and at once see his granddaughter wherever she might be. I think I must try to invent some
such Granddaughter-Seeing-Machine."

The letter was typewritten in three colors—red, pur-
ple, and black. He wants the child to ask her mother
"why this letter of grandpa's is like the coat Bible-Joseph
wore."

In another letter—eight pages in length, written with
the pen, and in a hand more like that of a man of forty
than of a man now in his eighty-first year—he undertakes
to tell the little grandchild how much he loves her. "I
love you a lot—if by *weight* I love you ten tons; if by
distance I love you enough to span the space between
Minneapolis and the sun; if by *value* I love you more
than the worth of a bushel of diamonds."

He wonders how soon she will take up Latin and
algebra and English literature. "A good way to begin
that last study—English literature—is to make some of
it yourself. And that you can most easily and profitably

do by writing a letter every week to your grandfather. . . ." And in this same letter she is to tell him all "there is to tell about herself—what you do, and where you go, and what you think." To him this will be genuine English literature.

CHAPTER XIX

THE OXFORD LEAGUE

As an illustration of John Vincent's inventiveness we might take his plan for a society to be known as The Oxford League. It was conceived in 1884, but has long since ceased to exist, if indeed it ever really existed in the sense of taking a strong hold on the young people of the Church.

One cannot help wondering why a scheme that was so picturesque, so attractive in form, and so genuinely educational should have failed. It was sanctioned by the authorities, was well advertised, had its own textbooks and its official organ (a sixteen-page weekly called *Our Youth*) and seemed at first in a fair way to succeed. The name may have hindered rather than helped it. Few young people care much about history or historical associations. Many of the young people for whose benefit the League was designed may have asked what Oxford had to do with *them,* and why, as Methodists, they should be curious about the famous English university.

The projector had such as they in mind when he founded the league. If they did not know what Oxford had to do with them it was high time they learned. Methodism began there, though it was to undergo a thousand permutations before settling into its present form. One ought to know how it began, who was responsible for

[234]

the movement, what were its immediate and after effects, and in what way that which was primarily local and English became international. These points were of supreme interest to the student of social and religious life. Of equal interest was this paradox. A movement that originated in the informal meetings of a group of young scholars captured the lower ranks of society, the illiterate toilers, a people to whom books and learning meant nothing.

When John Wesley, a fellow of Lincoln College, returned to Oxford in 1729, to fulfill certain obligations attaching to his fellowship, he found that his brother Charles and two other graduates had acquired the nickname of "Methodists" because of the exactness of their habits of study and devotional exercise. The name was not new; other enthusiasts for order and regularity had been dubbed the same. Wesley joined them. Having a gift for leadership, he became their head. As often in American colleges of to-day an excessive application to textbooks awakens ridicule, so it was at Oxford. And these four, a fellow and three undergraduates, were not merely enamored of study; they were enamored of religion. This was an even greater offense.

Before long another epithet was applied to them; they were called "The Holy Club." The mocking appellation is said to have originated at Merton College. Wesley, being their acknowledged chief, was known as the "Curator of the Holy Club." Their doings were made the subject of hostile comment in a weekly paper. This led to the printing of an anonymous pamphlet in defense of their practices.

These practices were not subversive. What the young

men mainly did was to search the Scriptures, in the original, and to help their fellow man. The latter occupation has of late years become fashionable and popular. Dickens satirized its extravagancies in his account of the farcical Mrs. Jellyby and Borriboola-Gha. But that was seventy years ago. Since then even philanthropy has reformed. When the Wesleys and their friends began visiting the wretched prisoners at the Castle, the common jail of Oxford, a mission of that sort was far from fashionable; it was hardly respectable. That it was an absurd way of spending one's time few doubted.

Nevertheless it was in work of this and a similar sort that the members of the Holy Club busied themselves in the intervals of reading and attending lectures. They spent some part of every day with the prisoners, read prayers at the Castle twice a week, preached on Sunday, and administered the communion once a month. They collected money for the poor—often stinting themselves in order to obtain it—and looked after the school children. The Bishop of Oxford, John Potter, thought their proceedings a little irregular, but admitted that they did good. John Wesley's father made a journey from Epworth to learn what his son was about, and professed himself well pleased with what he saw and heard.

The movement was local, confined to one university city, and the young men identified with it were all Anglicans as a matter of course. They came from various colleges—Exeter, Merton, Pembroke, and Christ Church —but Lincoln was the place of meeting. The rooms that Wesley occupied during a nine years' residence are still pointed out. The only portrait in existence that shows how he looked as a young man may be seen in the Hall.

In the ante-chapel stands the pulpit from which he often preached when he was a resident fellow. In marked contrast with this academic relic is the grassy natural amphitheater near Redruth, Cornwall, where Wesley used to preach to the miners.

The story from first to last has something of the charm that attaches to a romance. It always fascinated John Vincent, the initial chapter above all the others. He liked to dwell on the semi-monastic life of that small group who were primarily scholars, and only later became reformers and philanthropists. John Wesley lectured on philosophy and on Greek. In his private studies he gave the first two days of the week to the classics, the third day to what would now be called physics, the fourth to Hebrew and Arabic, the fifth to logic and metaphysics, and the sixth to rhetoric. He and his brother agreed to converse only in Latin; they kept up the habit for years. Neither declined into a pedant; the circumstances of the life they led at Oxford made it impossible. They were very human and very cheerful. John Wesley was an admirable *raconteur*. He never minced his words. Even when preaching he was surprisingly colloquial.

The more John Vincent reflected on the history of the so-called "Holy Club" of Lincoln College the more convinced he became that young Methodists should go into the subject, that they should know it not merely in outline but in detail. The study would be as useful as it would be entertaining. To this end he planned what he called The Oxford League. It was to be distinctively a young people's society.

He went at the business with his customary vigor, issued circulars, set two or three clerical friends of his at work on the textbooks, and himself gave innumerable talks on the theme. The textbooks, seven in number, were brief—the longest of them runs to twenty pages—and were sold at a price that barely covered the cost of making. Possibly these pamphlets erred on the side of brevity.

Each was a monograph. The first dealt with the Wesley family, the second with the Holy Club, the third with Oxford as the birthplace of Methodism, and the fourth with "Methodist Converts in High Places." Of the remaining three in the series one outlines (with not enough of detail, say in the way of bibliographical facts) the literary work of the Wesleys; the others discuss the place of education in English and American Methodism. All seven pamphlets are exactly the sort of thing one would have expected John Vincent to inspire. The ideas they contained were common property; they could be obtained from books that every library contained. The novelty consisted in their being so collected and presented as to focus attention on a few striknig facts in the history of the Church. In every number of the series the value of a regular training is taught, if not directly then by implication.

One sees that the Oxford League was conceived in the same spirit as were the Palestine Class, the Sunday-School Institute, and Chautauqua. Unlike these, it aimed to supply a denominational need; it was to be *the* young people's society, one comprehensive organization with many chapters.

The main purpose of the Oxford League was to commemorate the original Holy Club of Lincoln College by studying its history along with that of the Church as a whole. Presumably one might do as much collateral reading in ecclesiastical annals and biography as one liked. The fourfold object of that first club may be stated thus: a devout study of the Scriptures; an energetic personal piety; a quickening of the intellectual and literary spirit of the Church, and a word of practical benevolence. The Oxford League would not try to exact more from its members than they were willing and able to give. There were to be only four regular and four special meetings in the course of the year. And the required readings were so arranged as not to press heavily on those who can devour a novel in any number of pages, yet are appalled at the sight of a textbook of the most diminutive sort.

The League would emphasize the fact that Methodism began in an ancient university and that its founders were scholarly young men who, with one exception, came of families in which learning was an inheritance. Well born, they were bred in academic surroundings. From the halls and colleges of Oxford these young men went out into the town to do good, and then into the country, to the mining districts and the neglected rural parishes, and to that wilderness of slums of which, in the Eighteenth century, a large part of London was composed. Their mission was practical, not cultural, but something of the amenity and charm that culture gives its devotee must have made itself felt.

The members of the newer Oxford clubs would not only study the entire history of the movement but would also make an effort to apply its methods to modern social problems. No chapter of the League could be like the original group nor should it wish to be, but it

[239]

should be informed with the same spirit. Made up of earnest and intelligent young people who came from refined homes, and who were "thoughtful students in the school of Christ," each club, or chapter, would dedicate itself to the service of the race.

By dedication John Vincent did not mean separation. One was to live one's life as usual, though with less of self-absorption and with an eye to the needs of those about one. While strictly denominational from the nature of its organization, the League, in respect to the work it did or attempted, would be as catholic as could be asked.

Many flourishing chapters sprang up. The Oxford League was never feeble; it simply never became popular. More and more the opinion prevailed that neither its form nor its avowed purpose, to say nothing of the name, fitted it for the place the founder hoped it might occupy. There had been a great multiplication of clubs and societies throughout the country, all admirable in their several ways, yet ineffective because there was no union for a common end. One English name is as good as another; it is difficult to see why Epworth should have proved attractive and Oxford not. In 1889 the unaffiliated societies came together to form the Epworth League. The Oxford League was practically merged in the new body, and while it still had official countenance, the newer league had official support.

I suppose that Bishop Vincent—he had by this time been raised to the episcopacy—was disappointed and even annoyed. He saw that a compromise of some sort had to be made, but he hoped that it might be made in a way to keep virtually intact the society to which he had given so much of his time during the five years just past.

To the organ of the Oxford League, *Our Youth,* a word or two must be given. It was a sixteen-page weekly, attractive in appearance, printed from new type on excellent paper, the matter cleverly arranged, and the subscription price put absurdly low. How the publishers were able to part with fifty-two numbers for one dollar is a mystery that unfortunates who live at a time when a dollar buys little or nothing will not attempt to solve. *Our Youth* was not founded for the purpose of making money; it was thought quite enough if it paid its expenses.

Practically all the leaders were written by the founder of the League. As assistant editors he had the help of two young men who were recently graduated from Yale, his son, George E. Vincent, and James R. Joy, the present editor of *The Christian Advocate.* Their influence was paramount in all that related to the secular departments. Nothing flabby or sentimental found its way into their columns, or, for that matter, into any other column of *Our Youth.* The tone was healthy, robust, and decidedly modern. There was a department of "Recreation," a department called "The School at Home"— always lively, as when it attacked the English of George Saintsbury—a department of foreign affairs headed "The Outside World," and one that bore the caption "Jest and Youthful Jollity."

It is quite possible that these sections of the paper were more popular than the continued stories and tales that held the place of honor—these together with such articles as the ones contributed by Schwatka, E. S. Nadal,

W. H. Rideing, C. T. Winchester, Charles Barnard, and some twenty more or less readable authors. As the organ of the Oxford League the paper gave in every issue a column or more to the activities of the society: as a denominational paper for young people another column, "Our Berean Homily," to the lesson for the coming Sunday.

On turning over the pages of the weekly one is struck by the fact that although it lived its brief life nearly thirty-five years ago there is nothing old-fashioned about it. A few of the stories have a somewhat faded air; the great majority of the articles are instructive and entertaining still. It is rather a pity that *Our Youth* could not have been well subsidized, continued, and kept up to the standard its founder set for it. There is need for such a denominational paper. But nothing lasts long. The great dailies perish or are swallowed up by dailies greater than themselves, and why expect all the periodicals designed for a limited audience to live on indefinitely?

The Oxford League was one of those dreams that Bishop Vincent never saw come true. Nevertheless he liked to dwell on the idea, to recall what had been done, and to speculate on the possibilities of doing yet more. As late as 1910 he drew up a precise plan for the founding of Oxford Clubs within the Epworth League, a part of it, yet having a distinctive life. The most marked feature of the plan is the emphasis laid on education. "The club is to promote a higher appreciation among its members of a true scholarship as a factor in religious and Church life, answering thoroughly the superficial and false idea that high scholarship is hostile to deep and fervent piety."

Members were to be urged to take a regular collegiate course of training. Such of them as doubted the possibility of meeting successfully the obstacles, mainly financial, that stood in their way were to be helped to see that these obstacles might be overcome. Where the thing was manifestly impossible a pledge was to be exacted that the members would at least pursue a course of reading at home; in that way they might obtain the broader outlook of the scholar.

The persistency with which John Vincent dwelt on this subject of education is remarkable. Early and late he preached the necessity of the sort of training that is to be had through the printed page. One should know books. They are indispensable in this age and in this country of ours. To be sure culture won't save your soul, but you are the better for it and of greater use in the world.

CHAPTER XX

HIS POSITION ON CERTAIN POINTS

JOHN VINCENT was tolerant of shades of belief and of religious practices that differed from his own. His Protestantism was, to be sure, deeply ingrained; he could be depended on to speak with entire frankness in support of his convictions. But he was not one of those who are forever going out of their way to be frank. It has been thought with his fondness, up to a certain degree, for liturgies and the ceremonial side of religion he would have made a first-rate Episcopalian, and I dare say he would. But by no stretch of the imagination is it possible to conceive of him in the rôle of high churchman.

He was bound to be tolerant, for he firmly believed in denominationalism. He might and often did rally an acquaintance on his devotion to certain tenets, yet he would have been the last man in the world to assume that the acquaintance would be the better off for taking his own point of view. He held that denominationalism, with its different phases of belief and contrasting methods of work, was on the whole a power for good. Society, the State, and the Church profited thereby.

"It is better so," he writes, "than if there were but one society, one set of officers, and one administrative center. People differ. Civilizations differ. Policies must differ. It is better for a score of reasons. It is better for the city or the town to be made up of families living in separate houses rather than in one huge hotel, eating in one dining room, sleeping under the same roof. Individuality is as important as general and organic unity."

That was a good saying of his which runs somewhat like this: "There is a difference that makes for unity. A great truth is the greater when it has been looked at from two, three, or more sides." The context shows that he had in mind truths so indisputably great that however minutely studied they can never be gainsaid. Their very greatness will, nevertheless, give rise to critical schools and to sects. Denominationalism breeds "discussion and experimentation," and these contribute to such unity as is worth while.

He always insisted that Methodism was "the reproduction of the essentials of the Christianity of the first century: supernatural doctrine and experience; Christ in men as a source of life; the Holy Spirit of God controlling men and giving witness to men." It was not a new ecclesiastical establishment or a new theological system. It was "primitive Christianity revived."

His claim is sweeping. To what extent he had gone into the historical aspects of the question cannot now be known. He may have dipped into Lord King's book and read the Bampton lectures of Edwin Hatch. On the other hand he may have been struck by the salient points of resemblance between the ancient and modern forms of organization, and have cared little for the details. In its beginnings the Primitive Church was not much troubled with ecclesiastical machinery. The leaders—

known as presbyters or elders—were simply the shepherds of the flock. We are told that no proof can be found of the existence of "a specially set apart ministry." Any man might speak to the congregation so long as he spoke in accordance with the oracles of God.

Certain features in the polity of his own denomination had John Vincent's unvarying support; the itinerancy for example. He believed in it as a theory of government and he admired its practical results. By reason of it no flock was for one minute without a pastor. "The incumbent of the present is removed only as the name of his successor is announced." He thought that Methodists might safely declare that theirs was "the church of the perpetual pastorate."

Possibly he believed a short term preferable to a long one. He may even have agreed with that minister who, when the question came up of substituting an indefinite period of service for the limited term, remarked jocosely that in three years he had told his people all he knew, besides having learned enough about them to make him willing to move elsewhere.

As to revivals John Vincent's position was clear and consistent. He recognized their value and at the same time made careful distinctions. He certainly did not approve of them as, in the old days, they used to be conducted. When he entered the ministry, revivals were held to be essential to the health of the Church. It perplexed and disturbed him to find that he had no skill in promoting them. He need not have been perplexed. Temperamentally disqualified, as he certainly was, for achieving success by the time-honored methods, he also had doubts as to the wisdom of those methods. That special efforts should be made to persuade people to become Christians he freely granted. He simply objected to the form, often reprehensible, that such efforts were sure to take. The young should be safeguarded against all that savored of superficiality and sensationalism.

For the professional revivalists who employed unseemly antics to attract attention he had a contempt that he made little effort to conceal. Buffoonery, he thought, could be depended on to draw a gaping crowd—as an aid to genuine religion it was valueless. No man was ever really converted by seeing another man jump.

His aversion to all this sort of thing was in part instinctive. He was also firmly convinced that the method was objectionable in that it degraded what it professed to exalt. In short, he was opposed to introducing either into revivals or into the regular service anything that smacked of the music hall. He had witnessed queer performances in his day. Unfortunately he did not live long enough to learn that the evolutions of barefooted dancers were, in some quarters, to be looked on henceforth as a means of grace. One can imagine with what finished sarcasm he would have commented on this twentieth-century conception of a religious exercise.

He was opposed to yet another element in the old-fashioned revival. In his boyhood and youth he had seen many a convert made through the agency of terror, and he knew the evil of it. He puts the matter thus: "Terror may arrest attention. So far so good. But terror must be allayed before its subject is able calmly, deliberately, and effectively to make the choice that tells on character." As for seeking religion for private ends—

to insure one's personal safety and secure a comfortable berth in the next world—he would none of it. Self-interest was surely an ignoble motive for embracing Christianity and joining the Church.

He was so brief a time in the pastorate, about twelve years, and so happy in his choice of the means for promoting a vigorous church life, that the problem of revivals cannot have much disturbed him. Any congregation that he served was certain to be revived at least once a week throughout the year, and in the sanest of ways, by an appeal to the head and the heart, not by a playing on the nerves.

A question of greater moment than that of revivals, "past, present, and possible," was the question of the home training of children. "Home, as it is the first, is the most important of all schools." Parents should make a study of the problem of education and apply what they have learned to the training of the young animal in their charge. If the prayer meeting occasionally resolved itself into a sort of educational conference it would not be unprofitable. Men who were known to have sound ideas on pedagogy might be asked to fill the pulpit from time to time. "This is a subject which the pulpit can well afford to discuss, and *should* discuss, even if the congregation have reason to imagine that the parsonage would do well to consider these problems."

After the home comes the public school. John Vincent devoutly believed in our system of secular education and in keeping it free from outside interference. "But in our age and in our land we need to make the home the first school of reverence, of manners, of social good will, of the history of the race and its gradual development, of the civilizations under which the largest measure of popular education has been encouraged and the freedom of the individual most safely and effectively secured."

So the home is paramount after all, and the responsibility is thrown on the shoulders of parents rather than on those of professional teachers. The latter can do something, even when the home influence is against them; but they are sadly handicapped.

John Vincent defined his position on the subject of amusements in the editorial columns of *Our Youth*. These leaders were afterwards reprinted in a little book entitled *Better Not*. The title exactly expresses the spirit of the volume. It is neither "Should Not" nor "Must Not," but "Better Not."

The author held by the teachings of his Church. Its body of laws contained a specific proscription of certain forms of amusement. The phraseology of the General Rules differed in one edition of the *Discipline* from that in another. The meaning was always the same. Whether or not the law was too sweeping, and in some respects unjust, does not concern us. It stood for years; to be sure it had become a dead letter to a considerable extent. For that reason alone many efforts were made to repeal it. They were unsuccessful up to 1924. The law might well have been preserved as is preserved an ancient boundary or milestone, the sign of what was once regarded with respect and is now only a curiosity.

As to dancing, John Vincent's attitude, as stated in the little volume, is denominationally correct. The grounds of his disapproval are, however, his own. When he quotes certain positive utterances against the amusement (one from a physician) he grants that they may

have been too strongly put. But where there is so much
smoke must there not be a little fire? He honestly believed that there was both folly and fire in this form of
diversion.

When he comes to the question of card-playing he does
not discuss it in its relation to those who are known
as worldly people. Such people have their own standards. The point is "Shall Christians countenance the card
table?" He answers the query with a "Better Not."
That cards meant a prodigious waste of time he was perfectly satisfied. He quotes with evident relish this passage from Addison: "I think it very wonderful to see
persons of the best sense passing away a dozen hours
together in shuffling and dividing a pack of cards, with
no other conversation but what is made up of a few
game phrases, and no other ideas but those of black or
red spots ranged together in different figures. Would
not a man laugh to hear any one of this species complain-
ing that life is short?"

His homily on the stage is emphatic. He might have
summoned Jeremy Collier as a witness; Collier is very
entertaining. He denies that one's attitude towards theatrical entertainments is to be influenced by the opinions
of cultured people. "Culture, as it is understood, is no
standard by which to test moral and religious questions.
Culture is often spiritually blind and intensely selfish.
But what is the verdict of spiritually minded and devout
souls who sustain the Church? You all know the answer."

He had of course to deal with the problem of amusements in concrete. Even then, his son says, he did
not lay down the law, but used reason and persuasion.
The Methodist ban in relation to so-called worldly amuse-

ments, always rather irksome to one who had, presumably, a leaning towards the drama, proved little less than intolerable during the four years that the son spent at Yale.

The father expressed himself in this wise: "I do not say that these things are in themselves and always wrong. Good people differ in their judgments about them, but my official position is clear. If you were to do these things it would be an embarrassment to me. I also personally believe that they have aspects that would be dangerous to you. In everything about which there is no question I try to stand by you and give you opportunities for pleasure. And I should appreciate it very much if you would stand by me until you are twenty-one, even if you do not look at things as I do. When you are twenty-one you must decide for yourself and I shall have nothing further to say."

As the son rightly observes, an admonition worded in this manner could have but one effect. No boy of any decency would fail to play the game fairly. There would be no satisfaction in doing otherwise. A dictatorial attitude on the part of the father might easily have produced a different result. A proposition so reasonably put must be assented to, and the compact, a gentlemen's agreement, scrupulously kept.

One of the indulgences forbidden by the Church was the use of intoxicants, and the Church was thought narrow-minded in the extreme on this account. By the General Rules as printed in the *Discipline* of 1856 no one could remain a member of the society unless he refrained from "Drunkenness, buying or selling spirituous liquors, or drinking them, unless in cases of extreme necessity."

The last clause is often overlooked. The rule was not so very narrow at that epoch. It admits that there may be "cases of extreme necessity." As for the buying and selling, nothing was supposed to justify it. What was once forbidden by a few religious societies is now forbidden by the State. Men still traffic in intoxicants, but they do it *sub rosa*.

In his little book John Vincent advises letting wine alone. He was addressing himself to young people who might, he thought, fall into a questionable practice because it had the sanction of the social world. He admits that very worthy people have differed in opinion on this subject. Wines and liquors were once to be found on most sideboards in America. "Clergymen drank wine at parties and in private, after preaching and before it, at weddings and at funerals. They saw no harm in it." In England and Scotland to-day you will find wine (and much stronger beverages, he might have added) on the tables of those who deem themselves Christians. But if a great deal that is plausible may be adduced in support of the practice, more can be brought forward to prove its unwisdom. And so, on the whole, "Better Not."

The entire essay is a temperance tract, differing mainly from the ordinary tract in point of urbanity and reasonableness. The author has no patience, however, with parents who permit or encourage their children to drink in moderation at home, to the end that they may not be tempted to drink *ad libitum* elsewhere. He would hardly have been able to contain himself had he seen what the present writer once saw—a clergyman (of what denomination matters little) pouring out a tiny glass of claret for his small son, aged three and a half, and patting the youngster on the back as he gravely sipped it. A bishop who sat opposite applauded the boy for being able at so tender an age to take his liquor like a man. A certain other bishop would have said, "Better Not."

A paper meant to be read by boys and girls who have been bred in refined homes can deal with only one part of a subject, the elements. This paper has the tone of fatherly warning. If positive it is also genial. It was no part of the writer's design to take up aspects of the problem such as are brought out in the novel of *Joseph Vance*. De Morgan can hardly have meant his book to be a tractate on the evils of intemperance. The book becomes that to some extent by reason of the extraordinary realism of the treatment. That endless procession of men and women staggering into and out of public houses is a disquieting spectacle.

George Eliot, who rarely touches on the subject, except in the case of Dempster, makes clear what her attitude would have been had she written a novel of purpose with intemperance as a leading motive. Speaking of a corner of Hertfordshire in which she was spending the month of August, she says, "I prefer a country where I don't make bad blood by having to see one public house to every six dwellings. . . . My gall rises at the rich brewers, in Parliament and out of it, who plant these poison shops for the sake of their million-making trade, while probably their families are figuring somewhere as refined philanthropists or devout evangelicals or ritualists."

She tacitly assumes that the laboring classes will steep themselves in liquor if the stuff is to be had, and reserves her contempt for those who get rich by seeing that it is provided. The ghastly delirium tremens scene in *Janet's Repentance* is a particular case artistically treated, and essential to the development of the narrative. No general conclusions are forced on the reader as they seem to be in *Joseph Vance*.

CHAPTER XXI

RELIGIOUS VIEWS AND PRACTICES

WITH John Vincent religion was a matter of everyday life, not of fast days and Sundays. To be sure one kept the Sabbath by certain observances, not alone because of immemorial custom based on the Commandments but because such observances were fitting and salutary. The mere act of public worship was civilizing though there might be a shade of perfunctoriness in it.

But a religion that was summed up in decorous behavior and churchgoing one day out of every seven, together with the usual giving of gifts for this cause or that, necessarily lacked the vital qualities. There was no conscious hypocrisy about it; the worshipers were quite sincere—for that one day. They threw their influence on the right side. So long as their conduct during the other six days did not neutralize whatever good came of their formal observances there was a profit for all concerned. There people would be in a somewhat better case than the man mentioned by Doctor Johnson, the man who never by any chance entered a church but who never passed one without taking off his hat.

On the whole, a religion of this character can only be described as a simulacrum. It has no substance. Were the forms so scrupulously gone through with on Sunday repeated on Monday, and on each succeeding day, they would still be forms. It may be that the sort of religion

[255]

they stood for would become even more diluted because of the mere repetition of prescribed phrases.

Religion, then, must find expression in some other way than through set forms, beneficial as these are; and it must have qualities that fit it for common use. There are three hundred and sixty-five days in the year, and the religion that counts is the one that is available for all of them, not for a particular number; the usual estimate is fifty-two. John Vincent was never tired of inculcating the truth that every day in the year is not only a working day; it is "a holy working day." Grant, as we must, that there is nothing very novel in this saying, that it comes near to being a truism, we cannot help being impressed by the sincerity with which the idea is set forth, by the frequency with which it occurs in his public discourses, and by the aptness and variety of the illustrations used to enforce it.

A religion that will bear any test that worldly affairs may put it to cannot be made up of abstractions and theories. The man who professes it may at one time have puzzled his brain over intricate doctrinal points and got nowhere. As a consequence he falls back on that tangible side of his belief that principally concerns conduct. The celebrated man of letters who defined religion as "morality touched with emotion" failed to satisfy many readers whom he would have been glad to convince. But he undoubtedly described the sort of religion that a large part of humanity has embraced. Morality is its substance, but it is morality touched with emotion.

The emotional element in John Vincent's conception of religion was very marked. Temperamentally and by the circumstances of his upbringing he would be inclined

his younger compeers, lay and clerical, because he felt that the man had something that met their case. It did not follow that the author in question stood as high in his own private estimate as he once had.

On the whole it would appear that his theological position was somewhat advanced when he was a young man, though he sensibly refrained from shouting the fact from the housetops, and that it became more advanced as he grew older. The flurry over what was called the New Theology interested him. He was curious as to its exact aim and possible influence, and even made inquiries of a clerical friend as to the probable outcome of the movement. But he never went into the subject as one might do who was eager to have the old boundaries thrown down, or who regarded any stir in the world of religious speculation as necessarily a sign of progress.

Some theorists are for having no boundary at all. John Vincent was as far removed from these as from that large section of the Church which is reluctant to part with anything. On certain articles of belief he took his stand in the beginning and never changed. As to the immortality of the soul he had no doubt—I am speaking of the doctrine as it would have been taught him in its simplest form by his mother—nor of the existence of heaven. An attempt to define the nature of a departed spirit or the place of its abode he is likely to have regarded as futile, a mere exercise of the imagination and not necessarily pleasing or profitable. That we may meet in another world those we have known in this he was confident. One can see how deeply he would be moved by the closing lines of Browning's *Prospice*. Here a poet of massive intellect had put into powerful rhyme what he himself held to be an indisputable truth.

From his mother he would have obtained at an early age a conception of prayer in its noblest form. Mrs. Himrod Vincent, a practical woman in every way, set apart an hour of the morning for private devotion. Alone in her room she read from the Scriptures, from some book dealing with Christian experience, and then prayed. "No company, no domestic cares (the illness of her family alone excepted) could induce her to vary from this established order. . . . She saved time and gained strength by retirement from the busy world. In this hour of prayer she saw the true meaning of life and the relative value of things temporal and spiritual."

Once when her eldest son was leaving home for his first long journey her parting words were, "Live near to God, live near to God." Prayer was one of the means through which she attained what she so earnestly desired for him and for all her children. If there was something of quietism in this it was consonant with a piety that never lost itself in mere raptures and yearnings. The weekly talks that she had with her boys, at twilight on Sunday, were the better remembered by them because she dwelt on the ethical side of religion.

Two of these boys entered the ministry. Their testimony as to their mother's personal characteristics and influence coincided. Their attitude towards her was that of veneration. The younger of the two was not eighteen when she died, the older had reached the age of twenty. Their recollections of her were almost preternaturally vivid, and that after the lapse of nearly half a century. That she largely determined the course that each was to take seems a reasonable conclusion—not so much the profession as the attitude towards life.

It is a little singular that these two brothers—so unlike in many ways—should have arrived independently at the same philosophical position. Both were distinctly liberal. Both were open-minded in their attitude towards the teaching of science. (I well remember the day when I saw the younger brother throw down a book that he had been reading and exclaim, "From now on *I* am an evolutionist.") And both believed in a religion that would stand the wear and tear of everyday life. No system of ethics, however beautifully designed and successfully applied, would have satisfied either. God was very real to them. Christianity was so great a truth that not to embrace it seemed folly. For the wrangling of theological disputants over unimportant questions they had a contempt that could not always be hidden.

CHAPTER XXII

IN THE EPISCOPATE

At the meeting of the General Conference in May, 1888, John H. Vincent was raised to the office of a bishop of the Methodist Episcopal Church. He speaks of it as though it were a surprising thing that he should have been elected. Certainly it was no surprise to the public. He was as well known outside the limits of his denomination as within. The feeling that the honor had been fittingly bestowed was general.

Apart from the satisfaction arising from this proof that his colleagues thought him worthy of the highest office in their gift was the very great pleasure due to the opening of a new field. His habit had been to give himself with his whole soul to any project that he undertook, and not to relax his efforts until it was brought to a successful issue. Even then he was somewhat loath to hand over the business to his coadjutors; he liked to keep a guiding hand on it.

But there came a time when it bored him not a little to be known only as "a Sunday-school man." His interests were wide. Many schemes were fermenting in his brain. To what one of them he should devote himself was probably a question. By a rather odd coincidence the adoption of the International Lessons and the founding of Chautauqua, in its first crude form, were almost simultane-

[268]

ous. Within a year or two the Assembly had become John
Vincent's favorite enterprise. When presently he saw
in it the means for popular education he bent all his energies to making it a success. The Assembly grew with
astonishing rapidity, and as it grew his conception of what
might be made of it expanded. Under his management
—I am speaking only of the platform, the Reading Circle, and the schools, not of the business administration—
it attained the point of fullest development. It might be
changed in this respect or that (not always to advantage), new features might be added, and the attendance
doubled, but the form was practically determined. It was
the form that John Vincent gave it, and that it must keep
if it is to be a permanent institution.

To take for granted that his interest in Chautauqua
ever declined is wrong; he cared more for the Assembly
than for any other one project or enterprise with which
he had had to do. To say that he was not unwilling, at
the age of fifty-six, to spend his time and force on work
of a different character is a fair statement of the case.
And his election to the episcopacy gave him what he required—the change of occupation for which he was
more than ready.

A man of his repute in his own denomination would be
spoken of as a potential bishop long before he actually
became one. At the General Conference of 1884 he
polled a large vote on the first ballot. His friends were
sure that he would be elected sooner or later. He himself
says that he thought it an impossibility. Perhaps he had
in mind the current criticism to the effect that he was not
so good a Methodist as he might be.

In 1888, when it came to the voting, he was **chosen**

on the third ballot, along with J. N. Fitzgerald; by the rule then in force the suffrages of two thirds of the delegates were required to elect. He would wear his new title as one who had a right to it, being of the same mind as John Wesley, who said: "I firmly believe that I am a Scriptural *episcopas* as much as any man in England or in Europe; for the uninterrupted succession I know to be a fable, which no man ever did or can prove."

The Bible used at the consecration of John Vincent and his fellow bishops is a relic of singular interest. It once belonged to Wesley. A small octavo volume, in a coat of black leather, bearing the date 1671, it is bound up with the book of Common Prayer, the latter of an earlier date. The Bible came into the possession of Samuel Danks Waddy, Q.C., of the Inner Temple, and was by him put into the hands of Bishop Matthew Simpson as a gift to the Methodist Episcopal Church. The press clipping from which these facts are taken says that it was first used at the opening of the General Conference of 1884, at Philadelphia, and that from then until the present time it has regularly figured in the consecration ceremonial.

Newly elected bishops have no great liberty in the choice of residence. There being no diocesan system the plan is employed of fixing on certain points throughout the country as episcopal stations. What towns shall be so designated is (or was) left to the General Conference. The bishops decide for themselves who shall go where. The seniors, in point of election, have the first choice.

Bishop Vincent was disposed to congratulate himself when it was settled that Buffalo was to be his home.

Besides being attractive in itself, the city was within a few miles of Chautauqua. His amusement may be guessed when he saw himself described in the press as "The Bishop of Buffalo," or referred to as "a distinguished prelate." The newspapers contain many diverting things in addition to the headlines.

The principal duty of a bishop is to preside at the Annual Conferences. These are held in the spring or in the early fall. For example, in the spring of 1889 Bishop Vincent presided at conferences in Kansas and the Northwest. On his return to Buffalo he began a series of episcopal visitations throughout the city and the suburbs, preaching two or three times on Sunday and holding a service every night of the week excepting Saturday. The object of this intensive work was to promote the feeling of unity among his people.

At the Annual Conferences he made an innovation that proved useful and popular. Taking charge of the devotional service himself, he distributed copies of a leaflet containing Paul's Epistles to Timothy. These two letters, "so wonderfully adapted to the needs of the present time," he made the theme of the hour. His talks gave life to a service that had become perfunctory and was often ill-attended.

In yet another way he relieved the dull routine of administrative business and debate; namely, by providing a course of afternoon lectures by scholarly representatives of the Church. Biblical, theological, and scientific questions were discussed. This was a first step towards the founding of "The Itinerants' Clubs," of which he speaks in the *Autobiography*.

Designed primarily for ministers—young ministers in

preference to old—the "Itinerants' Clubs" were open to the public. The addresses were practical. Here are a few of the titles: *The Minister's Care of his Physical Health; The Noble Possibilities of Country and Circuit Work; Weekday Bible Teaching; The Pastor's Interest in Higher Education; Out-of-School Culture; The Art of Memory Training; The Possibilities of Adult Education; The Preacher's Library.*

In this list of eight titles—a list far from exhaustive— one notes the preponderance of themes of a distinctively educational sort. In any single talk or series of talks that the man might give before a body of his colleagues, the value to a minister of what is vaguely called "culture" was sure to be dwelt on. His definition of the thing itself was not narrow. As a means to its attainment the best books must be read, the literature of knowledge no less than the literature of power. He probably laid more emphasis on books than on any other one instrument.

Of science he would have less to say; but the little that he did say would show where he stood. He was "on the side of the angels" (as Disraeli once remarked, with a covert sneer, that he himself was), but he had a well-founded conviction that science was not necessarily on the other side.

"Your theory of Evolution does not make against Christianity," said Tennyson to Darwin. "No, certainly not," was the reply. Somehow one cannot imagine Bishop Vincent declaiming against the evolutionary doctrine because it failed to square with the Mosaic account of creation. Whatever may have been his actual position, he would have regarded as inept and futile any meddling on the part of amateurs with a subject on which only men of science have a right to speak.

What authors, and what books of those authors, he recommended to his "Itinerants' Clubs" cannot be made out from the brief note in the *Autobiography*. Only a few names appear—he was writing in haste and the printer waited. Ruskin and Browning are mentioned. We know that he was a devotee of the great Victorian poet, a man so unlike the classical versifiers (Campbell, for instance) whom he diligently read in his youth. To Ruskin he would be drawn by the splendor of the rhetoric and the moral passion. Optimist that he was, he would not be depressed by the jeremiads, and those outbursts of "rabid Protestantism" that Ruskin declared should be suppressed in later editions of his works would rather entertain him.

Robertson and Bushnell he is forever bringing to the notice of young preachers. Bowne the "Itinerant" would know perfectly. Many of them had studied under him. But to advise a re-reading of the books of one's professor is not always a work of supererogation. The list, as I have said, is not complete, and the outlines of the lectures, or lessons, would need to be gone over with care if it was proposed to write more than a paragraph on the "Itinerants' Clubs."

The circumstances are conceivable under which Bishop Vincent would be forced to carry the whole burden of the meeting alone; to act both as presiding officer and faculty. He preferred a different arrangement. At a "Club" held in Buffalo (April 10-14, 1890) he had ten assistants, all clergymen but one, and all men of reputa-

tion in their several lines. There were two hundred ministers in the audience. From a report¹ that appeared in
an English paper, *The Methodist Times,* one gathers
that he himself made only the opening address. It emphasized the ideal outcome of the "Club," namely, the
making of each of its members larger in intellectual
power, more sympathetic with struggling humanity, a
more prayerful man, and a more nearly perfect Christian
gentleman.

The influence that Bishop Vincent exerted over his
clerical juniors was of two sorts; one general, the outcome
of sound advice applicable to them as a body; the other
specific, growing out of a direct personal appeal to this or
that young man who, he felt sure, needed counsel and
would take it, when offered, in the right spirit. Here is
a case in point:

Talking privately with a young preacher he said, "You
are too promising a man to go on indefinitely in the way
you are going." He meant by this that the training was
not proportional to the gift; that the man was hampered
in his work now, and would continue to be hampered.
The upshot of their talk was that the young preacher
declined the excellent appointment that he might have
had, entered a theological school, went through the
course, and was graduated. From then on his career
was of a sort fully to justify the sacrifice he had made.
Pulpits were open to him that must have remained closed
but for the discipline to which he had subjected himself.
He became the head of a college. His success there led
to his being called to the presidency of an older and larger
institution.

¹ Written by H. A. Reed.

All of which sounds like one of those familiar anecdotes intended to show how, by minding one's book, one
may achieve worldly success and a respectable bank
account. Bishop Vincent's advice would have been the
same in all circumstances. The bank account had nothing to do with it. He believed in making the intellect
free and flexible by the only means through which it
could be done—education without pedantry. He would
have urged it though the ministerial novice were not
promising, and nothing better were in sight than a country pastorate.

So many young preachers were turned through his
cogent arguments into a course they would not otherwise
have taken that they may be said to have formed a
"school" of ministerial thought and practice. Bishop
Vincent's experience was very like that of an artist of
marked individuality, who so affects his pupils, perhaps
without actually intending it, that in course of time they
form a "school of painting." Throughout their work,
however varied and distinctive it may be, the master's
idiosyncrasy can be felt.

In 1893 he made an episcopal tour abroad. He sailed
on May 20 (accompanied by his friend F. W. Hyde of
Jamestown, New York), crossed to the Continent, and
at La-Chaux-de-Fonds, Switzerland, held the first of the
nine European conferences that had been assigned him.
The Germans met at Bremen, the Danes at Copenhagen,
the Norwegians at Arendal, the Finns and Russians at
Helsingfors, the Swedes at Norrköping. The nine-hour
journey by rail from Abo to Helsingfors gave him a
new idea of that corner of the world; he had not expected
to be so well pleased with Finland. At Helsingfors he

had the good fortune to meet an old acquaintance, Andrew D. White, then Minister to Russia.

In August he went to Bulgaria and held a Mission Conference at Varna. The Italy Conference met in early September. While in Rome he laid the corner stone of a new building that the Methodists were to erect there; it was to consist of a chapel, publication offices, a house for the superintendent of the missions, a theological school, and a school for boys.

In the course of this episcopal tour Bishop Vincent assigned to their several stations some three hundred and fifty ministers, effected the division of the unwieldy German Conference into two distinct bodies (one embracing the northern part of the country, the other the southern), preached many times, and gave an address on Chautauqua at the Union Religious Conference at Lucerne. Returning by the *Campania,* he reached New York on September 23. It was his fourteenth crossing. "Every passage stormless and delightful."

He had already been appointed a preacher to Harvard University for one year; his duties there began in November. What is expected of one who serves in this office may be learned from the autobiography of a man who, among other literary virtues, had the gift of concise and accurate statement. During the period of his incumbency "He conducts prayers in Appleton Chapel every morning, leads a vesper service on Thursday afternoon, and preaches in the Chapel on Sunday evening." [2] He lives at Wadsworth House, and it is assumed that at certain hours of each day he will be at home to such students as may wish to consult him. His term of

[2] Washington Gladden: *Recollections,* p. 324.

[276]

service is divided into two periods of three weeks each.

That Bishop Vincent enjoyed his work at Harvard, after getting fairly started, I know from remarks he dropped when I once called on him at Wadsworth House. That all who came under his ministrations profited thereby may be taken for granted. It is, of course, left to the students themselves to decide whether they will be ministered to or not.

When it was first proposed to him to take the office he raised a variety of objections. He was not qualified for the post, he said, and the undergraduates would not care for such talks as his; it would be "a dismal failure." And when at last he was persuaded to yield he did so with great reluctance. Some of his friends wondered a little at his using notes. He was never hampered by them, and probably discarded them as soon as he felt at home with his audience.

What impression he left can best be learned from a letter written by a member of the faculty shortly after the close of one of his periods of service:

> ". . . Your success here has been really no-table. You have given us something distinctive, something which no other preacher has given. Altogether simple and without pretense, your words at chapel have had that veracity about them which a rich life and fine insight lends. They have gone into our fellows' hearts as words of friendly cheer, assuring, enlightening, stimulating. And may I also add how much I—and others who have remarked it to me—have enjoyed the perfection of your literary

form. Each little talk has had its clear topic and its finished unity. You have made yourself loved and respected by all." [2]

Bishop Vincent was reappointed to the same post in 1894-95 and in 1895-96, making three terms in all. He was urged to take a fourth term. Official duties in the form of episcopal visitation made it impossible for him to accept. In recognition of his services Harvard conferred on him, at the Commencement of 1896, the degree of S.T.D.

He filled the office of university preacher at yet other colleges—Yale, Cornell, Chicago, and Wellesley, for example. The length of his term of service would depend on the custom that obtained at each of these institutions. He might be called on for a day only or for a fortnight and more. When at Cornell, in February, 1899, he preached twice and gave three addresses at vespers. Ten days would have been enough for carrying out the program. All five discourses were so planned as to come under the general heading of "Thoughts about God." What might be the conceptions of the statesman, the man of letters, and the man of science formed the theme of the vesper talks; Lincoln, Matthew Arnold, and Lord Kelvin were the three characters from whose writings and spoken words he drew his illustrations.

On December 1, 1896, he sailed for South America to inspect the missions and hold conferences; John Searles, of Brooklyn, was his traveling companion. The boat was small, the weather rough, and the discomforts arising therefrom many. They were eight and a half days

[2] From George H. Palmer to John H. Vincent, April 14, 1895.

in making the passage to Barbados; from there to the mouth of the Para River took six days more. They had planned to go up the Amazon as far as Manáos, where one of the missionaries was stationed, but were dissuaded from making the attempt.

Changing to a larger steamer they left Para on December 18, and arrived at Pernambuco on Christmas morning. The ocean behaved well if the cook did not. A worse table than that furnished by this company it would have been hard to find. The Bishop slept on deck in his steamer chair—preferring out of doors to a malodorous stateroom—and lived on such Spartanlike fare as could be picked up at one or other of the ports at which the boat called. At Pernambuco (Recife) he and his companion were able to live in the manner of American Christians.

He was interested in the attitude of foreign residents towards religion in general, not towards missions. Here is an extract from one of his letters. "Went to the English Church again last night (Sunday). About six people there. Eighty young Englishmen, Scotchmen, and Americans live here, clerks, etc., who *never* go to church and who fall into most miserable ways of living. I don't wonder they don't want to go to such a service as the English Church has *here,* but they ought to have some principle about it."

On January 2, they were off again, this time by a first-class boat, the *Liguria,* had one day at Rio, and arrived at Montevideo on January 10. Bishop Vincent gives his first impressions of the Uruguayan capital in this paragraph: "The finest city I have yet seen. The houses are well built, covered with stucco, tastefully decorated.

. . . Everything is clean. The people are superior. The women dress well. The children are like the better class of American children. A revolution is on, and trouble impends. . . . But we have seen nothing of it. It is said that the storm may burst at any moment. There are two U. S. gunboats in the Harbor."

Having satisfied himself that the state of affairs in the Church was a credit to those in charge (for the episcopal visit was not a mere formality) Bishop Vincent went on to Buenos Aires. There he preached, met the clergy and the people, inspected the schools, and did what he could to compose certain differences that had arisen. The monotony of ecclesiastical life in the Argentine was at that moment being relieved by disputes over the higher criticism. "Conservatism, narrow and intense, is arrayed against modern views." And there were other questions that could only be settled by the exercise of common sense and a most tactful firmness.

The South America Conference met at Montevideo on February 7, held a five-day session, then adjourned to meet again, at Santiago in Chile, for the concluding deliberations. To the uninstructed mind of a layman it seems an odd arrangement whereby one half of a meeting takes place on the Atlantic coast, and the other half at a point nine hundred miles away, within easy reach of the Pacific. One assumes that the entire body of ministers did not migrate, only the officials. The trip entailed two nights on the sleeper, a night at a hotel in the mountains (at Las Cuevas), a carriage ride, and a final stage by rail.

Bishop Vincent arrived at Santiago on the night of February 18. Conference began the next day, with com-

paratively little to do because so much had been done on
the other side. It closed on February 25. There remained but one more official duty—a visit to a school
at La Concepción, three hundred and sixty miles to the
south. On March 7 began the long voyage to Panama.

The bare outline of the trip gives but an imperfect
idea of the amount of work done—the places visited, the
sermons preached, the lectures and addresses delivered,
the consultations held, the calls made and received, and
the social affairs participated in, some of which were
as exacting as any platform performance. Bishop Vincent was now sixty-five, but from the tone of his letters
home you would say that he might have been about forty-
five, or even less. He was never tired, except in circumstances when any man would have been tired; from
an unduly protracted journey, say, or insufferable heat,
or too many public appearances within a given twenty-
four hours. As for being ill he hardly knew the meaning of the phrase. I will qualify the statement. He *did*
omit one evening sermon because he felt a little out of
sorts; but he had already preached in the morning.

The notebook that he kept during this long journey
is yet another witness to his insatiable curiosity about
things, his passion for collecting and classifying facts,
his eagerness to learn and to condense what he had
learned into a portable shape. The book contains three
maps of South America, one showing the political divisions, the other two the physiographical characteristics of
the country. There are pages of description of the various districts and states, much of it set down from personal observation, much more of it culled from trustworthy histories and travels. By using abbreviations he

managed to pack into a small space all that he especially needed to know about the races, manners, and government, or lack of government.

There are notes on the mountains, the rivers (very copious on the Amazon and its tributaries), the plant and animal life, the industries, and the natural products. Several pages are filled with lists of words, Spanish and Portuguese, chiefly names of objects in common use. Of impressionistic pictures, for the making of which the diarist had a real gift, there is no great number. The anecdotes, though few, are always of a sort worth recording. On running through the eighty pages of the book, one sees that it was not compiled merely to serve as a *vade mecum,* a convenience, but that a genuine zest for the gaining of knowledge informed it.

The account of the tour that was printed in *The Epworth Herald* is readable. Four of the papers were brought out in a pamphlet at Buenos Aires. They are vivacious. Take for example the paragraph apropos of the disputes that had arisen over doctrinal points. "The theological school is doing excellent work. Some stir was caused by rumors concerning the teaching of what is called the 'higher criticism,' and a few of the younger students, looking through smoked glass for the first time, made more of the spots on the sun than was necessary, and gave the impression that the principal thing taught in the institution was the scientific theories concerning spots. And some good people were afraid that the School of Theology had damaged the Sun, and that it might go out entirely."

It was, of course, the writer's view that the orb of day, as old-fashioned poets called it, was none the worse for a few blemishes. On the other hand, little was to be gained by specializing in spots.

Because of Bishop Vincent's well-known doubts as to the merit of revivals of the emotional type, and his firm belief that converts might be made by an appeal to the head, he was asked, along with Bishop Warren, to conduct at one of the downtown churches of Denver a series of meetings of the sort he advocated. This was in March, 1900. Evangelistic services in the orthodox manner had failed, so it was said, to make a lasting impression on the public. What one gathers from certain articles in the religious press is that people flocked to this church because of the personal popularity of the regular incumbent. They gladly attended the services; they were not so ready to become members.

The Vincent-Warren meetings made considerable talk. One of the odd features of the affair was that meetings designed to be free from sensationalism were heralded in the newspapers with headlines of the most strident character. Bishop Vincent was mildly reproached by a cleric of his own denomination because the program of these special services was "printed in ecclesiastical colors." What those colors might be is not told. The program, by the way, was not of the Bishop's devising. Another criticism was called out by the discovery that the old form of making a public profession of the desire to lead a new life would be done away with. And there was a solemn shaking of the head over the name given to the meetings as a whole; they were described as a "mission" and not as revival.

That it was a revival cannot be questioned, but a revival shorn of all those elements that repel the modern sophisticated man or woman. Bishop Vincent was invited by a pastor who believed in the new methods—the Bishop's own methods—to apply them in the hope that good would come of it. In addition to the public addresses, arrangement was made for private consultation; for this certain hours were set apart. Profession of faith was made through the sacraments.

How Bishop Vincent affected a not wholly sympathetic auditor may be learned from the following sketch:

> "He was the center of curious attention. It is easy to see that he is a master of assemblies. The prominent impressions made on one as he appears in the pulpit or on the platform are that he is a brave, true, sincere man, with a constitutional antipathy to anything uncouth and improper, a sense that amounts almost to instinct for anything scholarly and advanced, and the highest disdain for any kind of superstition or anything that has a tendency to lower the intellectual dignity of men. His voice is strong, and is made pleasant by a kindly resonance; his manners are elegant and full of energy and earnestness. He has a clear, strong grasp of thought, and he presents it in terse, incisive language that any one can readily understand. He is manly and commanding. In tones clear and strong he announces the purpose of the meetings to be to win men to righteousness. . . . In doing this they must consent to give up sin. . . ."

The rest of the long article is devoted to an analysis of the content of the addresses, in which, from the writer's point of view, something was wanting. The part here quoted has value in that it gives a fairly vivid picture of the man as he appeared on the platform.

At the time this "mission" was held Bishop Vincent's official residence was at Topeka, Kansas; the change from Buffalo had been made in 1893. The general superintendents of the Church are itinerants, and have been known to move one another about; this by virtue of certain privileges accorded seniority. It was of course permitted them to exercise self-denial if that chanced to be their favorite virtue. Bishop Vincent was sorry to leave Buffalo; he never regretted having gone to Topeka. At the time the next change was made he went overseas.

CHAPTER XXIII

RESIDENT BISHOP IN EUROPE

WHEN the episcopal roster for 1900 was made up John Vincent was assigned the duties of resident bishop in Europe, with headquarters at Zurich; he was the first to hold this office. Nothing that his *confrères* might have done could have pleased him more. His zest for foreign travel had in no degree abated, and he was deeply interested in the little centers of Methodism scattered about the Continent.

He sailed on June 9, and was in Milan for the opening of the Italy Conference on June 20th. With an eye to the needs of American tourists—needs of which they are seldom conscious—he sent out announcements of a vesper service, with an address in English, to be held on the fourth day of the session.

In one respect the work that he had to do in Europe differed little, if at all, from that he had already done on a former episcopal visitation. In another way it differed much. The business had increased in volume, was at once more complicated and more various. As resident general superintendent he would be drawn into affairs that as a mere presiding officer he would only have glanced at. In short, the arrangement was very nearly that which would have existed had the Continent been an actual diocese and he its accredited head.

An idea of his work—not an adequate idea but sufficient for the purposes of this sketch—may be gathered from his notebooks and from the printed leaflets that he sent out from time to time. One finds that he was at Bucharest in early May, 1901, and his letters show that there were difficulties of one sort and another to be straightened out. The Bulgarian mission was perfectly human and required adroit management. There had been too much talking back and forth, perhaps recrimination. He recommends "silence and kindness."

In another letter he applies to some friend who understands the Balkans, and the work there, for trustworthy facts and an honest expression of opinion. "Tell me frankly why we have not succeeded better up to this time? And what *have* we accomplished that ought to encourage us?" The friend—his name is not given in the notebook—was to come out strong in the matter of statistics in his reply. To be sure figures were available in any gazetteer, but Bishop Vincent wanted those same figures interpreted by somebody who knew the country and the people.

There is frequent mention of schools in the notebook. "My private opinion is," he writes, "that the work in Bulgaria, to be effective, must be largely promoted by the power of the educational work now going on there and a new educational work to be begun there." The sentence occurs in a long letter to the then head of the School for Girls at Loftcha. On at least one occasion he voluntarily undertook the thankless task of procuring teachers, or a teacher—one who should have the ability to double parts. Writing to one of his coadjutors, he says: "Do you know a young woman who is an accomplished French scholar, who could easily learn the Bulgarian-Sclavonic language by living among the people, and who is also a really fine teacher of music?" He grants that such a paragon will be difficult to find. Nevertheless the school must have her if she exists. Unfortunately the pay "will not be large."

The leaflets that he sent out were of two kinds, official greetings and messages to his clergy, and printed circular letters to friends in America with whom it would have been impossible otherwise to communicate. He had great faith in the virtue of printers' ink, whether it was used for business or for pleasure or for friendly correspondence. The sending out of the circular letters was an act of pure kindness, as was the sending out of the calendar that he issued year after year. Orders for these calendars to the number of a hundred or so would sometimes come from him when he was on tour; this was one of his many ways of remembering the people whom he had met.

The first pastoral letter to his preachers in Europe is simply a résumé of what he had long been teaching—the necessity of system, especially in the matter of church finance, the need of coöperation, since no pastor can do single-handed all the work of the society, and the need of watchfulness; if the people are neglecting duties that are theirs rather than the pastor's, they must be told about it. "It is the alert pastor who has an earnest people." The tone is paternal both in encouragement and in warning. In point of style the address might be thought lacking, but its unadorned simplicity would make it easy to translate. Versions probably appeared in French, German, Italian, and in the Scandinavian tongues.

Supplementary to these papers were certain brief essays to which he gave the name of "After-Conference Memoranda." The first of these is on the opportunities every pastor has to do good by conversation. He recommends "conversation sermons" by which he means giving an evangelical turn to casual talk. In that way a pastor might reach many people who do not attend church regularly. Another of the "Memoranda" is on smoking. He evidently thinks the clergy are too much addicted to pipes and cigars. He is plain-spoken but temperate; his essay is no counterblast against tobacco. Fearing, however, that some of his comments might be softened in the translation, he writes at the bottom of the manuscript: "Don't modify that tobacco item."

From another of his circular letters I give a short extract. He is remarking on the surprise of certain good people at the presence of the Methodist Episcopal Church in Europe, a field already occupied by ancient Protestant churches. From their point of view it was an "obtrusion." He might also have remarked that these same good people had had time to recover from their surprise; the missions had been there a full half century. There was really nothing much to be "explained"; one had only to understand the situation:

> "A Church with apostolic ideals and impulses," he says, "and with a New Testament message on its tongue, will be universal in its horizon and aspirations. It *must* 'go into all the world.' We are in Europe and dare not leave until we find a reason sufficiently strong to neutralize the reasons that led hither the founders of the mission more than fifty

years ago. We are compelled by . . . the providential leading of our fathers, by the inward impulsion, the urgent invitation, the exigent need. . . . It is not a question of human policy but of providential purpose. We are needed to coöperate with the other evangelical forces of Europe in their efforts against materialism, rationalism, an unscriptural ecclesiasticism, and the deadly apathy which everywhere imperils the Christian Church."

Certain practical questions had to be considered. An aggressive evangelistic and educational effort had resulted in building up a constituency respectable for size though composed of plain people. The little chapels must be kept in repair and made attractive. If debts burdened the societies they must be cleared off.

The sympathetic interest shown by Bishop Vincent in the simple and unfashionable folk to whom he ministered on the Continent recalls his attitude towards the farmers and mechanics who made up his congregations when he was a young circuit rider. He has something of the enthusiasm of one who is beginning a new career rather than of one who is rounding out the work of more than half a century. He describes two or three of the societies. That at Schneeberg was composed of miners, collar makers, embroiderers, color grinders, laundrymen, and so forth. There were five hundred of them all told. At Reichenbach was a smaller society, about three hundred, made up largely of flannel weavers, bakers, seamstresses, and peddlers; this unaristocratic body could boast of one merchant who owned his shop and one farmer who owned his farm. Their pastor supported a family on the far from munificent stipend of three hundred dollars a year.

At Zurich affairs were in a most prosperous state; a membership of a thousand and Sunday-schools with an attendance of more than two thousand. The young people were very like those to be found in other towns. They came from the working class. Among them were "telegraph and telephone operators, clerks, bookkeepers, milliners, silk-factory employees, and representatives of all trades." A few school-teachers were enrolled as members or regular attendants. Professional men could hardly be expected to take an active part in the work of an American mission.

That these societies led a vigorous if socially obscure life, that the number of them was increasing, and that each separate body was adding daily to its membership seemed to Bishop Vincent a proof that Methodism had a field of its own on the Continent. He says that he found in some quarters "a slight objection" to the name of the Epworth League because it was English. "I told them that if Americans, with all their independence, were willing to accept an English name, certainly there was no sacrifice of self-respect on the part of Germans and Scandinavians who do the same." Hoping to remove their prejudice, he explained the historical significance of the name, and told how it came to be adopted.

Of his activities during one of the busy months we may learn from a four-page letter to friends at home. It is dated January, 1902. He had just completed a pastoral tour that lasted nearly a month; it began at Berne, Switzerland, and included Christiania, Upsala, Stockholm, Copenhagen, Munich, and Berlin. In the course of this journey he had given twenty-seven sermons and addresses, the latter on the training of young people.

He had to preach through an interpreter, and seems to have enjoyed doing so. A sermon delivered in this manner would be robbed of much that makes spoken discourse pleasing, continuity for example, and a swift progression from an idea to one that grows out of it or may be introduced by way of contrast. With an interpreter by his side the least wordy of orators would be forced to part with everything but the essentials.

Bishop Vincent learned that many members and some ministers of the State Church were in his audience from time to time. He himself played the respectful and sympathetic listener on several occasions. When in Berlin he went to the University to hear a lecture by Harnack. He had long wanted to see the man whose distinctive characteristic was "his claim for absolute freedom in the study of Church history and the New Testament." The American visitor sat between two American students, one of whom came of a German Methodist family in Denver, and followed the discourse through their notes. Of more immediate interest to him than Harnack's theme of the hour was Harnack himself. "I watched his movements, studied his face, and felt the spell of his strong personality."

On the last page of the leaflet is a reference to journeys to be made in May and June, one to Turin for the Annual Conference, the other to Ireland. The leaflet dated March, 1902, gives an account (less detailed than one would like) of an official trip to Geneva and Lausanne. On the Sunday that he spent in Geneva he preached in the church, or hall, of the little congregation of Italian Methodists.

In the early summer of this same year (1902) he returned to America for a three months' visit. His reception at Chautauqua was memorable. The present writer thought at the time, and still thinks, that one of the testimonials he received over-emphasized the fact of his having reached the age of three score and ten. He is a philosopher who can bear with equanimity being told by so many friends, all speaking in concert, that they know how old he is. To be reminded of the inevitable by one's own family is quite sufficient.

The testimonial in question consisted of seventy autograph letters, each from a professional associate or personal friend, the whole richly bound in a small quarto, the cover stamped with the Bishop's name, unencumbered by titles of any sort, and the dates 1832-1902. The separate leaves had been distributed long enough beforehand to admit of their being inscribed, returned, and inserted in their proper place in the book. There were no failures, I believe, and the binder had the volume ready against the day of its presentation. Many of the letters deserve to be quoted in full. That being impossible, there remains the alternative of giving a pithy sentence from a few of the more striking tributes.

Richard G. Moulton wrote: "As half an American, I admire your splendid gifts for organization; as an Englishman, I rejoice to see realized, in the newest of worlds, the old-world ideal of the close relation between education and religion." William T. Harris wrote: "I congratulate you upon the completion of so many years of high usefulness. . . . You hold a place of honor

in the noble band of worthies who have labored to extend
and improve the education of our people." At the close
of Richard T. Ely's letter occurs this paragraph: "I want
to add that the opportunity I have had to serve under
you at Chautauqua and to make your personal acquaintance has been one of the fortunate circumstances of my
own life."

Here is an extract from Melvil Dewey's letter: "You
have given a new word to language, and Chautauqua is
now known throughout the civilized world. . . .
Your service to the public and to education in its broad
and best sense is greater than that of any single college
or university, for you have sown seeds far and wide
that will yield an abundant harvest far and wide because
of the stimulus to better reading and thinking." The
letter from William R. Harper should have been especially grateful to the recipient: "It is remarkable that a
man who has accomplished so much should, at your age,
still have the vigor of youth. . . . It is the earnest
desire of your many friends that still greater things
shall be done by you in the future than any that have
yet been done."

Lyman Abbott wrote: "Sacred indeed is that fellowship which binds together those of different creeds and
different vocations, who are one in the sincerity of their
desire to do Christ's work in Christ's way, to serve God
in the service of their fellow men. This, my dear Doctor
Vincent, has been my fellowship with you." The letter
signed by Charles W. Eliot contained a graciously worded
tribute to the Bishop's work when preacher to Harvard
University. Said the writer: "We have never been able
to fill just your place, and probably never shall be."

Edward Everett Hale wrote: "How well and how often do I remember thankfully the morning when you called upon me in my underground cell, and explained and opened to me the system of Chautauqua, and made me see that the Lord had need of me there. God bless you, dear Friend."

In choosing the seventy people who were to contribute to this memorial great care was taken. It was intended that the book should be representative. A few of those who had helped to make the early Assembly a success were no longer living. More than a few were yet very much alive, and to that fact their letters bore witness. Not all of the instructors in the first schools of language and literature could be included, but only those who had helped to create those schools. Certain members of the later faculty, the trustees and officials, the presidents of various classes, and a number of personal friends were asked to send letters. The mere signatures, apart from the text, had a meaning for Bishop Vincent. Each name stood for a distinct contribution to the religious, the educational, the administrative, or the social side of Chautauqua. He could have gone through the book page by page and told accurately what every one of these coadjutors of his had done to make the Assembly what it was at a given moment. It must always be cause for regret that he never took the time to make a series of pen portraits of the men, *and* women, to whom he owed much and to whom he was everlastingly grateful. He was always ready to talk about them when the subject came up, and was apt at a characterization, but he refrained from writing.

On December 3 he sailed for Liverpool, and enjoyed

one of those perfect winter crossings the account of which is a source of unutterable chagrin to voyagers who have known the ocean to be at its worst in July and August. One of his table companions was Hall Caine, the novelist. "I enjoyed several delightful conversations with him. He is a charming man."

In 1903 was made another regular tour of the European Conferences. The papers at hand mention no incident worth recording here. In February, 1904, on the eve of his return to America (the period of service being about to end) the Bishop brought out the last of his circular letters to friends on this side of the water. The leaflet is twice the length of its predecessors. A distinctive feature is the map on the first page, showing, in color, what countries of Europe had been reached by the mission. Bishop Vincent has been heard to say, "Nothing but a telegram will wake up So-and-So"—meaning some able but sluggish correspondent. He also held that there was nothing like a map for emphasizing any point capable of being so emphasized.

The letter begins with a justification of the existence of the Church in Europe; a part of this has already been quoted. All else is in the nature of a report. The writer deals in figures—the number of conferences, preachers, members, probationers, Sunday-school officials and pupils who compose the European Church. When speaking of the number of converts believed to have been made through the efforts of his people he does not say that they have been gathered into "our fold," but characteristically, that they have been gathered into some one of the evangelical folds, State or Free Church as the case may be.

The "November Conversations" mentioned in the letter were without doubt instituted by him. A topic for discussion was assigned to one month of each year. It was to be the set theme for private and public discussion in all of the Methodist centers throughout Europe. In an article printed in *The Sunday School Chronicle* he described these talks as "conventions that did not convene." "The theory of the November Conversations," he says elsewhere, "is that in order to be efficient workers people must be intelligent." Giving them a definite subject to grapple with is one of the best ways to make them so.

It was taken for granted that each topic would in turn be brought up at the various church meetings, and that the pastors would preach on it. But the scheme as a whole would have no distinctive merit unless it prompted the laity to talk among themselves. Bishop Vincent believed that it possessed this merit in a high degree, and that many a man who had neither the inclination nor the courage to speak in public was more than ready to talk over the prescribed topic with a friend. He asked for reports from all the centers. The documents came in in such large numbers as to astonish him. He found in them "a wealth of material . . . revealing to me the needs of my people."

The European Reading Circle was another of the agencies by which a good deal had been accomplished. Its aim was not so much the spread of bookish knowledge as religious truth.

Bishop Vincent found many things to admire in European Methodism. The Church over there, he thought, had been saved from extravagancies of any kind. There was little to criticize in the mode of conducting the service, and the revivals were none the less fruitful for being dignified. In some parts of the field there was need of a higher ideal of ministerial culture, a little more liberality of thought, and a warmer sympathy with "the advancing yet duly conservative Biblical scholarship of the age."

Of the deeper significance of his work during the four years that he spent on the Continent only the men who were associated with him are competent to speak. Points of a technical character are involved in the question of what he actually accomplished. It was his gift to do some things better than the experts, whether at home or abroad, could do them. That peculiar power of his for inspiring men—not alone those who made up his audiences but those who were his superiors in mastery of detail—is difficult to analyze. No one doubts that he had the power to an extraordinary degree.

It is natural to think that he might have been hampered in dealing with his Continental hearers, both ministers and public, by the necessity he was under of using only English. But his presence and manner were in themselves eloquent. He could be authoritative without being dictatorial. He looked the sort of man from whose lips wise counsel must certainly come. The interpreter did not incommode him. He could hardly have said that he enjoyed the arrangement that involved speaking a paragraph and then waiting for the echo to come in another tongue, unless satisfied that his effectiveness was not appreciably diminished. The impression he made on people was never better expressed than by a celebrated Anglo-Irish journalist who met him in London some years after his retirement from official work. Says this writer: "I never met an old ecclesiastic to whom I thought one could apply more justly the title of saintliness. Sweetness was in his face, in his manner, in his conversation; he was a true father in God, to whom you could imagine the most abandoned sinner going with certainty of the promise of forgiveness and the hope of salvation."

CHAPTER XXIV

IN RETIREMENT

BISHOP VINCENT'S term of service in the episcopate began in 1888 and ended in 1904. Remarking in his *Autobiography* on the well-known fact that a bishop is elected for life, he adds, "and when unable to work is placed on the retired list." It could not in fairness be said of him that he was unable to work at seventy-two, but it was the opinion of the General Conference (held at Los Angeles in May, 1904) that younger men than he were needed for the trying task of presiding over deliberative bodies such as were the Annual Conferences, or, for that matter, any gathering of the clergy. Three or four of his colleagues were retired at the same time.

Amazed though he was by the decision he accepted it with a show of equanimity and at the same time he chafed under it. To the many correspondents who wrote expressing regret at what had occurred he replied by a circular letter. Of the action of the Conference in respect to himself he said, "I am quite certain that it is not justified by a single fact the force of which could not have been broken by a careful and impartial investigation."

He seemed to think that the adverse vote of the Conference was due to a general misconception as to the state of his physical health. It was due to a sense that he had grown forgetful when dealing with cabinet affairs—details that appeared to be petty and yet were essential to the transaction of business. The difficulties almost certain to be encountered when an attempt is made to decide a number of cases on their individual merits were peculiarly trying in 1904. One result was "to compel the Church to devise an automatic method of retirement for age."

Bishop Vincent had now to determine where he would live and how he would spend his time. He chose to make his home in Indianapolis, largely for personal reasons. There he would be in easy reach of his son, and the central location of the town made it a convenient point of departure; he foresaw that numerous journeys, eastward and westward, were before him. Of supreme importance was the question of his wife's health. Mrs. Vincent had grown frail and much anxiety was felt on her account. It was assumed that the climate of central Indiana, reputed mild and equable, would have a beneficial effect.

So far as he himself was concerned retirement simply meant increased activity in fields that he had always cultivated. In the above-mentioned circular letter he gave, as a matter of purely personal interest, the list of his engagements for the following summer. The list included a sermon at Yale, another at Wesleyan University, Middletown, addresses at the Illinois State Sunday School Convention, and an extended series of lectures at the numerous Chautauqua assemblies throughout the country. He probably had no intention of being ironical, but it was as though he had said, "You observe that I have been relegated to the limbo of noneffectives."

He speaks of certain meetings held from time to time during this period of his career under the name of "A Seven Days' Study in Church Life." They differed a little from the "Itinerants' Clubs" over which he used to preside while in active episcopal work. The "Clubs" were expressly designed for ministers, though in some circumstances the public was admitted. The "Seven Days' Study" was open to everybody.

Three sessions were held each day. The audience for the evening lecture would tax the capacity of the church. The morning and afternoon conferences would, as a matter of course, draw a relatively small number of people—such laymen as were minded to leave business for an hour or two in the heart of the day, a few ministers, and the usual quota of interested women. The topics discussed were the home, the public school, the Sunday-school and other departments of the Church, political responsibility from a Christian point of view, the value of self-culture, and similar themes.

The first meeting of this sort was held in Baltimore.[1] The morning ministerial conferences dealt almost exclusively with the pastor and his work. The afternoon meetings, described in the program as conversations (which they actually were, Bishop Vincent acting as chief interlocutor) took up such subjects as "The Measure of a Layman's Responsibility," "Woman's Place in the Church," "Neighborhood Morals," "What is 'Worldliness'?" and so forth.

One can believe that Bishop Vincent was at his best in meetings of this character. He had no warring elements to compose, and there were no decisions to be made ex

[1] At the Strawbridge Methodist Episcopal Church, February 14-20, 1905.

his power to encourage those who were genuinely interested in the Chautauqua idea we may take the following
incident; if not very striking, it is at least characteristic.

The managers of an obscure and struggling Assembly
in the South wrote him to ask whether it would not be
possible for him to make them a visit, to break the journey there when he was *en route* to one of his more important engagements. They could pay almost nothing,
but they wanted the encouragement of his presence for
a day; it would be of inestimable value to them. He at
once accepted their invitation, though he was not then
planning for summer work and had no expectation of
being anywhere near this remote place. They might
count on him, he wrote; he would make the trip for the
sole purpose of speaking from their platform. His coming was therefore widely and jubilantly announced.

A day or two before he arrived, a clergyman of some
standing went to the managers and said: "There has
certainly been a mistake made in this business. You are
all wrong in thinking that the Chancellor of Chautauqua,
a man accustomed to speak before immense audiences,
is going to travel several hundred miles in the middle of
July to talk to the handful of farmers and village folk
that you are able to muster. My belief is that you have
been corresponding with the wrong person!"

The doubter was quite sincere and could hardly be
convinced that he was in the wrong, even when shown
the correspondence. It is said that after the Bishop
arrived he was still skeptical as to whether it was *the*
Bishop Vincent, the one he had in mind.

The five years' residence in Indianapolis had been
agreeable in many ways. It was brought to a close by

an event not wholly unanticipated. Mrs. Vincent died on March 30, 1909. Her last illness was long drawn out and extremely painful. She endured it with a stoicism rarely equaled. No complaint ever escaped her lips. She kept her mind occupied to the very last. During the tedious waking hours she read incessantly, the book propped up before her, and continued to read until she had barely strength to turn the leaves. The least that can be said of her is that she was a woman of heroic temper.

For the remainder of his life (eleven years were still left to him) Bishop Vincent lived in Hyde Park, Chicago. He would naturally elect to make this city his home, his son was then Dean of the University and he had a host of friends throughout that section of the country. Moreover, he liked the bustle of town existence. The over-praised quiet and serenity of the country had no charm for him.

The home was presided over by his sister-in-law, Miss Caroline Dusenbury (who for many years had been a member of his family) and his own sister, Mrs. James Farovid. He was surrounded by all the comforts that a reasonable man could ask and he deserved them. Whether he was entirely happy in his environment is a question. The one thing lacking was the necessity of going at a piece of work that must be done by a given time; if another task succeeded the first, with no interval to speak of between, so much the better. The man was only himself under continuous pressure.

Engagements were not lacking. He was the orator of the occasion when Grant's birthday was celebrated at Galena on April 27, 1911. Fifty-one years had elapsed since the day when, a young minister of twenty-seven, he had said farewell to Grant and his company as they were starting for Springfield. I quote one typical passage from the address:

"Ulysses S. Grant will live in history. He was American to the core, democratic in every instinct, an avowed enemy of every system, political, civil, and ecclesiastical, that attempts to curb personal liberty in any direction; he was the embodiment of resoluteness and persistency, and yet he had a tender and sympathetic heart. . . .

"He was sound in judgment, an incarnation of common sense; if not always the wisest judge of men in private life he did know men as by intuition when his powers of judgment were stimulated by present emergencies.

"He was loyal to the last to personal friends, devoted with a most beautiful tenderness to his family. His domestic life was stainless, his love for his wife and children steady and ardent. He was profoundly in earnest, conscientious; silent under abuse; pure in speech and thought; magnanimous to the foes he defeated; reverent and trustful as he bowed before the God of his father and mother, honoring the day of God and the house of God. . . .

"Grant is often called 'the silent man.' As a matter of fact he was an admirable talker. Some one has described Wordsworth thus: 'You would have said that he was an unusually taciturn man, and yet he seemed glad to unlock himself to an

audience sympathetic and intelligent when such offered itself.' In like circumstances Grant's utterance was free, his manner simple and direct, his
vocabulary ample and excellent. His reserve arose
in part from natural timidity, but for the most part
from wisdom. He knew when to be silent. And he
knew when and how to speak."

On this occasion bronze medals were presented to the
sixteen survivors of the Jo Daviess County Guards.
Twelve men out of the sixteen were able to answer the
roll call and receive their medals in person.

Bishop Vincent visited Galena once again, in 1915,
and preached in his old pulpit. He might have filled
every moment of his time, so many were the requests
that poured in on him for talks, lectures, and sermons.
But there was an element of great uncertainty in his
movements during these latter days. Once on the platform, with his notes before him (notes had become indispensable) he was eloquent and inspiring, not the
shadow of his old self, but that old self at very nearly
its best. But the difficulty was, so to say, in piloting him
to the platform, and occasionally he forgot what address
he had agreed to give.

He was hard to control because so vivacious and
strong and self-willed. Nothing about him suggested
weakness. He remembered more after his memory
began to fail than the majority of people remember in
a lifetime. But his forgetfulness in respect to trivial
things, such as railway tickets, luggage, and destination,
led to more than one amusing *contretemps*. He was
finally persuaded to accept no more engagements to

speak; he was simply to rest, an occupation of which he knew little other than that he heartily loathed it.

How he came by his enormous vitality, or rather, how he came to retain it so long, is a puzzle. His mother died at the age of forty-nine. His father, at seventy, was a confirmed invalid. On the other hand he himself at eighty-seven—he was just that when I saw him last—had the bearing and the quickness of movement of a man hardly past middle life. His step was firm, he walked rapidly, and he retained the genially magisterial air that so well became him and of which, I believe, he was quite unconscious.

His voice was never so rich and sweet as at this time. At family devotions he used the Collects. His reading of the prayers was deeply impressive, as noble as it was sincere and heartfelt. One had a renewed sense of how much religion—that is to say, Christianity—meant **to** this strong man.

CHAPTER XXV

THE gift of superb bodily health was his virtually for a lifetime. A few illnesses he had, but only one that was serious, a violent attack of influenza followed by a temporary loss of the voice; that is, for public speaking. I met him somewhere in the West shortly after he had begun to recover, and well recall the sarcastic tone in which he quoted an unsympathetic compeer of his who had been heard to remark that "Vincent was breaking up."

The truth is that he was doing nothing of the sort. He regained his strength—his voice came back, and it continued strong and resonant to the very end.

He conserved his physical powers in sensible ways, ran no needless risks, and, though not puritanical, gratified no desire that stood for mere personal enjoyment. He kept reasonable hours and was temperate in his eating. The practice of light indoor gymnastics morning and evening he found beneficial and never gave it up, but in middle and later life he took no exercise of a strenuous sort other than what rapid walking afforded. His brother, younger than he by two and a half years, was not only a walker but also an incorrigible bicyclist, and rode his wheel when he was eighty-three. Both died the same year (1920) and within a few months of each other.

I retain a vivid mental picture of the two old men, as they would then have been accounted, striding at a rapid pace up the hill at Chautauqua on their way to the trolley station. It was difficult to overtake them. A hotel porter, laden with no great amount of hand luggage, toiled in their wake far behind. Such an exhibition of octogenarian animation and vigor did the heart good. One could fancy their both living to be ninety-five at the least.

Bishop Vincent was fortunate in that he suffered no long illness during the closing months of his life. He had hoped that when it came time for him to go he might go easily and quickly. For a week, or possibly only a few days, prior to his death he complained a little of a pain in the chest; it was not so troublesome as to prevent his going about his affairs as usual. His appetite was good, he slept well, was cheerful, and the day before he died he took his regular walk both in the forenoon and the afternoon. He spent the evening in reading aloud in the family circle as was his custom. So far as is known he had a quiet and restful night.

When he failed to appear at the breakfast table the following morning (Sunday, May 9) his sister-in-law went to see what was the matter. He confessed to being ill and asked to have a doctor sent for. The physician came at once, made a careful examination, prescribed a remedy, and told the patient not to attempt to go out of the house that day. Shortly afterwards the Bishop was heard stirring about his room. In response to a rap at his door he called out that he needed no help, but that he was getting up because he "could not lie still."

Having dressed completely (the white tie that he

always wore was scrupulously exact) he came out into
the drawing room and lay down on a sofa. His sister,
Mrs. Farovid, sat by his side, her hand in his. Presently he remarked that he was suffering from the heat.
Miss Dusenbury went in search of a fan and was gone
but a moment. When she returned she saw that he was
dying. "He passed away quickly and quietly. Not above
fifteen minutes had elapsed since he came from his
room."

He had his wish—the end had been painless. It is said
that the expression of his face in death was very lovely.
The benignant look, so eminently characteristic of him,
may well have been intensified at this time.

His son was at once communicated with. As there
had been no warning of a sort to cause alarm about the
state of his health, all the members of his immediate
family were in the East. The observances at the home
in Hyde Park were private, only relatives, the clergymen who officiated (or were there as representatives of
the General Conference) and a few intimate friends
being present.

The body was taken to Portville, New York, to be laid
beside that of the Bishop's beloved wife. A service was
held at the house of one of Mrs. Vincent's kinsmen. The
ritual at the grave was read by the Reverend Jesse L.
Hurlbut, an intimate friend of many years' standing.

On the afternoon of the funeral the public offices, the
places of business, and the schools at Chautauqua were
closed for the hour. The bell in the Miller Memorial
Tower was tolled. The villagers and the school children
gathered in the square, where the flag was flying at half
mast, and joined in a simple but touching service ex-

pressive of their affection and sorrow. The formal memorial meeting at Chautauqua took place in the midseason, on August 1. Of the several addresses that were made, either in the Amphitheater or at the Hall of Philosophy, two at least stand out prominently. In the first, emphasis was laid on Bishop Vincent's influence as a churchman; in the second, on his work as an educator.

The tributes in the press were many and generous. The three or four quoted here are typical of what might have been found in most of the well-known journals. *The Public Ledger* said: "The death of Bishop Vincent removes a man who probably did more for the promotion of education in America than any other one man that the country has known." *The Outlook* said: "He was a true progressive; he combined an inspiring breadth of view with intensity of conviction." The next is from *The New York Sun:* "John H. Vincent made the name of Chautauqua immortal, and he made thousands of men and women happy by showing them that education should not end with youth, and that vacations need not imply vacuity of mind. He was a strong man, an impressive figure of a purposeful age."

The following tribute appeared in *The Chicago Evening Post:* "Bishop Vincent will be remembered by America chiefly because he founded one of the distinctive features of its life—the Chautauqua movement. . . . And whatever the supercilious may say of Chautauqua, or however the movement itself may at times have strayed from its higher aims, beyond cavil it has brought millions of Americans, in towns and rural communities, into con tact with the richer and finer things of the soul and the spirit. Bishop Vincent helped America. He believed in God and in man, and was the friend of both."

Personally he was one of the most attractive men of his time. He had great charm. Affectionate, loyal, scrupulously honest, incapable of envy, winning of address, charitably disposed towards every one, democratic in the finer sense of the word, he was also generous to a fault, more ready to praise than to blame, to give than to receive. That he had a weakness for offering advice he laughingly acknowledged. In the *Autobiography* he confesses that all his life he "preached" too much. But they who came in contact with him were the better for it; the dullest person might have discovered that Bishop Vincent's preaching out of season was more profitable than that of many another man in the pulpit.

And he was a man of great gifts, a born leader, an orator of high rank, and so inventive that he was able to conceive and set in motion a system of popular education that has produced incalculably good results. One may say of him, in words borrowed from an address by an eminent English man of science, that "he had the wisdom of which knowledge is only the servitor. And that wisdom enabled him to see that ignorance is one of the roots of all evil."

INDEX

Abbott, Lyman, 137, 153, 294.
Arnold, Matthew, 215-217.

Beckwith, Colonel, 70-71.
Bench Street Church, Galena, Ill., 48.
Berean Sunday-school lessons, 107.
Better Not, by J. H. Vincent, 249-253.
Bible, The, used in consecration of bishops, 270.
Bienville, Céleron de, 115-116.
Blackall, C. R., *note* 88.
Borrow, George, 125-126.
Broomall, Jesse, 19-20.
Buffalo, N. Y., 270, 273, 285.
Bushnell, Horace, 264.
Bryant, W. C., 157.

Caine, Hall, 296.
Camptown, N. J., 40, 42.
Chalmers, Thomas, 264.
Charente Inférieure, 1.
Chase, Sidera, 34.
Chautauqua, first Institute, 117; characteristics and growth, 118-120; classes and conferences, 121-125; non-sectarian standards, 126-127; financial support, 127-129; Sunday observance, 129; a rival institution, 130; lectures and lecturers, 145-155; Society of Christian Ethics, 166-167; *also* 91, 268-269.
Chautauqua Lake, 115.
Chautauqua Literary and Scientific Circle, general activities, 132-139; required readings, 139-144.
Chautauqua Movement, The, by J. H. Vincent, 187-188.

Chautauquan, The (magazine), 125.
Chicago, Ill., 44, 306; *see also* Trinity Church, Chicago.
Chicago Sunday School Teacher, The, 88.
Chillisquaque, Pa., 13, 14, 19.
Christian Commission, The, 93-100.
Church of England Sunday School Institute, 114.
Church of the Future, The (lecture), 180-182.
Circuit riding, 29-32.
Court Street Church, Rockford, Ill., 53, 80.

Dana, Mrs. M. S. B., 23.
Debue, Esther, *see* Vincent, Mrs. Levi.
DeMorgan, William, 253.
Dewey, Melvil, 294.
Doremus, Elizabeth, *see* Vincent, Mrs. John.
Drummond, Henry, 153.
Dusenbury, Caroline, 306.
Dusenbury, Elizabeth, marriage, 45-46; *see also* Vincent, Mrs. John Heyl.

Eggleston, Edward, *note* 88, 110, 111.
Eliot, C. W., 137, 294.
Eliot, George, 253.
Elliott, John W., 29.
Ely, R. T., 294.
Epworth League, 240.
Eugénie, Empress, 67.
Evarts, W. W., 86.

Fair Point, Chautauqua Lake, 116, 117.

INDEX

Farovid, Mrs. James (Mary Elizabeth Vincent), *note* 14, 220, 306.
Fitzgerald, J. N., 270.
Fort Freeland, Pa., 4.
Fort Niagara, 4.
Freeland, Jacob, 4.
Freeport, Ill., 86.

Galena, Ill., 44, 48-49, 51, 53, 101-103, 306-308.
Garfield, J. R., 155.
Gilly, W. S., 70.
Gladstone, W. E., 218.
Grant, U. S., first meeting with J. H. Vincent, 49-51; letters to J. H. Vincent, 52-53; return to Galena, 101-103; birthday celebration, 306-308; *also* 51, 98, 155, 220-221.
Grant, Mrs. U. S., 51-52.
Gray, James, 112, 113.
Green, Mrs. M. F., 34.

Hale, E. E., 137, 144, 295.
Hall, John, 222.
Hammond, H. L., *note* 88.
Harnack, Adolf, 292.
Harper, W. R., 130-131, 294.
Harris, W. T., 293-294.
Harvard University, 276-278.
Henson, P. S., 225.
Himrod, Martha (Mrs. Bethuel Vincent), 3.
Hogan, J. B., 5.
Holy Club, The, 235-237.
Holy Land, The, incidents of travel in, 75-78.
How to Have a Small Class, by J. H. Vincent, 186.
Hurlbut, J. L., 312.
Hyde, F. W., 275.

Indianapolis, Ind., 111, 301, 305-306.
International Sunday School Convention, 5th, 111.
Irvington, N. J., 40.

Itinerants' Clubs, 271-274, 302.
Jacobs, B. F., 89, 111.
Janes, E. S., Bishop, 38.
Jo Daviess County Guards, 49, 51, 308.
Joliet, Ill., 44.
Jones, Sam, 222-223.
Joy, J. R., 241.

Lewisburg, Pa., 13, 19.
Lewistown, Pa., 27.
Libby Prison, 100.
Lincoln, Abraham, 98, 100.
Lincoln as a Student (lecture), 179, 262-263.
Little Footprints in Bible Lands, by J. H. Vincent, 185-186.
Livermore, Mrs. M. A., 137, 146.
London Sunday-School Union, 186.
Lowell, J. R., 149.
Luzerne Circuit, Pa., 29.
Lyon (publisher), 110-111.

Mahaffy, J. P., 153, 154.
Martineau, James, 264.
Maurice, F. D., 264.
McCabe, C. C., Bishop, 226-227.
McVeytown, Pa., 27.
Mechanicsville, Pa., 28.
Methodism, beginnings in England, 234-235; defined, 245; in Europe, 296-298.
Methodist ministry, required preparation for, 28, 41-42.
Miller, Lewis, 116, 127, 187.
Miller, William (Adventist), 24-25.
Milton, Pa., 3, 5.
Modern Sunday School, The, by J. H. Vincent, 113.
Mont Cenis route, 69.
Montour Ridge, Pa., 14.
Morisonians, The, 58.
Moulton, R. G., 152, 153, 293-294.
Mount Morris, Ill., 44, 48.

Napoleon, Louis, 66-67.

[316]

INDEX

[317]

INDEX

Freemasonry, 13; life at Chillisquaque and vicinity, 13-15; personal characteristics, 16-17; home
life and religious practices, 18-19,
21-23; *also* 33, 44, 189, 198.
Vincent, Mrs. John Himrod (Mary
Raser), life at Tuscaloosa, 8-9;
death, 17, 32-33; personal characteristics, 17-18, 265-266; favorite
books, 22; *also* 9-11, 188-189; *see
also* Raser, Mary.
Vincent, Levi, 1, 2.
Vincent, Mrs. Levi (Esther Debue),
1.
Vincent, Mary Elizabeth, *see* Farovid, Mrs. James.
Vincent, Thomas Raser, *note* 14.
Vincent and Pitcher, 6, 9.
Vincent-Warren meetings, 283-285.

Waddy, S. D., 270.
Waldensians, The, 70-71.
Ward, Phebe, *see* Vincent, Mrs. Cor-
nelius.
Warren, H. W., Bishop, 283.
Warrior Run Creek, Pa., 3, 4.
Washburne, E. B., 102.
Watson, Richard, *Theological Insti-
tutes,* 30, 41, 42.
Watsontown, Pa., 26.
Webber, Wolpfert, 2.
Wesley, John, 235-237, 270.
Wesleyan Institute, Newark, N. J.,
33-34.
White, A. D., 276.
Whitney, G. H., 35-36, 92.
Wilkinson, W. C., 63, 65, 106.
Willard, F. E., 123, 146.
Wise, Daniel, 91, 104, 186.